October
1989

ECONOMIC
POLICY A European Forum

Senior Editors
GEORGES DE MENIL
RICHARD PORTES

Managing Editors
DAVID BEGG
CHARLES WYPLOSZ

Assistant Editors
JOHN BLACK
DAMIEN NEVEN
PAUL SEABRIGHT

Board of Governors
GEORGES DE MENIL *Co-Chairman*
RICHARD PORTES *Co-Chairman*
FRANÇOIS BOURGUIGNON
JEREMY HARDIE

Cambridge University Press and
Editions de la Maison des Sciences de l'Homme for
Centre for Economic Policy Research and
École des Hautes Études en Sciences Sociales

Panel

Charles Bean
London School of Economics

Lars Calmfors
Institute for International Economic Studies, Stockholm

Pierre-Andre Chiappori
DELTA, Paris

Jean-Pierre Danthine
University of Lausanne

Jeffrey Frankel
Harvard University

Henrik Horn
Institute for International Economic Studies, Stockholm

Alexis Jacquemin
Commission of the European Communities

Jean-Paul Lambert
CORE, Louvain

Richard Layard
London School of Economics

Edmond Malinvaud
College de France, Paris

Colin Mayer
City University Business School, London

James Mirrlees
Nuffield College, Oxford

Manfred J. M. Neumann
University of Bonn

Victor Norman
Norwegian School of Economics and Business Administration, Bergen

Horst Siebert
Institut fur Weltwirtschaft, Kiel

Luigi Spaventa
University of Rome

Anthony J. Venables
University of Southampton

Statement of purpose

Economic Policy provides timely and authoritative analyses of the choices which confront policy-makers. The subject matter ranges from the study of how individual markets can and should work to the broadest interactions in the world economy.

Edited in London and Paris, *Economic Policy* offers an independent, non-partisan, European perspective on issues of worldwide concern. It emphasizes problems of international significance, either because they affect the world economy directly or because the experience of one country contains important lessons for policy makers elsewhere.

All the articles are specially commissioned from leading professional economists. Their brief is to demonstrate how live policy issues can be illuminated by the insights of modern economics and by the most recent evidence. The presentation is incisive and written in plain language accessible to the wide audience which participates in the policy debate.

Prior to publication, the contents of each volume are discussed by a Panel of distinguished economists from Europe and elsewhere. The Panel rotates annually. Inclusion in each volume of a summary of the highlights of the Economic Policy Panel discussion provides the reader with alternative interpretations of the evidence and a sense of the liveliness of the current debate.

The Panel meeting of April 1989 was funded in part by a grant from the European Commission. Financial support from the Esmee Fairbairn Charitable Trust and the Scaler Foundation is gratefully acknowledged.

Subscriptions: *Economic Policy* (ISSN 0266-4658) is published in April and October, volume 4 (issues 8 and 9) subscription prices, which include postage, valid until 31 December 1989, are per volume £19.00 UK, £21.00 elsewhere (US $38.00) for institutions, £11.00 (US $19.00) for individuals ordering direct from the publisher† and certifying that the journal is for their personal use. Single issues cost £10.50 (US $19.00) plus postage. US dollar prices apply to USA and Canada. Copies of the journal for subscribers in USA and Canada are sent by air to New York to arrive with minimum delay. Orders, which must be accompanied by payment, may be sent to a bookseller, subscription agent or to the publishers: Cambridge University Press, The Edinburgh Building, Shaftesbury Road, Cambridge CB2 2RU, UK or 40 West 20th Street, New York, NY 10011, USA.

† When exchange control regulations permit, individuals may pay by any of the following methods: Cheque (made payable to 'Cambridge University Press'), UK Postal Order, International Money Order, bank draft. Post Office Giro (a/c no. 571 6055 – *advice of payment should be sent with the order to the Press*), Barclaycard/Visa/BankAmericard or Access/MasterCard/Eurocard.

Contents

9

Editors' introduction

This issue contains the five papers discussed at the ninth panel meeting on 20–21 April 1989 in Paris. The papers have a common theme: the impact of the 1992 programme on Western Europe. Since this is so predominantly the focus of the current policy debate in Europe, we felt it appropriate that both this issue and the next issue of *Economic Policy* should be devoted to this single topic. As usual, each paper is preceded by a summary of the argument and principal conclusions. In addition we report a roundtable discussion on yet another aspect of 1992: the appropriate framework for regulation once the internal market has been completed. In this Editors' introduction we place the panel discussions in the context of the wider policy debate.

The Single European Act sets out the commitment of member governments to complete the internal market in Europe by 1992. A host of small non-tariff barriers will be removed as standards are harmonized, as government procurement policies no longer provide implicit protection for domestic producers, and as suppliers licensed in one country become able to compete in other member states. 1992 is much more than a trade liberalization: in many markets there will also be substantial deregulation and enhanced competition.

1992 symbolizes a desire for much greater integration in Europe. Politically, it already has enormous significance. But what of its economic impact? The Cecchini Report has estimated that it will increase EC output by between 2.5% and 6.5%. Such an increase is not negligible, but it scarcely justifies all the rhetoric and excitement. We asked Richard Baldwin of Columbia University to reassess the potential benefits of 1992 to member states of the European Community.

Baldwin's answer is clear cut. The Cecchini Report focuses on the static, or once-off, efficiency gains from market liberalization: these are well understood and reasonably easy to quantify, though of course debate will continue about the precision of the Cecchini estimates. But static gains will always be modest. The enthusiasm for 1992, in business as well as government, is based on the judgement that it will lead to growth. Yet there has been little attempt to analyse, much less quantify, these dynamic gains from 1992.

Baldwin examines two sources of dynamic gain, both of which are triggered by the static effect of higher efficiency, productivity and output. First, higher output and savings will enable higher investment and a once-off rise in the capital stock, even though the growth rate is not permanently affected. Baldwin shows that this 'medium-run bonus' may be at least as large as the static effects identified in the Cecchini Report. Second, the 'new growth theory' argues that scale economies may translate a once-off market enlargement into permanent sustainable growth. In a pioneering attempt to quantify such effects. Baldwin argues that this growth bonus may dwarf both the static effect and even the medium-run bonus. If so, the optimism surrounding 1992 may indeed be justified.

Turning from economy-wide effects to effects in particular industries, market completion and market liberalization may have the most dramatic effects in markets that were previously heavily regulated. European airlines are an obvious example. The example is instructive for another reason: the US experience of airline deregulation since the mid 1970s provides one of the few live rehearsals for 1992. We asked Francis McGowan of the University of Sussex and Paul Seabright of Cambridge University what Europe can learn from the US experience, and how European airlines should be regulated after 1992.

McGowan and Seabright draw three lessons from the US experience. Deregulation can produce major gains for consumers (especially in lower prices) without damaging the long-run profitability of airlines, by forcing reductions in operating costs through the pressures of market competition. Second, congestion problems, especially in the availability of landing slots at overcrowded airports, need to be carefully managed if new entrants are to have any hope of challenging existing carriers. Finally, in this and many other ways, incumbent carriers retain significant opportunities to exercise market power even after deregulation. Vigorous competition policy, especially in the scrutiny of merger proposals, will be an essential supplement to European airline deregulation.

One of the most significant aspects of the Single European Act is the establishment of a European Financial Area with free capital movements and a single market in the provision of financial services. Beginning from a situation contrasting widespread regulation in most EC countries and the relatively light regulation in a few – chiefly the UK and Luxembourg, with neighbouring Switzerland to be kept in mind – this change could be dramatic. We commissioned two papers on the consequences of 1992 for financial markets: the taxation of capital income and the location of financial activity.

Alberto Giovannini of Columbia Business School highlights the lucrative tax avoidance activities to which existing tax structures give rise. By establishing subsidiaries for the right activities in the right places, firms can substantially reduce their tax liabilities. At present this strategy can be very sophisticated, and is practised to perfection only by very large companies. Giovannini shows that tax avoidance will become much easier and much cheaper after 1992. EC governments will, therefore, face a tax loophole of massive proportions. Closing the loophole will require an unusual degree of coordination across a complex range of issues.

Two guiding principles of taxation are available. The territorial principle holds that all income is taxed where it is earned, independent of the country of residence of the taxpayer. Essentially it means withholding taxes. Tax competition between different countries would then tend to lead to approximate harmonization of tax rates, possibly at a very low level as each country endeavoured to obtain a larger share of Community business. Alternatively, the worldwide principle holds that income is taxed by the country of residence regardless of where it is earned. To be effective, it requires truthful reporting or a considerable information exchange amongst tax authorities. Giovannini does not address this problem – in his comments Edmond Malinvaud sees this as a serious weakness – but rather offers an economic assessment of the two systems on the assumption they can be suitably enforced. He concludes that the territorial principle gives rise to much more serious distortions than the worldwide principle. The former distorts the international allocation of savings, which being extremely mobile are greatly affected, whilst the latter distorts the level of national saving which is notoriously unresponsive to changes in the net rate of return. Giovannini provides a blueprint of how to apply the worldwide principle.

Vittorio Grilli of Yale University tries to foresee how 1992 will affect the geographical location of financial services, particularly banking. He considers whether the Single European Act will reinforce the position of London, or whether Paris, Frankfurt, Milan and Brussels will challenge the City's supremacy. He concludes that London is fairly safe. History matters. An established financial centre enjoys 'thick-market externalities': each firm benefits from the presence of many others through networking, shared resources, and the presence of a skilled labour force. Such an advantage could be overcome if another government offered substantial inducements – chiefly tax advantages – but Grilli believes even aggressive attempts to compete with London are likely to fail.

His article focuses primarily on international bank deposits. What will happen once EC residents are allowed to hold deposits in the country of their choice? Will the banking industry be completely transformed? Grilli first tries to understand why people bank abroad. He concludes that 80% of international deposits are inter-bank and that banks mainly seek thick-market externalities. Non-bank depositors, on the other hand, look for tax advantages and secrecy. Unlike Giovannini, Grilli sees little serious threat of widespread relocation of bank deposits, though his analysis does not address the parallel question of the location of bank branches and subsidiaries.

The EC is not Europe. A number of Western European countries are watching 1992 from the outside, with a mixture of hopes and fears. The European Free Trade Area (EFTA) group already have important trade agreements with the EC with whom they trade extensively. 1992 will certainly affect the EFTA countries. Is it good news or bad? How should they best respond? These are the issues we asked Victor Norman of Bergen University to investigate.

He focuses on the Nordic countries and conducts a detailed study of two industries chosen because they have very different structures and links with the EC: the motor vehicles industry and the pharmaceuticals industry. His answer is most interesting. 1992 does matter a lot for EFTA countries, not because they stand to lose a lot as a result but because the gains to further integration with the EC would then be large. And if such integration did occur, the benefits to EC countries would be small in comparison with those reaped by EFTA countries. Importantly, the benefits would not be evenly spread. Norman's study essentially shows that consumers will almost always benefit, but EFTA firms will almost always lose since their ability to exploit a dominant position at home disappears with a truly single market in Europe.

A number of wider issues arise. Norman deals with one of them, namely how the industry effects of 1992 impact on resource allocation and costs. Such general equilibrium effects have been recognized in recent attempts to measure the effects of 1992, but Norman's is an early effort to put these into practice. These tend to dampen the effects of industry level studies, such as those forming the input for the Cecchini Report. But the general conclusion remains: after 1992 the EFTA countries would be better off within the EC than on the fringes. As the subsequent panel discussion made clear, much work still remains to be done to confirm this conclusion.

Norman focuses on the trade liberalizing aspect of 1992 but what other effects will it have? Will it bring about convergence of prices and the enhancement of competition? Given that the Nordic countries have actively used exchange rate policy, what would be the consequences of macroeconomic integration with the EC? Finally, how should the assessment be altered to take account of the growth effects which form the basis of the Baldwin analysis with whcih we begin this issue?

The final session of the panel meeting was devoted to a roundtable discussion of the appropriate form of regulation in Europe after 1992. What principles should guide the basis of regulation? How do we decide which regulatory activities are best conducted at local level, which at national level, and which on a community-wide basis? Manfred Neumann of the University of Bonn contrasts the instinct to centralize and the determination to decentralize, and favours the latter where possible. Competition between regulatory jurisdictions will often enhance efficiency and choice, but cannot be an invariable principle, for example when adverse externalities such as acid rain cut across local and national boundaries. Neumann tries to spell out both general principles and specific illustrations of how the structure of regulation should be designed.

Michael Emerson of the European Commission emphasizes the importance of recognizing the legal and institutional framework in which such decisions will be made, and acknowledges quite frankly that politics as much as economics will shape the evolution of policy. He provides a useful guide to the political and institutional background against which he sets essentially the same analytical framework as that adopted by Neumann.

Colin Mayer of the City University Business School in London explores how general principles stand up in a particular example, the evolving regulation of the financial services industry. He emphasizes that different problems appropriately require different solutions, both across institutions and across countries. He cautions against simplistic harmonization of regulations and in particular identifies activities which will be overregulated if the current direction of policy continues.

To conclude the roundtable, we invited Judge Stephen Breyer, who played a leading role in the legislative reforms deregulating US airlines, to give a transatlantic perspective on European regulation after 1992. Like Emerson, he stresses the shifting institutional power balance in the Community and its effect on the way regulatory decisions will in fact be taken. Like Mayer, he identifies common analytical themes but foresees no way in which these can be translated into simple decision rules. The appropriate form of regulation can be usefully guided by some robust economic principles, but their application will always depend on difficult judgments about the particular case in hand.

Economic Policy   October 1989   Printed in Great Britain

The growth effects of 1992

Richard Baldwin

Summary

The Cecchini Report estimates that 1992 will raise the output of the European Community by between 2.5 and 6.5%. If the effect is so small, why is everyone so excited? These numbers are so small because the Cecchini Report only measures 1992's one-time effects on productivity and output. It does not attempt to quantify the growth effects. Yet if the latter exist, they are likely to dwarf the one-time gains.

The growth effects can be described in theory and measured in practice. Even if 1992 has no permanent effect on European growth, it will bring a medium-run growth bonus. Higher productivity will improve the savings and investment climate in Europe. The resulting extra investment will provide a medium-run output effect proportional to the one-time efficiency gain. This effect is likely to be of the same order of magnitude as the one-time effects measured by the Cecchini Report.

With scale economies, completing the internal market may also permanently increase Europe's growth rate. Attempts to quantify this effect suggest that it could be the largest of all.

The growth effects of 1992

Richard Baldwin
Columbia University and NBER

1. Introduction

The aim of the 1992 programme is to eliminate all barriers to the movement of goods, people and capital within the European Community. To this end, it will remove border controls, liberalize financial markets, harmonize VAT rates, standardize industrial regulations, open up govenment procurement and generally remove barriers to competition among EC firms. The Cecchini Report (1988) estimates that, by allowing a more efficient utilization of productive resources, the programme will lead to a once-off rise in EC income of between 2.5 and 6.5%. The mismatch between the radical nature of the liberalization and the modest nature of the estimated gains is striking. There is a standard reply to this mismatch. 1992's greatest benefits may be found not in its once-off effect on resource allocation but rather in its *dynamic* effects: more innovation, faster productivity gains, greater investment and higher output growth. The Cecchini Report ignores these dynamic effects for the simple reason that they are poorly understood and supposedly impossible to measure.

This reasoning brings to mind the person who one night loses their wallet in a dark car park but looks for it on the street corner 'because that's where the light is'. Undaunted by the lack of empirical illumination, the EC's political leaders have emphasized the dynamic or growth effects of 1992. Lord Cockfield in his foreword to the Cecchini Report states 'the completion of the internal market will open up: opportunities for growth, for job creation, for economies of scale, of improved productivity ... in short a prospect of significant inflation-free growth

I gratefully acknowledge comments and suggestions from the Managing Editors, Charlie Bean, Ricardo Caballero, Pierre-Andre Chiappori, Alberto Giovannini, Assar Lindbeck, Rich Lyons, Jim Mirrlees, Torsten Persson and Tony Venables. The Institute for International Economic Studies in Stockholm provided a fertile environment for the completion of this paper.

and millions of new jobs.' This stress on growth is understandable. Small increases in the growth rate soon lead to large increases in the material standard of living. If 1992 raised Europe's growth rate even half a percentage point, it would chalk up an extra 5% real income not just once but every 10 years. If it permanently added one percentage point to the growth rate, Europe's real income would triple in an average person's lifetime rather than doubling as under current growth rates.

Traditional thinking about the growth effects of liberalizations is guided by the neoclassical growth model which explains per capita growth entirely by technological progress. Since the determinants of this technological progress are not addressed, it is easy to see why the Cecchini Report found the growth effects of 1992 impossible to measure. Starting with Romer (1983), a number of economists have explored theoretically how competition, market size, and trade policy can affect growth rates. The 'new' theory stresses the role of economy-wide increasing returns to scale and profit-motivated technological improvements as the primary determinants of productivity gains and growth. At first blush, the new theory seems the ideal tool with which to address the growth effects of 1992. However, the nascent literature has yet to converge upon a consensus model. Nor has it been developed with an eye for empirical testing or implementation. Indeed, no studies have tried to gauge whether policy changes have large or small effects on growth.

This paper analyses some of the dynamic effects of the market liberalization implied by 1992. The theoretical part is relatively straightforward. The quantitative part is trickier. Many of the key effects in the new theory involve factors which are unobservable or on which data are unavailable or unreliable. To get round this, I apply the calibration methodology recently introduced into the trade literature by Dixit (1987) and Baldwin and Krugman (1987). The results should be thought of as rough, back-of-the-envelope calculations. Samuel Johnson's quip about a dog walking on its hind legs applies to my empirical work: the interest lies not in that it is done well, but rather that it is done at all.

My analysis suggests that the Cecchini Report significantly underestimates the economic effects of 1992, perhaps by an order of magnitude. In addition to the initial static effect, the focus of the Cecchini Report, there will be a substantial 'medium-run growth bonus' as the static efficiency gains induce higher savings and investment. This medium-run bonus will be achieved even if there is no permanent increase in the underlying growth rate. Furthermore, the 'new growth theory' suggests that growth rates may be permanently increased. My efforts to quantify this suggest that 1992 might add between 0.2 and 0.9 percentage points to the EC's long-term growth rate.

Section 2 introduces a framework for assessing scale economies and the dynamic effects of 1992. Section 3 presents evidence on the importance of scale economies. Section 4 looks at the policy implications of the new growth theory. Section 5 discusses how to calibrate these models and presents the empirical results. Section 6 summarizes and draws conclusions.

2. Scale economies and the growth effects of 1992

For a given labour force, extra capital raises output. In the absence of scale economies, there are diminishing marginal returns to extra capital. Eventually the return on extra investment is insufficient to bribe consumers to defer consumption in order to save and invest. Per capita growth stops.

How, then, does traditional theory explain the per capita growth the world has experienced since the industrial revolution? Simple; it assumes continuous 'manna-from-heaven' technological progress. This has two effects: it raises productivity and output directly, and, by raising the return on capital, it increases the incentive to invest. However, since growth depends ultimately only on unexplained technological progress, this is not a useful framework for addressing the growth effects of 1992. In particular, trade barriers and market size cannot possibly affect long-term growth. Several notable empirical efforts have been made to explain technological progress (see Maddison, 1987, and Denison, 1985). However, without a coherent theoretical framework, policy analysis based on such efforts is inevitably *ad hoc*.

In contrast, with economies of scale, the return to capital and, thus, the incentive to invest depend on the scale of economic activity. Thus, market size matters. Programmes like 1992 matter. Furthermore, if scale economies are sufficiently important, we may be able to explain sustained per capita growth without relying on inscrutable technological progress. I discuss these new growth theories in Section 4. As yet they are fairly undeveloped and completely untested empirically. Consequently, I begin with a simple extension of the traditional growth theory. My aim is to show that the one-time efficiency gains from 1992 will be multiplied into a medium-run growth bonus.

2.1. The medium-run growth bonus from 1992

Suppose the economy-wide relation between the amount of capital and labour employed and GDP can be described by

$$\text{GDP} = j(\text{capital stock})^{a+b} (\text{labour employed})^{1-a} \tag{1}$$

This formula says that a 1% increase in both the capital stock and labour force increases output by $(1 + b)\%$. Thus the number b is a measure of aggregate scale economies. The traditional model sets b equal to zero; the new growth theory lets b be positive. Specifying the micro foundations of why b might be positive is an important contribution of the new theory. Moreover, the discussion in Section 4 shows that certain policy implications depend upon the source of the increasing returns. For the moment, however, just take b as given. The number $(1 - a)$ is the percentage increase in GDP that would result from a 1% increase in employed labour, holding the capital stock constant. The parameter j measures overall economic efficiency. This can be affected by technical progress as well as policy changes like the 1992 programme.

To facilitate the exposition I shall ignore technical progress and changes in labour employed. Equation (1) is plotted as YY in Figure 1. Figure 1(a) is drawn for the case of constant returns to scale $(b = 0)$; Figure 1(b) for the case of scale economies $(b > 0)$. The marked curvature of YY in Figure (1a) reflects the fact that with b equal to zero, the returns to additional capital quickly diminish as we increase the capital stock (recall that we are holding the labour input constant). With some scale economies, the marginal return to capital falls off less quickly, so the curvature of YY is less pronounced. For the moment we consider only $(a + b) < 1$. Section 2.2 considers what happens when $(a + b)$ is greater than or equal to one.

To see how GDP grows, we must determine how the capital stock grows via savings and investment. There are many ways to do this. The simplest is to suppose that the economy invests a constant fraction of

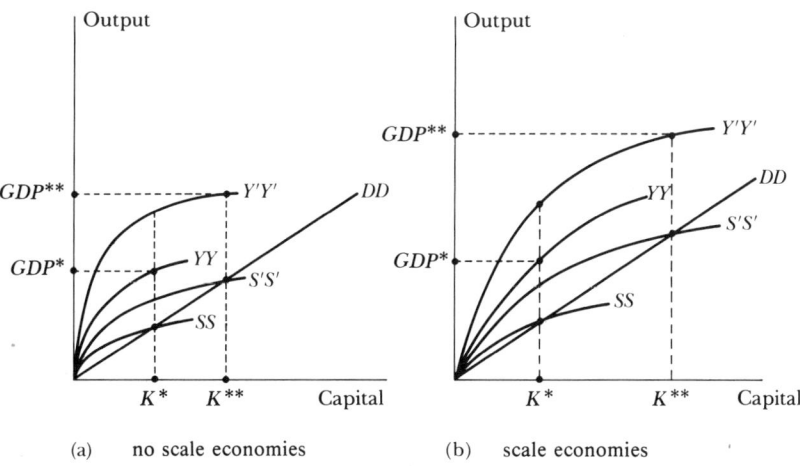

(a)   no scale economies   (b)   scale economies

Figure 1. The medium-run growth bonus

GDP (call this fraction s). This assumption enormously simplifies the exposition without fundamentally altering the conclusions. However, since the assumption disobeys a standing order in modern macro theory – 'if it moves, maximize it' – an optimizing model is sketched in Appendix A. This constant investment rate assumption can be plotted as SS in Figure 1(this curve is s times GDP).

From the economy-wide perspective, investment goes first to replacing the fraction of the capital stock that depreciates each year. If there is any investment left over after making up for depreciation, the capital stock rises. If investment is insufficient to cover depreciation, the capital stock falls. It is not hard to see that eventually the capital stock will settle down to the point where all investment is devoted to replacing last year's depreciation. In Figure 1 the capital stock at which this occurs is where DD and SS intersect (DD shows how total depreciation depends on the capital stock, i.e. DD plots dK where d is the rate of depreciation). Thus K^* and GDP^* represent the stable long-run equilibrium of the economy.

With all this on the drawing board, we use Figure 1 to demonstrate the medium-term growth effects of the 1992 programme. The first step is simple: the removal of barriers to the movement of goods, labour and capital will improve the overall efficiency with which the EC labour force and capital stock are combined to produce output. The result is a higher output for any given level of inputs. In terms of Figure 1, this is a once-off shift up in the YY and SS schedules (this corresponds to an increase in j in formula 1). The new curves are drawn as $Y'Y'$ and $S'S'$. The size of the upward shift is estimated to be between 2.5 and 6.5% by the Cecchini Report.

However, this is not the end of the story. The increase in efficiency leads to more savings and investment. In terms of Figure 1 this shows up as an increase in the stable long-run equilibrium capital stock (from K^* to K^{**}). Consequently, 1992 raises EC GDP in two ways: it directly boosts efficiency which means Europe can get more output out of the same amount of labour and capital, and it boosts savings and investment which raises the capital stock and therefore output. We call this second effect the medium-term growth effect. The size of this second effect depends on the magnitude of the initial efficiency increase and upon how quickly the marginal return to capital falls off (this in turn depends on the importance of scale economies). The second effect on the capital stock is larger in Figure 1(b), which allows for scale economies, than it is in Figure 1(a), which imposes constant returns to scale. To give a bit of a preview, Section 5 shows that even with constant returns to scale the medium-term growth effect is about 40% of the static effect. Scale economies can enormously magnify this effect.

In Figure 1, 1992 directly increases savings since the savings rate is constant. With or without scale economies, this raises the long-run equilibrium capital stock. In the Appendix A model, we get an identical effect for a different economic reason. 1992 lifts the marginal return on investment, leading consumers optimally to forego more consumption. The result is a higher capital stock. In a nutshell, in addition to raising per capita income directly, 1992 will boost savings and investment in Europe. This leads to a higher steady-state capital-labour ratio. As the economy moves towards its new steady-state capital-labour ratio, income will rise by more, perhaps much more, than the original static efficiency gain.

2.2. The new long-term growth bonus in Romer's model

Already we see that the Cecchini estimates substantially understate the effects of 1992. My argument so far relies on a strictly medium-run growth effect: once the economy settles down to the new stable level, K^{**} and GDP^{**}, there is no further growth. From the long-run perspective, we have not changed the growth rate but merely boosted the once-off effects.

Simple algebra shows that a liberalization can have long-run (i.e. permanent) growth effects only if $(a + b)$ is greater than or equal to one. As it turns out, if scale effects are large enough so that $(a + b)$ is greater than one, we should observe accelerating growth. Since this is pretty clearly not a fact of life in the modern world, we dismiss this theoretical possibility. On the other hand, if the scale economies are such that $(a + b)$ exactly equals one then a one-time market liberalization leads to permanently higher growth. It may seem a bit strange to think that $(a + b)$ would exactly equal any given number at all, much less one. However, Romer has presented a fairly reasonable model (see Romer, 1987) where this is true; furthermore he has presented some very crude empirical evidence that $(a + b)$ actually does equal one in the US. Although Romer's empirical methodology is faulty, given the present state of knowledge about economy-wide returns to scale, we cannot rule out conclusively the possibility that $(a + b)$ equals one. Since it has important new policy implications, I consider what the growth effects of 1992 would be, if $(a + b)$ does indeed equal one.

The principal difference between the Romer model where $(a + b) = 1$ and the Figure 1 case is that in the former the capital-labour ratio never reaches a stable level. (This should in no way be considered a drawback, since in fact the capital-labour ratio has risen for at least a century in the industrialized nations.) Basically, this is because the marginal product of capital is not diminishing when $(a + b)$ is one. A consequence of this property is that attempts to find the new stable level of K as in Figure 1 are futile. Nevertheless, translating the case of $(a + b)$ equal to one into a formula is straightforward.

As in Figure 1, the key is to see what is happening to the capital stock since we are holding labour input constant. Clearly, next year's capital stock equals last year's capital net of depreciation plus last year's savings. Plugging this back into the GDP formula and taking the ratio of next year's GDP to this year's gives us:

$$\begin{pmatrix} \text{long-run} \\ \text{growth rate} \end{pmatrix} = \begin{pmatrix} \text{savings} \\ \text{rate} \end{pmatrix}\begin{pmatrix} \text{GDP-capital} \\ \text{ratio} \end{pmatrix} - \begin{pmatrix} \text{depreciation} \\ \text{rate} \end{pmatrix}$$

$$g = s(GDP/K) - d \tag{2}$$

Consider what 1992 would do to the long-run growth rate. The one-time efficiency gain implies a higher GDP for any given capital stock, leading to a one-time rise in the GDP-capital ratio. With a constant investment rate this directly raises the rate of investment. Thus, the static gain from 1992 generates a *permanent* increase in the sustainable growth rate when $(a + b)$ equals one. This can be thought of as a long-run growth bonus. Again to give a quick preview of Section 5, if the savings rate is 10% then a 1% static gain will permanently add one-tenth of 1% to Europe's long-run growth rate.

3. The data versus the traditional growth model

In 'A Scandal in Bohemia' Sherlock Holmes tells Watson that it is a capital mistake to theorize before having the facts, since insensibly one juggles facts to fit theories, not theories to fit facts. It would appear that much of the empirical work on traditional growth ignored this wisdom. In this section I offer formal and informal evidence that the data is trying to tell us that scale economies are important.

Section 3.2 discusses some highbrow econometric results that tend to reject the traditional crucial assumption of constant returns to scale. However, to many analysts the more intricate the econometric methodology is, the less convincing are the results. I therefore first present some evidence against constant returns which does not rely on advanced econometric reasoning. The advantage of this type of evidence is its transparency. The drawback is that it is only suggestive, not conclusive.

3.1. Traditional theory and growth

The crucial assumption of the traditional theory is constant returns to scale. Taken literally, this assumption implies that each of us could have a personal economy in our garden, producing all the goods and services we consume each year. Moreover, constant returns implies that such an arrangement would be as efficient as the industrial structure that actually exists. Obviously in this unadulterated form, the assumption does not pass the laugh-test, much less any sort of econometric test. Nevertheless, rejecting firm-level constant returns does not let us reject the traditional model. What the model actually requires is that the aggregate economy act as if there were constant returns.

Suppose for example firms face first increasing then, after a certain point, decreasing returns to scale – the famous U-shaped cost curve. If the market is quite competitive, producers will be forced to operate at the minimum cost level of output (otherwise competitors would under-cut their price). Now at the bottom of the cost curve, but at no other point, returns to scale are constant. Thus, despite the fact that firms face increasing returns, competition (viz. contestability) forces them to operate at the point where returns are locally constant. Thus, with this add-on story, the fact of ubiquitous firm-level scale economies can be made consistent with constant returns to scale at the aggregate level. Moreover, the absence of firm-level scale economies does not imply an absence of economy-wide increasing returns. For instance, there may be technological spill-overs between firms, or economies of agglomeration. Or as Adam Smith argued, it is possible that larger markets can support finer division of labour (more on this in Section 4).

The next strike against constant returns can be found in world trade patterns. Two-way trade in similar products between similar countries suggests the importance of scale economies which are not exhausted by the size of the domestic market. What this says is that market size may matter. But it is not conclusive: scale economies may provide the motive for trade, but with relatively free trade, they may be exhausted as a result of trade, leaving few remaining scale economies for 1992 to exploit.

3.1.1. Some aggregate evidence against the traditional model. Now let's look at the assumption of constant returns to scale from another angle. Recall that the traditional model predicts that per capita output growth would grind to a halt without continual manna-from-heaven technological advances. In other words, according to the traditional theory we need a time trend to explain the growth in per capita output. It is simple to write down a formula for the traditional growth theory's explanation for growth. The formula divides growth into two parts: a part that can be explained by the growth in the K/L ratio (which itself is driven by the technological advances), and a part that is explained by a time trend which is labelled technological progress. In terms of per cent changes, this says:

$$\begin{pmatrix} \text{\% change in} \\ \text{output per} \\ \text{worker} \end{pmatrix} = \begin{pmatrix} \text{Technological} \\ \text{progress} \end{pmatrix} + a \begin{pmatrix} \text{\% change in} \\ \text{capital per} \\ \text{worker} \end{pmatrix} \qquad (3)$$

where a is usually taken to be about 0.3. The received wisdom of the traditional model is that, of the two parts, technological progress is by far the most important, accounting for 50 to 80% of growth. By contrast, some of the new growth models (for example when $a + b$ equals one) predict that per capita growth can be fully explained by growth in the capital-labour ratio without appeal to a time trend.

Let's see whether the data likes the traditional theory's idea that per capita growth is mostly explained by a time trend and not by the rise in the K/L ratio. Unfortunately it is impossible to get data on technological progress (indeed it is hard to be exactly sure how to define it). Data on the capital-labour ratio and output per worker, however, are readily available for the past 75 or 100 years. Figure 2(a)–(f) plot an index of GDP over a measure of the labour force against an index of the capital stock over the same index of the labour force for France, Germany, Italy, Japan, the UK and the US. (The index measures hours worked instead of employment to improve international comparability.) 1913 is the base year for all indices. If the data had its way, the value of a would be pretty close to one, not one-third. There would then be no need for a time trend to explain growth. Consequently the technological progress term would be largely extraneous.

Clearly, these figures suggest that it was not the facts that told us we had to juggle the theory to account for a time trend. Rather it was the traditional theory that told us we had to juggle the facts to get a time trend into the data. And it is pretty clear how the traditional theory accomplished this. Output per worker and the capital-labour ratio move one-for-one with each other in the real world. Since traditional theory dictates that a be a fraction like 0.3, there will be a lot of 'unexplained' growth left over to assign to conveniently unobservable technological progress. To graphically demonstrate this point, I have plotted what a time K/L looks like, taking a equal to 0.3. The difference between GDP/L and $(K/L)^{0.3}$ is exactly the amount of growth that the traditional model explains with unobservable technological progress.

3.1.2. The traditional model's rejoinder. A traditional growth theorist would point out that these figures can be made to be consistent with constant returns to scale. Figure 2 confirms the well known fact that the capital-

Table 1. Scale economies (econometric estimates of $(1 + b)$) (constant returns if $(1 + b)$ equals unity)

	Germany	France	UK	Belgium	US
Central estimate	1.22	1.59	1.13	1.42	1.37
95% confidence interval	0.70–1.74	1.01–2.17	0.17–2.09	0.42–2.42	1.19–1.53

Source: Caballero and Lyons (1989).

output ratio has been roughly constant for a century. Whilst this is a direct implication of the Romer model, it can also be derived within the traditional growth theory. With constant returns to scale, profit-maximizing firms will choose a capital-labour ratio that is inversely proportional to the real interest rate. If this rate is roughly constant over time, the capital-output ratio will also be roughly constant. The time trend reflecting technological progress then reconciles this theory with the observed behaviour of output and capital per head in Figure 2.

Plainly we have two competing explanations for the same set of facts. Next I turn to the highbrow econometric evidence.

3.2. Econometric evidence against constant returns to scale

Caballero and Lyons (1989a, b) and Hall (1988) have addressed the question of economies of scale using industry-level data on manufacturing. I focus on the work of Caballero and Lyons which is more general in that they distinguish between scale economies within the firm and external scale economies. External economies might arise from technological spill-overs which increase the productivity of one firm when the output of other firms rises. It is the total effect of internal and external scale economies in which we are interested.

We can interpret the results of Caballero and Lyons using Equation (1). If scale economies exist, $(1 + b)$ exceeds unity. Table 1 reports their estimates for $(1 + b)$ for France, Germany, the UK, Belgium and the US. The estimates for these countries suggest that scale economies exist in each country's manufacturing sector. However, the statistical precision of the estimates is such that only for France and the US can we clearly reject the competing hypothesis that scale economies do not exist.

In summary, the jury is still out on the importance of scale economies at the economy-wide level. This formal and informal evidence is well short of an airtight case against constant returns to scale. However, I

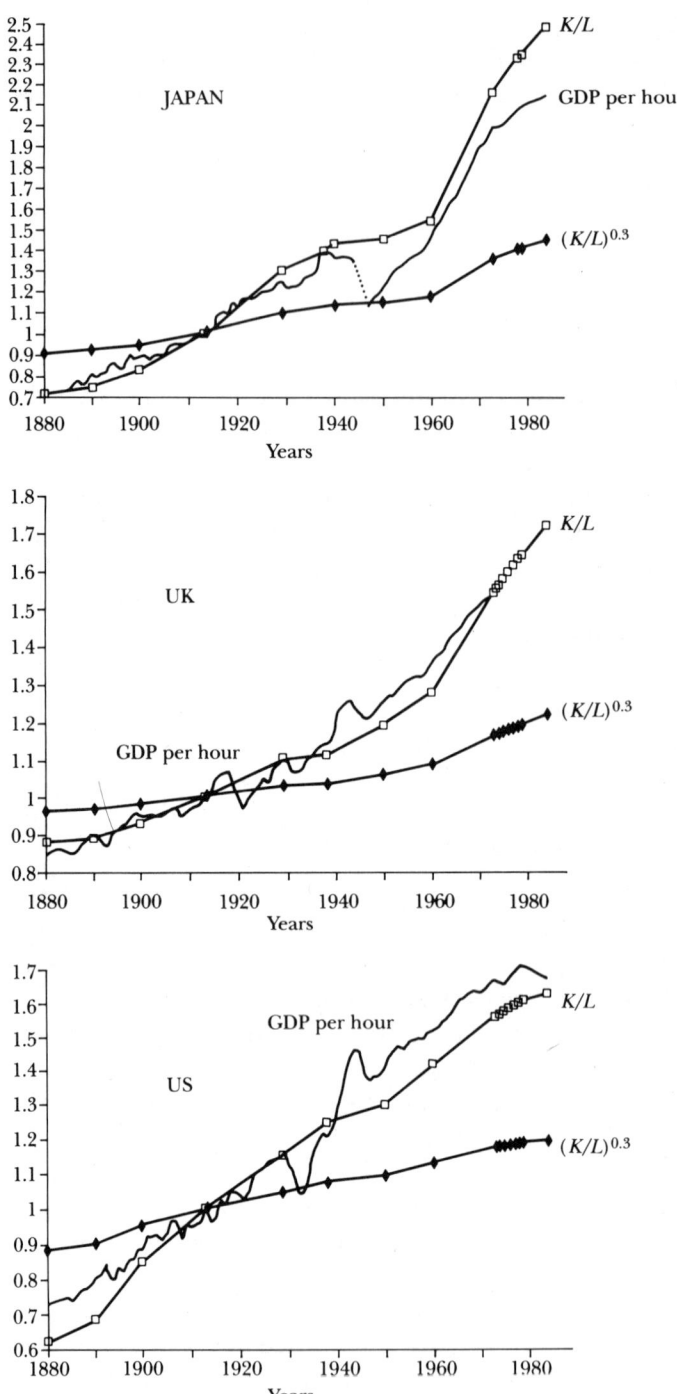

Figure 2. Capital, labour and productivity

Source: Maddison (1982)

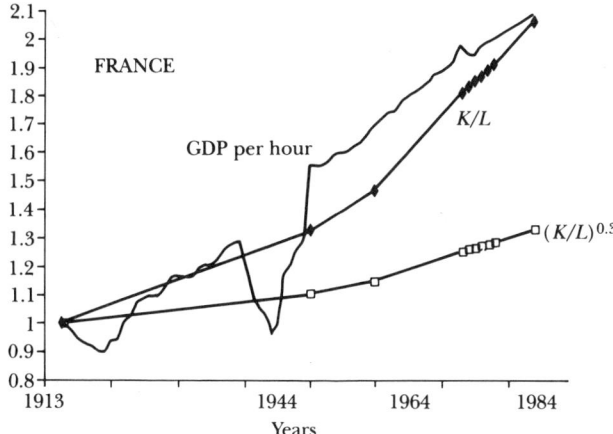

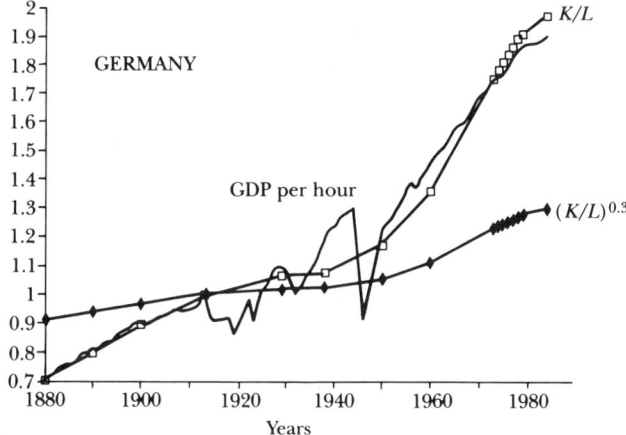

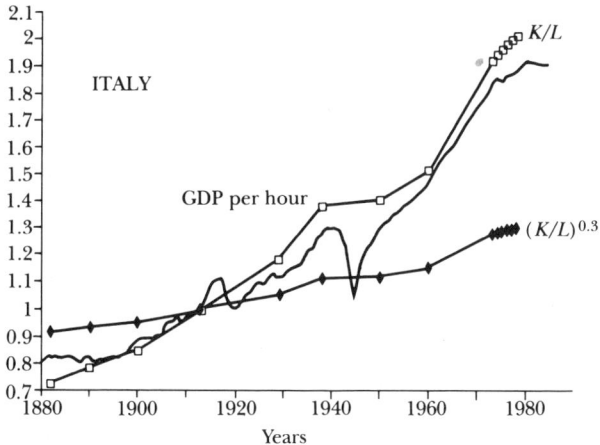

hope to have raised sufficient doubts to prevent analysis using the new growth theories being dismissed as empty theorizing.

4. Policy implications of scale economies

Scale economies can arise at the level of the factory, the industry, the region, the country or the world. The level at which they occur is critical for policy. I now discuss three standard sources and their implications for 1992.

4.1. Specialized inputs

Adam Smith argued that the division of labour is limited by the extent of the market: a finer division of labour allows greater specialization and efficiency. Romer (1986) and Young (1928) have shown that a larger market can also lead to higher output growth. A larger market increases efficiency and profitability, and the rate at which productivity-boosting inputs are developed.

1992 will expand the market in this way, and may therefore lead to faster introduction of new specialized inputs which increase productivity and output growth. However, 15% of EC output is exported to non-EC countries whose output will not be substantially altered by 1992. This dampens the market-expanding effect. Moreover, growth from this source depends on growth in the number of specialized inputs available to firms in the EC. It does not require that the specialized inputs (e.g. advanced microprocessors) be produced in the EC. Thus, 1992's impact on worldwide growth of new specialized inputs will be further dampened by the fact that it will not significantly affect profitability for the large fraction of developers outside the EC.

4.2. Technology spill-overs

A second source of scale economies is technology spill-overs. Why do firms cluster in places like Silicon Valley or the high-tech area outside Cambridge, England? The advancement of knowledge is often facilitated by the presence of many innovators concerned with similar problems. Advances by one firm spill over into another. Hence a larger, more open market can lead to faster growth.

But how should one define market size? Information may be exchanged and informal contacts maintained among innovators who are geographically dispersed. Maybe the relevant market is the world industrial economy. The growth effects of 1992 will therefore be dampened significantly unless it affects the rate of knowledge creation outside the EC, and especially in the US and Japan. Moreover, any move towards Fortress Europe might hinder the dissemination of knowledge from elsewhere.

4.2.1. Euro rust belts. Alternatively, face-to-face interaction, or a buyer-seller relationship may be the key to technology spill-overs. In this case the relevant market size seems to be the amount of activity in a city or region (like Lyon or the Ruhr Valley). If this region-size definition of scale economies is correct, the completion of the internal market may lead to 'Euro rust belts'. Without national borders to restrict them, EC firms may find it worth while to concentrate geographically at the EC level rather than just at the national level. Thus, instead of having 12 separate industrial regions (Germany's Ruhr Valley, Italy's Pianura Padana, England's Spaghetti Junction, etc.) after 1992 there may be only a handful of such regions; bad news for those in the contracting regions.

4.3. Profit-motivated innovation, growth and 1992

Of the three commonly cited sources of scale economies, the most appealing is that of endogenous technological change (typically associated with Schumpeter and Schmookler). The basic idea is simple. The effectiveness with which inputs are combined to create value is constrained by managerial and technical know-how, itself largely the product of profit-motivated firms. Basic scientific advances (CERN's finding the z-particle or the discovery of room temperature superconductors) may be insensitive to commercial motives. Yet their application to enhance productivity is a task inevitably undertaken by firms. An innovation usually gives the innovator a temporary edge over the competition, thereby boosting profits. From the macro viewpoint, the effect of these profit-motivated innovations is growth (see Grossman and Helpman, 1988). In this framework, it is easy to see how 1992 might lead to faster growth. The removal of hundreds of small trade barriers could allow a potential innovator to spread the R&D costs over more units of output, making innovation more profitable.

This is not a new idea. The contribution of the new growth literature has been to crystalize it into precise relationships, allowing us to check for subtle logical inconsistencies and providing a basis for quantification. Grossman and Helpman (1988a, b) have studied product innovation; Shleifer (1986) and Krugman (1988) process innovations. I now develop Krugman's approach.

4.3.1. A model of endogenous innovation and growth. Growth models with endogenous innovation view R&D spending on innovation as investment. In a nutshell, the amount of innovation done each period depends on two things: the profitability of innovating and the willingness of people to invest, i.e. postpone consumption. The equilibrium rate of innovation (or more precisely spending on R&D) is the level at which the profitability of an extra innovation is just high enough to prompt the necessary amount of consumption postponement. To be more precise we examine the two aspects separately, starting with the savings-investment decision.

If the economy is to innovate and grow faster, more investment in R&D is required. This of course means more consumption must be postponed. To induce people to postpone the extra consumption requires a higher rate of return on their savings (savings of course is just postponed consumption). People will want to save more: (i) the less impatient they are for current consumption, (ii) the more future consumption is a good substitute for current consumption, and (iii) the greater the rate of return on their savings. Saving more means planning a consumption path which rises more quickly over time. Since there is a good deal of evidence that in the long run real consumption and real output grow at the same rate g, this analysis means that output growth is faster the lower the rate of impatience or time preference ρ, the greater the elasticity of substitution σ between current and future consumption, and the greater the rate of return on innovation investment[1].

Let me turn now to investment in innovation. To simplify, I assume that a cost-reducing 'typical' innovation can be developed by investing F units of resources this period which achieves a given percentage reduction in production costs next period which the innovating firm alone enjoys because of a patent. In the following period the innovation becomes public knowledge and is adopted by all firms.

The innovation gives the innovating firm a clear advantage during the patent life. The corresponding profit is worked out explicitly in Krugman (1988). The key results are that, in the absence of trade barriers and regulations, the profit margin and expenditure per innovation are constant. Trade barriers mean that, in addition to producing the good, the firm must devote resources to overcoming these barriers. A convenient way to capture this is to assume Samuelson's 'iceberg costs': trade barriers are viewed as 'melting' a certain fraction of

---

[1] Since I shall want to calibrate this model empirically to quantify the relevant magnitudes, I need to assume a particular relationship to fit to the data. Making standard assumptions about the intertemporal utility function, I obtain:

$$1 + g = (1 + \rho)^{-1} \, (\text{profitability of innovation})^{(\sigma/(1-\sigma))}$$

where g is the rate of output and consumption growth, ρ the rate of time preference (consumer impatience), and σ the elasticity of substitution between present and future consumption.

potential output. Let the profit margin including trade barriers be $(1 - T)$. In fact, we can include in T not merely the trade barriers but all the other costs of non-Europe.

We can now make more precise what goes into the determination of the profitability of innovation, which we know will crucially affect the growth potential of 1992.

$$\begin{pmatrix} \text{profitability} \\ \text{of} \\ \text{innovation} \end{pmatrix} = \begin{pmatrix} \text{profit margin net} \\ \text{of trade and} \\ \text{other barriers} \end{pmatrix} \begin{pmatrix} \text{resource} \\ \text{expenditure} \\ \text{per good} \end{pmatrix} \Big/ \begin{pmatrix} \text{fixed} \\ \text{R\&D} \\ \text{cost} \end{pmatrix} \qquad (4)$$

This relationship allows us to analyse the long-run growth effects of 1992. Any aspect of 1992 that affects the profitability of innovation can affect long-run growth.

Trade opening, arising from the removal of small non-tariff barriers, boosts profits by effectively increasing the size of the market over which R&D costs can be spread. It increases the net profit margin $(1 - T)$.

Fortress Europe, an increase in external protection, would tend to offset the liberalization of the internal market. Since EC exports are split roughly 50–50 between EC and non-EC countries, a tit-for-tat retaliation could entirely negate the market expansion effects of trade opening under 1992.

Pro-competitive effects, which are judged quite substantial by the European Commission, would tend to offset the growth effects of market expansion. They cause a fall in the net profit margin on innovation, and hence reduce savings and investment because the rate of return is reduced. However, we have sensible theories which show that extra competition might increase the incentive to innovate, and other sensible theories which show that it might further impede innovation. To date, empirical research has been unable conclusively to identify whether competition helps or hinders innovation.

Standardizing regulation might lower the fixed cost of innovation, most obviously in the innovation in new products. It will tend to increase profitability, and hence saving, investment and growth.

Finally, it is worth pointing out that, since innovations eventually become public knowledge, 1992 could lead to faster growth for countries outside the EC. In turn this would enlarge the market available for EC exporters, and might have second-round effects on EC growth.

5. Calibrating the growth effects of 1992

Empirical evaluation of the new growth models is inherently difficult for two reasons. First, there is no general agreement on which model to use. The tractable models focus only on one aspect of the scale economies-growth link. There are more complete models, such as Grossman and Helpman (1989); however, I have not been able to calibrate these. Second, much of the relevant data are unavailable, incomplete or unreliable. Moreover, many of the key aspects, such as the rate of dissemination of technology and the appropriability of innovation, are intrinsically unobservable.

I have no answer to the first problem. The calibration methodology helps with the second. This technique involves specifying a simple model, borrowing some estimates from the work of other researchers, and imputing the remaining parameters so that the theoretical relationships just fit a set of historical data. The calibrated model can then be used to simulate policy changes. Clearly this approach is far from satisfactory – for example we have no idea of the precision of the results – but at present it appears to be the only option.

5.1. Quantifying the medium-term growth bonus

Figure 1 showed that the initial static efficiency gain is augmented by a medium-run growth bonus: higher productivity and output raises savings and investment thereby raising the long-run capital-labour ratio. The size of this bonus depends on the curvature of the YY curve (what we have called $a + b$). Table 2 shows estimates of $(a + b)$ for several European economies taken from a variety of studies. Prior to the emergence of the new growth literature, it was widely assumed that $(a + b)$ was equal to capital's share of income (an implication of constant returns to scale and perfect competition). The first four rows of Table 2 show a number of estimates based on this assumption. Maddison (1987) takes 0.3 as the consensus estimate.

A number of researchers have attempted econometric estimates using industry data. This is widely interpreted as an effort to measure scale economies. As discussed, Caballero and Lyons (1989a) have done so for France, Germany, Belgium and the UK.[2] Since these are only estimates, I show the effect of increasing or decreasing their estimates by one standard error.

Table 3 uses the high and low Table 2 estimates (for each country) to compute the medium-run growth bonus. The most important point to emerge from Table 3 is that *all* estimates of the bonus are considerable. That is to say, by ignoring the indirect effect of 1992 on the steady-state capital-labour ratio, the Commission's figures significantly underestimate the total impact of 1992. We cannot determine the exact

---

[2] Caballero and Lyons (1989) have estimated scale economies (effectively estimates of $(1 + b)$) for various countries. To recover $(a + b)$ I multiply their estimates by capital's share of output.

Table 2. Estimates of the output capital elasticity ($a + b$)

Source	France	Germany	Netherlands	UK	Belgium
Denison (1967); Denison and Chung (1976)	0.23	0.26	0.26	0.22	
Maddison (1987)	0.31	0.30	0.30	0.26	
Kendrick (1981)	0.38	0.35		0.35	
Christensen, Cummins and Jorgenson (1980)	0.40	0.39	0.45	0.39	
Caballero and Lyons (1989)	0.37	0.48		0.34	0.43
minus 1 standard error	0.29	0.39		0.20	0.28
plus 1 standard error	0.44	0.57		0.48	0.58
Summary:					
low estimate	0.23	0.26	0.26	0.20	0.28
high estimate	0.44	0.57	0.45	0.48	0.58

Source: First four rows from Maddison (1987), fifth through seventh from Caballero and Lyons (1989a).

Table 3. The output increase from 1992 (static effect and medium-run bonus)

	France	Germany	Netherlands	UK	Belgium
medium-run bonus as % of static effect:					
low estimate	30	36	35	24	38
high estimate	80	129	124	93	136
medium-run effect: % increase in GDP					
low range	0.8–2.0	0.9–2.3	0.9–2.3	0.6–1.6	1.0–2.5
high range	2.0–5.2	3.2–8.4	3.1–8.1	2.3–6.0	3.4–8.9
total effect: static + medium-run, % increase in GDP					
low estimate	3.3–8.5	3.4–8.8	3.4–8.8	3.1–8.1	3.5–9.0
high estimate	4.5–11.7	5.7–14.9	5.6–14.2	5.8–12.5	5.9–25.4

Source: Author's calculations.

extent of this underestimation without knowing $(a + b)$ exactly. The first row in Table 3 represents a lower bound on the size of this indirect effect. Consequently we can conclude that the Commission's estimates of the economic benefits of 1992 are *at least* something like 30% too low. The high estimates of the bonus indicate that the Cecchini Report numbers should be more than doubled.

The Cecchini Report identified a static output gain of between 2.5 and 6.5% from 1992. To get the medium-run growth effect, this range of estimates must be multiplied by the range of the medium-run growth bonus. The third and fourth rows of Table 3 show the results. In all cases the medium-run growth effect is considerable. At a minimum, the induced rise in saving and capital accumulation will boost UK output by a further 0.6%. At a maximum, it will boost output in Germany, the Netherlands and Belgium by over 8%. The centre of this range implies that the medium-run growth effect is about the same order of magnitude as the static effect estimated in the Cecchini Report. Loosely, we could say 1992 will have about twice as big an output effect as previously anticipated.

To emphasize the sensitivity of these estimates, I calculate what would be implied if the new growth theory is much closer to being correct than the above estimates imply. In the spirit of Figure 2, I simply explained the historical rise in output per head by increases in labour and capital inputs with no time tend to reflect technological progress. I obtained a central estimate of 0.975 for $(a+b)$, which of course is much higher than the estimates embodied in Tables 2 and 3. Simple arithmetic confirms that the medium-run growth bonus would then be 38 times the size of the original static increase in output! This is not a realistic estimate, but it does serve to establish an upper bound.

Even if the bonus is much smaller, say of the order of magnitude implied in Table 3, one should ask how long it might plausibly take for the economy to reach the new long-run equilibrium. Equation (1) can be used not just to calculate the new long-run equilibrium but also to quantify the speed of dynamic adjustment. Taking the depreciation rate d as 12% and $(a+b)$ between 0.3 and 0.5, half the adjustment would be achieved within 8–12 years. The medium run will last a long time. Notice this means that, even after the event, it will be difficult for a long time to distinguish between medium-run effects of 1992, which eventually tail off, and permanent effects on the growth rate.

5.1.1. The plausibility of the medium-run bonus. The estimates of Table 3 depend both on the Commission's estimate of the static effect and on the capital-output elasticity $(a+b)$. How plausible is the Cecchini Reports's range? Let's look at estimates of other trade liberalizations. The Tokyo Round tariff cuts reduced *ad valorem* tariffs by 7 percentage points (Harris and Cox, 1982). The removal of hundreds of small non-tariff barriers within Europe under 1992 might have a roughly equivalent effect, certainly no greater. Deardorff and Stern (1979, 1981) estimate that the Tokyo Round increased world GNP by one-tenth of 1%. Brown and Whalley (1980) put the gain at 1.6% of world output. The Commission's estimates for 1992 are massively larger. However, the earlier studies did not allow for static gains due to industry-level scale economies which are the source of much of the Commission's estimated gains. Such scale economies are, however, included in the seminal work of Harris and Cox (1982) who estimate that a move to free trade with all trading partners would increase Canadian GNP by 8.6%.

In summary, if one made the mistake of viewing 1992 merely as a trade liberalization, the high side of the Commission's range would appear unjustified. Intra-EC trade accounts for only half total EC trade, and this trade is already substantially liberalized. Nevertheless, the readily observable behaviour of EC and non-EC firms indicates that those at the cutting edge believe that 1992 will have large effects. In addition, it is probably more important to view 1992 as a massive market liberalization *and* deregulation rather than as a mere trade liberalization. From this perspective, the Cecchini Report range seems more plausible.

Another revealing source of market expansion estimates comes from survey data reported in European Commission (1988a). Firms were asked to quantify the overall effect of 1992 on unit costs for the firm's main product line. On average firms felt the completion of the internal market would lower unit costs by 2%. In principle, this would allow output to rise by 2% if current input levels can be sustained. In the same survey, firms expected sales to increase on average by 5% after 1992. If all firms expand together, output might rise by something on the order of 5%. Thus the survey data gives a 2–5% range, which is similar to the Cecchini range.

5.2. Long-term growth effects of 1992

So far I have been discussing effects that eventually fade away. Now I want to turn to permanent changes in the growth rate. To compare the two, we need a common measuring stick. The concept of discounted income serves this role well. Suppose ρ is the discount rate and g the initial growth rate. It is easy to show that a 1% gain of the type measured by the European Commission increases discounted income by 1%. In contrast, if the growth rate rises by one percentage point, discounted income is boosted by $(1/(\rho - g))\%$. Taking ρ as 5% and the initial growth rate as 1.8%, we see that an extra percentage point of growth for ever is equivalent to a once-off GDP rise of 31.25%. To put it differently, a rise in the growth rate of 0.16% would have the same impact as a 5% once-and-forever output gain.

5.2.1. Calibrating the Romer model.
Equation (2) presents the simplest version of the Romer model which assumes a constant labour force. Taking the static increase in output implied by the Cecchini range and a savings rate of approximately 10%, Equation (2) implies that, if the Romer model is correct, 1992 will increase the growth rate by between

one-quarter and three-quarters of one percentage point. Converting this back into its equivalent as a once-off gain in discounted income, it would be worth between about 8 and 24% in extra discounted income.

These formulae assume a constant labour input. In fact it is possible to generalize the model to allow for changes in labour input. I calibrate the more general model in Appendix B. I then obtain an increase in the estimated growth rate of between 0.28 and 0.92 percentage points, or between 9 and 29% in discounted extra income. This is little different from the simpler model's results, since EC labour input has been fairly constant during the last decade.

5.2.2. Calibrating the endogenous innovations model. This model, summarized in Footnote 1 and Equation (4), relies on larger markets to spread the fixed costs of R&D, thereby raising the return on innovation. The extent to which this raises saving and investment depends on σ, the extent to which current consumption is a substitute for future consumption. Hall (1988) summarizes evidence on this substitutability and concludes that it is low. This reflects the stylized fact that aggregate savings rates are unresponsive to changes in the real rate of return. I shall take σ to equal 0.1.

In addition to the static effects of 1992 discussed earlier, harmonizing industrial regulation may affect the profitability of innovation by reducing the cost of developing new products. The only direct estimate I could find is that for European pharmaceuticals in the EC report *The Economics of 1992* (1988a) which estimates cost savings at between half and four-fifths of 1%. I add this to the direct static effect to obtain an estimate, admittedly very crude, of the effect of 1992 on the profitability of innovation.

On this basis, I calculate that 1992 will add between about 0.3 and 0.8 percentage points to the permanent growth rate. Again these can be expressed in equivalents of a once-off increase in output: between about a 10 and a 25% increase.

5.3. Adding up the output effects

Lastly, how should we add up these various effects? The direct static effects are at the base of all the numbers so they should always be added in. After this we have to hedge. Not all the effects are consistent (due to the lack of a consensus model). In the end we get three different ranges of the total effect (static plus dynamic). If $(a + b)$ is less than one, we get the medium-term growth bonus. We obviously cannot add to this the long-term growth bonus predicted by the model when $(a + b)$ equals one. Consequently if $(a + b)$ is actually less than one, the total effect will be something like twice the size of the Cecchini Report's estimates, namely 5 to 13%. The static part of this would be spread over the five to seven years following the completion of the internal market. As for the medium-run growth bonus, it would take about 10 years for half this effect to be realized.

If Romer or the endogenous innovation model are right, 1992 could permanently raise Europe's growth rate. To get both static and growth effects into one number we must focus on 1992's impact on the discounted sum of EC income. (Recall that this has the nice property that a one per cent static increase in GDP raises the discounted income by one per cent. Thus we can directly compare our ranges to the Cecchini Report's range.) Using this measure, 1992 is estimated to increase discounted income by between 11 and 35% (adding the static 2.5 to 6.5% to the dynamic 9 to 29% from the Romer model). Thus according to this model, by ignoring dynamic effects, the Cecchini Report range underestimates the true impact of 1992 by approximately 450%. Finally, if the endogenous innovations model is right the range is 13 to 33%, so the EC numbers are about 350% too low.

These numbers from the long-term growth effects are certainly bigger than the Cecchini Report's range of 2.5 to 6.5%. Are they believable? The answer must certainly be yes, if 1992 does indeed change the long-term growth rate in Europe. Even tiny growth effects easily dwarf static effects. However, the estimates of the long-term growth effects were based on models that have a long way to go before they become part of the received wisdom of economics. Therefore, the specific numbers may very well prove to be way off the mark. However, even leaving aside these exploratory models, we still have the medium-term growth bonus. This rests on well accepted principles. The only controversy is on the importance of scale economies at the economy-wide level. The low end assumes constant returns. The high end of the range requires substantial economies of scale at the aggregate level. An increasing number of economists agree that these are important; however it should be said that there are still many dissenters.

6. Conclusions

By focusing exclusively on the static effects of 1992, previous studies of 1992 have seriously underestimated its economic impact. My analysis suggests that simply taking account of the medium-run growth effect would roughly double the Cecchini estimates of 1992's impact on EC income, and might add considerably more. I expect roughly half of the medium-run growth effect to be realized in the first 10 years after the completion of the internal market.

More tentatively, my findings suggest that 1992 might permanently add between one-quarter and nine-tenths of one percentage point to the EC growth rate. Certainly, the high side of this range seems to require more than the usual suspension of disbelief. Given the exploratory nature of the new growth theory (on which the growth numbers are based), I make no claim as to the precision of the estimates. Nevertheless, an important conclusion emerges. The most important impact of 1992 may well be its growth effects, not its static effect on resource allocation. This paper shows that it is possible to quantify, at least roughly, several types of dynamic effects of the 1992 liberalization. Dynamic effects may still be poorly understood. They are not, however, impossible to measure.

Hopefully, the estimates I have presented here shed enough light on the quantitative importance of growth effects to suggest that it is time to start looking for the wallet where we suspect it is – not where the light is the brightest.

Discussion

Pierre-Andre Chiappori
DELTA, Paris

The paper presented by Richard Baldwin raises an interesting point: 1992 may, in addition to the static gains already mentioned elsewhere, have a positive effect upon long-term growth rates in the EC. Baldwin argues rightly that such long-term consequences, though rather difficult to estimate in a precise way, may well exceed all the once-and-for-all benefits that have been extensively analysed so far. I am quite sympathetic to this view. I do believe, for instance, that the existence of the EC had had, during the last 35 years, a non-negligible impact upon growth rates in Europe. If economists, in the early 1950s, had tried to estimate the consequences of the European Market from a purely static viewpoint, the benefits would have been significantly underestimated.

The theoretical question is whether (and through what mechanism) a one-time efficiency gain can significantly affect long-term growth. Such effects are excluded by classical growth theory; economy-wide increasing returns to scale have to be invoked to rule out the traditional convergence toward a 'natural' steady growth path. Unsurprisingly, Baldwin refers at that point to the so called 'new growth theory' to support his claim. Two models are presented in this line. The first model assumes a traditional Cobb–Douglas technology with economy-wide increasing returns to scale, while the second elaborates on the idea that increased market size may lower the cost of innovation, hence boosting growth in the long run.

According to the first model, the dynamics of capital accumulation are given by:

$$K_{t+1} = (1-d)K_t + sjL_t^{1-a}K_t^{a+b}$$

Since Baldwin is essentially concerned with long-term effects, it is natural to investigate the asymptotic properties of this system. The problem is that the dynamics involved are rather tricky. Assume, for simplicity, that labour supply is constant in the long run – not an unrealistic assumption, after all. The system's properties essentially depend on whether the parameter $a+b$ is under or above 1. The case $a+b<1$ is illustrated in Figure A1. Unsurprisingly, K_t converges to some long-term equilibrium level K^*; as a consequence, the GNP growth rate tends to zero. Obviously, no static efficiency gain can modify this conclusion: the growth benefits of any institutional innovation must vanish in the long run. Of course, the result might be different, should some exogenous productivity trend be introduced; but the effects of trade policies upon the trend would then become crucial, and would consequently require modelling explicitly.

Consider, now, the case $a+b>1$. Figure A2 shows that, for a sufficiently high initial stock, capital – and hence GNP – will grow more than exponentially. As a consequence, the GNP growth rate will tend to infinity. Here, though a one-time efficiency gain may actually boost real growth, the exact status of this conclusion is not clear, since growth is unbounded in any case; clearly a diverging model is not the right tool for analysing the long-term behaviour of the economy.

The last case, which Baldwin uses to calculate Romer's long-run growth bonus, is $a+b=1$. Then the economy grows at a constant rate,

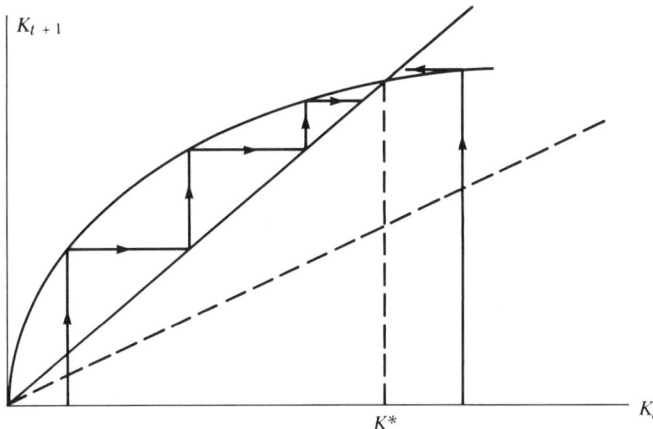

Figure A1. Convergence with $a+b<1$

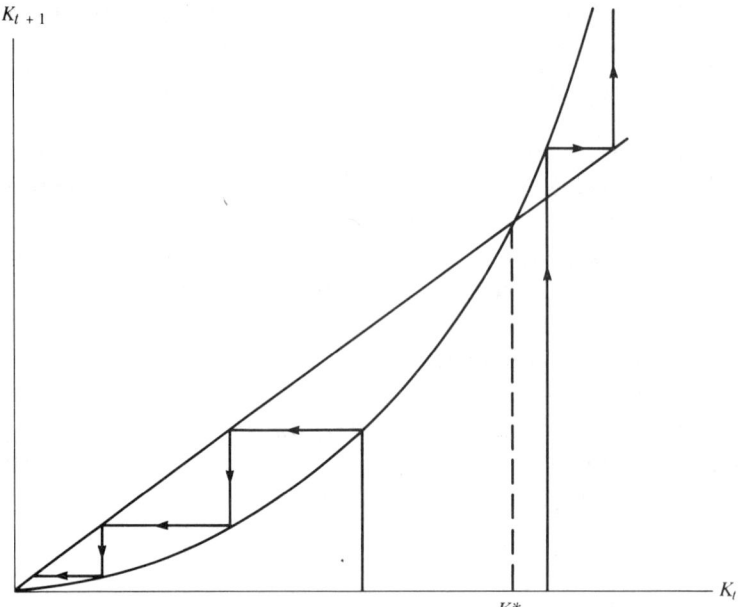

Figure A2. Divergence with $a + b > 1$

equal to $(sjL^{1-a} - d)$; in particular, any gain in efficiency (say, a higher j) will increase long-term growth. The problem is that this case is non-generic. The dynamic system defined by (1) *bifurcates* at $a + b = 1$; hence, if the real value of $a + b$ is either $1 - \varepsilon$ or $1 + \varepsilon$, with ε arbitrarily small, growth rates will tend respectively to zero or to infinity. In other words, the assumption implicitly made here is not that $a + b$ is *approximately* equal to one (which might perhaps be an acceptable hypothesis), but that it is *exactly* equal to one. This kind of miracle is quite difficult to believe in and the point sheds doubt upon the robustness of the conclusion.

I have fewer problems with model 2, the micro foundations of which are much sounder. Here, the amount invested in R&D exactly reflects the willingness of agents to postpone their consumption. Should an increase in market size reduce unit costs, this would boost innovation, hence real growth.

How 1992 affects incentives to innovate will depend not just on how it affects unit costs but also on how it affects market structure. Greater competition may reduce average profit margins, which might be thought to reduce incentives to innovate. But this conclusion may be based on a confusion of average and marginal. Even if profits on average are lower, the marginal return on innovation need not be reduced. Being the only competitor in a race can hardly be seen as an incentive to run fast, even with higher prizes. After all, a (non-contestable) monopoly that does not invest in R&D will simply lose opportunities of making more money, whereas a non-investing competitive firm will be turned out of the market. A number of micro models of R&D investment actually suggest that competitive pressures typically boost, rather than dampen, innovation, for several reasons. The optimal innovation pace of a monopolist may be quite low, but will accelerate under the threat that actual (or potential) competitors may reach the patent first. R&D expenditures of new entrants are often higher than those of existing firms. Also, the innovation process may require a variety of different lines to be independently pursued, only a few of them being eventually fruitful; and, of course, the natural selection mechanisms associated with competition are in general needed to eliminate inefficient innovators. In the same way, several historical studies have shown that most innovations, in the long run, are due to small firms belonging to a competitive fringe rather than to major oligopolies (see the recent book by Francois Caron on the innovation process in France). Lastly, even if monopolies could be more efficient in *producing* innovation, they may well be socially less efficient in *using* the corresponding patents; monopolies also have dynamical welfare costs. Hence, I would believe that the pro-competitive effects of 1992, if any, are more likely to *favour* real growth in the long run – in which case the results are probably underestimated.

Anthony Venables
University of Southampton

Completion of the internal market is essentially a one-off set of institutional changes, so it is not surprising that most economic analyses of its effects have used comparative static techniques. This paper studies how a one-off change might have continuing dynamic effects. For such a change to lead to continuing economic growth, it must affect either the rate of capital accumulation in the economy, or the rate of technical change. This paper develops two models, one to deal with each of these possibilities.

Baldwin's treatment of capital accumulation can be understood by reference to the simplest of growth models. Abstract for the moment from depreciation. The rate of growth of the capital stock is equal by identity to the savings ratio times the output-capital ratio. Baldwin obtains estimates of the savings ratio (which he assumes constant) and of the output-capital ratio. He then takes the output expansion effects of 1992 as estimated in the Cecchini report and assumes that this extra output can be produced without any increase in the capital stock, so giving an increase in the output-capital ratio. Inserting these numbers into the growth identity gives an estimate of the increase in the rate of growth of the capital stock, and this increased rate of growth of capital stock feeds into production, raising the rate of growth of per capita income.

Much emphasis is placed in the paper on the contribution of economy-wide increasing returns to scale, but it is important to note that the story so far is independent of assumptions about economy-wide returns to scale. The force initiating extra growth is not some interaction between increasing returns and market enlargement, but merely the savings implications of the Cecchini output estimates. However, with constant returns to scale, the increased rate of growth of capital stock would translate into capital deepening and convergence to a new steady state. There would be extra growth, but it would not continue indefinitely. The role of economy-wide increasing returns to scale is to permit the increment in the rate of growth to be larger for longer. Indeed, in the Romer model the social marginal product of capital is a constant, regardless of the economy's capital stock. Growth is then sustainable in perpetuity, and the increment to output growth is (after minor adjustment for changes in the labour force) equal to the increased rate of growth of capital stock discussed above.

It is worth remarking how sensitive Baldwin's estimates are to assumptions about the savings ratio. Changes of one or two points in this ratio could easily dominate the other effects discussed. The assumption that it is constant is justified by appeal to the steady-state solution in the Appendices, where it is determined by the rate of depreciation. But changes in the short to medium run could still have important effects on the overall growth bonus. And *a priori* 1992 seems to me just as likely to change savings behaviour (by affecting either preferences or depreciation) as to affect the capital-output ratio.

The second model contained in the paper analyses growth by endogenizing the resources devoted to R&D. Demand for R&D depends on the private returns to the activity. Supply of resources for R&D depends on the willingness of consumers to forgo present consumption. Putting this together gives an equation linking the rate of growth of the economy to the private rate of return on R&D projects. There are several problems with this model. One concerns the rudimentary modelling of the supply of R&D. Essentially, consumption can be transformed into R&D at a fixed rate, and furthermore, the *only* way the economy can postpone consumption is by investing in R&D. The supply of R&D therefore depends only on parameters of the consumer's utility function. I think that a richer structure would have been desirable here. A second problem concerns the goods market equilibrium. It appears that the model has price competition, trade barriers, and the same unit costs everywhere, except for firms that have innovated in the last period. If this is so then there is no international trade going on, except by the firms who have just innovated.

Given the equation linking the private rate of return on R&D to the growth rate, the next question is, what is the effect of 1992 on the rate of return on R&D? The model is structured such that each firm that innovates succeeds with certainty, and the innovation affects a fixed share of total consumption. Since both the probability of success and the market share of a successful innovation are assumed fixed and unchanged by 1992, the most significant positive contribution 1992 makes to the rate of return is by increasing *total* EC consumption. Baldwin feeds in the Cecchnini estimates to quantify this effect. It seems to me that this does not adequately capture the possible effects of 1992 on the return to R&D. There may be mergers of European firms, joint research ventures, or less duplication of national research effort. Each of these would either increase the probability of a research project succeeding (or winning the patent race), or mean that a successful research effort would reach a larger *share* of the market. I would expect this to have a much greater effect on the private return to innovation than would growth in the EC market as a whole. But these effects seem to be precluded in the construction of the model which Baldwin uses.

I am particularly sceptical about the results of this second model. In applied work it is essential that the model employed gives an intuitively acceptable description of the economy as we all observe it. The second model described in this paper may be an elegant way of building a growth model based on R&D, but it is not rich enough to capture the policy change which it is trying to study.

General discussion

Several panellists thought that the paper exaggerated its criticisms of earlier growth models. Victor Norman said that Baldwin sounded like Nicholas Kaldor 30 years ago. But it was hard to see why the presence of economy-wide scale economies would be a more convincing explanation of the rough constancy of the capital-output ratio than were (say) vintage capital models. Charlie Bean agreed, and said there was a fundamental identification problem. Jim Mirrlees was not convinced by the model's central claim that the long-run growth rate would be sensitive to the savings rate. For this to be true required $(a + b) = 1$, but there was no reason to think that economies of scale would be precisely of the magnitude necessary to generate this result. Measured productivity growth might be generated partly by scale economies and partly by a time trend. Edmond Malinvaud agreed that earlier theories had been misrepresented. Economy-wide scale economies had been recognised in the growth-accounting literature, though he believed Denison had over-estimated them.

Discussion turned to other means by which static income gains could have lasting growth effects. Georges de Menil though European integration could increase the economies' flexibility in responding to external shocks. Horst Siebert pointed to reductions in entry barriers, and to the associated stimulus to innovation. Lars Calmfors though that divergences between private and social returns to innovation were the main impediment to growth; he hoped that the EC would be able to avoid excessive regulation that would prevent these returns from being realized. He was struck by the disparity between the modest static gains that had been estimated as accruing from the 1992 programme, and the large public interest in the Single Market; only sustained increases in growth rates could reconcile the two. Manfred Neumann thought income gains would not be the only significant benefits to European citizens: they would also have greater freedom to move around the Community and to work where they chose.

The question was raised whether the Single Market would really raise the contestability of European industry to any significant degree. Luigi Spaventa remarked on the high current rate of mergers and acquisitions in Europe. Colin Mayer suggested that the available evidence cast doubt on there being major unexploited scale economies; on the contrary, there were often managerial diseconomies, and diseconomies arising from the actions of governments. Horst Siebert emphasized that the degree of contestability would depend on the nature of government regulation.

In conclusion, Richard Baldwin accepted that some technical progress was certainly exogenous and not due merely to scale economies; indeed, a consensus model might well have $(a + b)$ less than one. However, he said it was very hard to obtain evidence about the prevalence of economy-wide scale economies. One could not conclude that these were unimportant on the basis of firm-level studies.

Appendix A. A formal model and the medium-run growth bonus

The analysis of Figure 1 and Equation (1) made two simplifying assumptions: a constant savings rates s (and hence a constant ratio of gross investment to output), and the representation of the static effect of 1992 as a proportional shift in the output function. Whilst a constant savings rate may be plausible in the steady state, we may wish to allow both for adjustment dynamics and for the dependence of s on 1992 itself. The second assumption obscures relative price effects which are potentially important. The latter assumption will be correct in a broad class of well-specified models since the *ad valorem* tariff equivalents of many types of trade barriers enter multiplicatively into the first-order conditions of firms. I turn now to such a model which is based on Baldwin (1989).

A.1. The basic model

Since trade is already substantially free within the EC, I model the EC as a single goods market. The 1992 programme is interpreted as a general market liberalization rather than specifically a trade liberalization.

A.1.1. Technology and endowments. There is a constant labour supply L. There are N types of goods produced according to identical technologies. In each period firms incur fixed labour costs f to manufacture at all. A firm can then produce according to: $x_{it} = A_t K_{it}^a L_{it}^{1-a}$ where x_{it} is a representative firm's output of good i in period t and K_{it} and L_{it} are the amounts of variable inputs used. A_t is the total factor productivity in the economy which evolves according to $A_t = K_t^b B_t$ where $B_t = B_{t-1}(1+\eta)$. Thus B represents the productivity effect of basic scientific knowledge, evolving as a time trend. Firms take A_t and η as given.

Sticking as closely as possible to the Solow growth model, where investment is simply forgone consumption, we suppose output can be transformed directly into capital. A unit of capital requires some of each of the N goods: the gross amount of new capital created from output goods is $\prod_{i=1}^{N} I_i^{(1/N)}$ where I_i is the amount of good i used as an input for capital goods. Capital produced this period cannot be used till next period.

A.1.2. Preferences. Consumers have identical preferences summarized by

$$U = \sum_{t=0}^{\infty} \left(\frac{1}{1+\rho}\right)^t \left(\frac{1}{1-(1/\sigma)}\right) (u(c_{1t}, \ldots, c_{Nt}))^{1-(1/\sigma)} \tag{A1}$$

where $u(c_{1t}, \ldots, c_{Nt}) = \prod_{i=1}^{N} (c_{it})^{1/N}$

where ρ is the constant discount rate, σ the intertemporal elasticity of substitution, and c_{it} the consumption of good i in period t.

A.2. Within-period equilibrium

Taking as given that the representative consumer finds it optimal in period t to set expenditure at E_t, the optimal within-period expenditure pattern is to divide E_t equally among the N goods. With an income Y_t, the consumer's demand for new capital goods (the only store of value) is $Y_t - E_t$. The consumer demand for a typical good is $c_{it} = (p_{it})^{-1}(E_t/N)$ and investment demand is $I_{it} = (p_{it})^{-1}(Y_t - E_t)/N$. Aggregate demand, faced by firms, is the sum of these two demand curves.

Firms are price-takers in factor markets, and play period-by-period Cournot in the goods market. The typical firm faces a series of static problems:

$$\operatorname*{Max}_{q_{it}, K_{it}, L_{it}} (p_{it}q_{it} - w_t L_{it} - r_t K_{it} - w_t f) \text{ subject to}$$

$$q_{it} = x_{it}(1+\mu)^{-1} = A_t K_{it}^a L_{it}^{1-a}(1+\mu)^{-1} \tag{A2}$$

where q_{it} is the representative firm's sales, x_{it} its output, r the rental on capital, w the wage rate, and p the output price. μ measures what the EC Commission (1988b) calls the costs of non-Europe (the whole gamut of 'red tape' barriers, redundant regulation, and X-inefficiency). Since μ measures frictional barriers it does not generate revenue or any kind of directly appropriable rents. It simply 'melts' part of output, driving a wedge between output and income.

Firms play Cournot with m other symmetric firms (m determined by free entry) producing good i. The first-order conditions with respect to capital and labour are:

$$r_t = (a/K_{it})(1 - m^{-1})A_t K_{it}^a L_{it}^{1-a}(1+\mu)^{-1}$$

$$w_t = ((1-a)/L_{it})(1 - m^{-1})A_t K_{it}^a L_{it}^{1-a}(1+\mu)^{-1} \tag{A3}$$

Firms enter up to the point at which m is such that the marginal firm's markup over marginal costs just covers the average fixed cost, which implies that the number of firms m solves

$$m^2(w_t f) = (1 + \mu(1-m))(Y_t/N) \tag{A4}$$

If $\mu = 0$ this simplifies to $m = (Y_t/(Nw_t f))^{1/2}$. It is easy to show that m rises as μ falls. How does m change over time? If Y and w grow at the same rate, the number of firms m is invariant. I will show this is the case.

Aggregating across firms' first-order conditions

$$r_t K_t = a(1 - m^{-1})(1+\mu)^{-1}p_t X_t$$

$$w_t(L - mNf) = (1-a)(1 - m^{-1})(1+\mu)^{-1}p_t X_t \tag{A5}$$

where $X_t = \sum_{i=1}^{N} (m x_{it})$ and p_t is the common price of all goods, which I will set equal to 1. Output is divided among rental income, wage income of variable labour, wage income of fixed labour, and the wastage.

Aggregate income Y_t is the sum of $w_t(L - mNf)$, $r_t K_t$, and $w_t mNf$. Aggregate investment is $I_t = Y_t - C_t$ where $C_t = \sum c_{it}$. We also get an exact relationship between aggregate income Y_t, the factors of production, and technology: $Y_t = (1 + \mu)^{-1} A_t K_t^a (L - mNf)^{1-a}$. Lastly, we have an exact capital accumulation equation $K_t = K_{t-1} + Y_t - C_t$.

A.3. The steady-state, balanced growth path

Consumption and output will grow at a common rate g. The intertemporal allocation of expenditure must therefore satisfy

$$\frac{\partial U / \partial C_t}{\partial U / \partial C_{t+1}} = (1 + \rho)(C_{t+1}/C_t)^{1/\sigma} = (1 + \rho)(1 + g)^{1/\sigma} = (1 + r^*) \tag{A6}$$

where r^* is the steady-state real interest rate (a constant). Together with the first-order condition for capital, the constant real interest rate implies that the capital-labour ratio is constant on the steady-state path. Thus $\dot{K}/K = \dot{Y}/Y = g$ and from the aggregate output function

$$g = \dot{Y}/Y = \dot{K}/K = \eta/(1 - a - b) \tag{A7}$$

Note that the steady-state growth rate depends only on the capital-output elasticity $(a + b)$ and the exogenous growth rate of basic science η. In particular it is not affected by 1992 policy as measured by μ.

The capital accumulation equation and the fact that investment is proportional to income on the steady-state path imply $\dot{K}/K = \psi(Y/K)$ where ψ is a factor of proportionality. The first-order condition for K can then be used to derive the steady-state capital-output ratio (K^*/Y^*)

$$\psi = g(K^*/Y^*) = (a + b)\left(\frac{1 - m^{-1}}{r^*}\right)\left(\frac{\eta}{1 - a - b}\right) \tag{A8}$$

Thus the balanced growth path is characterized by (g, r^*, ψ). It is easily checked that the growth rate of w is

$$\dot{w}/w = \dot{A}/A + a\dot{K}/K = \dot{g} \tag{A9}$$

confirming that Y and w grow at the same rate, whence the number of firms m is constant along the balanced growth path.

Appendix B. The Romer model with a variable labour input

Imposing the Romer assumption that $(a + b) = 1$, the output function is $Y = AKL^{1-a}$ where A is a constant describing total factor productivity which will be increased by the static effect of 1992. Assume labour L grows at n per annum. Saving sY equals gross investment, and with a depreciation rate d next period's capital stock $K_{+1} = K(1-d) + sY = K(1-d) + sAKL^{1-a}$. Hence we obtain

$$(1+g) = (1-d+sAL^{1-a})(1+n)^{(1-a)} \tag{B1}$$

where g is the rate of output growth. In the model of the text, $n = 0$ and we recover $g = -d + s(Y/K)$.

To calibrate the more general model (B1) I proceed as follows. The depreciation rate d is taken to be 12% based on Maddison (1987) who reports this as the average for France, Germany, the Netherlands, Italy, and the UK. From the OECD *Employment Outlook* I calculate the growth rate of hours worked in the EC (minus 0.77% per annum) as the estimate of n. Suspending reservations about Romer's empirical work, I adopt his estimate of 0.32 for the value of $(1-a)$ in Romer (1987) – note that this makes a considerably larger than I have assumed elsewhere in the text. The growth of EC output is set at 1.8% per annum, its average during 1980–1987. In principle I could get separate estimates of L and s but since it is sAL^{1-a} that enters Equation (B1) I simply choose the value for sAL^{1-a} which makes Equation (B1) hold for the borrowed parameter estimates (d, g, a, n).

The implications of this calibration of the Romer model are discussed in Section 5.2 of the text.

References

Baldwin, R. (1989). 'Measurable Dynamic Gains from Trade', working paper.

Baldwin, R. and P. Krugman (1987). 'Market access and international competition: a simulation study of 16K RAM', in R. C. Feenstra (ed.), *Empirical Methods for International Trade*, MIT Press.

Brown, F. and J. Whalley (1980). 'General Equilibrium Evaluations of Tariff-Cutting Proposals in the Tokyo Round and Comparisons with More Extensive Liberalisation of World Trade', *Economic Journal*.

Caballero, R. and R. Lyons (1989a). 'Increasing Returns and Imperfect Competition in European Industry', Columbia University working paper.

—— (1989b). 'The Role of External Economies in US Manufacturing', Columbia University working paper.

Cecchini Report (1988). *The European Challenge 1992*, Gower.

Deardorff, A. and R. Stern (1979). 'An Economic Analysis of the Effects of the Tokyo Round of MLN on the US and Other Major Industrialized Countries', MTM study, US Senate.

Denison, E. (1985). *Trends in American Economic Growth* 1929–82, Brookings Institution, Washington DC.

Dixit, A. (1987). 'Optimal Trade and Industrial Policy for the US Automobile Industry', in R. C. Feenstra (ed), *Empirical Methods for International trade*, MIT Press.

Emerson, M., with M. Aujean, M. Catinat, P. Goybet and A. Jacquemin (1988). 'The Economics of 1992', *European Economy*.

EC Commission (1988a). 'The Economics of 1992'. *European Economy*.

—— (1988b). 'The Cost of Non-Europe: Basic Findings', EC Document.

Grossman, G. and E. Helpman (1988a). 'Product Development and International Trade', Princeton University Working Paper.

—— (1988b). 'Endogenous Product Cycles', Discussion Paper in Economics 144, Princeton University.

—— (1989). 'Comparative Advantage and Long Run Growth', NBER working paper 2809.

Hall, R. (1988). 'Intertemporal Substitution in Consumption', *Journal of Political Economy*.

Harris, R. and R. Cox (1982). *Trade, Industrial Policy and Canadian Manufacturing*, Ontario Economic Council.

Krugman, P. (1988). 'Endogenous Innovations, International Trade and Growth', Working Paper presented at SUNY–Buffalo conference on development.

Maddison, A. (1982). *Phases of Capitalist Growth*, Oxford University Press.

—— (1987). 'Growth and Slowdown in Advanced Capitalist Economies', *Journal of Economic Literature*.

Romer, P. (1983). 'Dynamic Competitive Equilibria with Externalities, Increasing Returns and Unbounded Growth'. PhD thesis, University of Chicago.

—— (1986). 'Increasing Returns and Long Run Growth', *Journal of Political Economy*.

—— (1987a). 'Crazy Explanations for the Productivity Slowdown', *NBER Annual*.

—— (1987b). 'Growth Based on Increasing Returns to Scale Due to Specialization', *American Economic Review*.

Shleifer, A. (1986). 'Implementation Cycles', *Journal of Political Economy*.

Young, A. (1928). 'Increasing Returns and Economic Progress', *Economic Journal*.

Economic Policy   October 1989   Printed in Great Britain

Deregulating European airlines

Francis McGowan and Paul Seabright

Summary

One of the industries with the greatest potential to benefit from the Single European Market is civil aviation, which has been highly regulated by European governments. The deregulation of civil aviation in the US since the late 1970s has provided valuable evidence about the nature of the airline industry and its response to the liberalization of conditions of entry by new carriers. We examine the US experience and look at the changing regulatory framework for the European industry. We also consider the main sources of market failure in air transport. The lessons of the US experience are threefold. First, deregulation can in principle produce major gains to consumers without damaging the long-run profitability of carriers, by reducing the high costs of operation of European airlines. Second, congestion problems, especially the availability of landing slots at airports, need to be managed effectively to prevent incumbent carriers squeezing out new entrants: we recommend a system of slot auctions to achieve this. Third, in spite of relatively low sunk costs of entry to the industry, there remain significant opportunities for the exercise of market power by incumbent carriers. Deregulation of entry needs, therefore, to be supplemented by a vigorous competition policy, especially with regard to the approval of mergers.

Deregulating European airlines

Francis McGowan and Paul Seabright

University of Sussex and University of Cambridge

1. Introduction

Previous experience provides very little basis for assessing the likely impact of developments of the magnitude of the Single European Market. Scheduled air transport is one of the few industries in which there has been anything even remotely in the nature of a rehearsal for 1992. The deregulation of civil aviation in the US since the late 1970s, though taking place in circumstances rather different from those of Europe, has yielded valuable lessons about the potential benefits of a more open and unified market, as well as some of the risks implicit in a comprehensive abandonment of economic regulation.

These lessons are of broader application than to air transport alone, even granted the major differences between the deregulation of a particular sector and the liberalization of trade within an entire region. Specifically, it has become evident that, even when industry sunk costs appear comparatively low, the removal of artificial entry barriers is only a first step in the process of making markets more competitive. The nature of the Single European Market by the year 2002 will depend not just upon the degree of entry by firms into new markets, but also on the degree of exit as a result of subsequent battles. If market power on a national scale is not simply to give way to market power on an

We should like to thank Nicholas Argyris of the Competition Directorate at the European Commission, Tom Bass of the Civil Aviation Authority and Frederik Sorensen of the Transport Directorate at the European Commission, for extremely helpful advice and information. Nicholas Argyris, David Begg, John Black, David Newbery and David Thompson made valuable comments on an earlier draft. George Bulkley, Paul Klemperer and Michael Levine gave us copies of articles or advice on particular points. Many panel members of *Economic Policy* made suggestions beyond those recorded in the printed discussion. We are grateful also to Carlo Cardilli for research assistance and to the Department of Applied Economics, University of Cambridge, for contributions towards research expenses. The usual disclaimer applies.

international scale, it is important that direct regulation of entry be replaced by an informed and vigorous competition policy.[1]

This paper is in two parts. The first notes developments in the reform of civil aviation regulation in the US and the EC. It assesses the experience of US airline deregulation, examining especially the way in which initial market entry by new carriers has been succeeded by a period of consolidation through exit and merger that has significantly increased concentration once again. Deregulation has, nevertheless, brought substantial benefits so far, but these may have been limited by the absence of a firm policy to regulate anti-competitive behaviour, including mergers. Such consolidation could even lead to a significant erosion of the benefits to date. We consider how far the lessons of the US experience are applicable to Europe, and look at the evolving regulatory framework for the European industry. We examine where the benefits of deregulation in Europe will come from, offering evidence that European airlines have high costs relative to those in the US, due particularly to high rents to labour and high levels of overhead costs.

Whether the consolidation of the US industry has disturbing implications for Europe depends on how 'contestable' is the market for air transport; that is, on the extent to which potential as well as actual competition constrains the exercise of market power. The second part of the paper addresses this and related questions by asking on what grounds the air transport industry requires regulation at all. It examines the sources of market failure in the industry, concluding that, in spite of claims to the contrary, there are substantial opportunities for the exercise of market power by incumbent carriers. Furthermore, regulatory policies to deal with other causes of market failure – such as congestion externalities, and asymmetries of information in computer reservation systems (CRS) – have important implications for the extent to which abuses of market power are possible. For example, different mechanisms for allocating airspace or airport landing slots can operate to different degrees in favour of incumbents. It follows that the design of regulation mechanisms must tackle the different forms of market failure in an integrated manner. We conclude with a series of recommendations about regulation design.

2. Regulatory reform in the US and Europe

Since the 1970s, the regulation of civil aviation in many countries has come under increasing scrutiny. The rules governing the industry's

---

[1] This point is emphasized in Smith and Venables' (1988) assessment of the welfare benefits of completing the single market.

conduct for the last 40 years were originally intended to ensure a safe, reliable and inexpensive service. But in the last 15 years they have come to be heavily criticized as inflexible and unduly protective of those they were supposed to control. This process has gone furthest in the US where economic regulation of airlines has been abandoned. There has been more limited liberalization in a number of other countries (notably in Europe), at the initiative of individual countries or pairs of countries; and the European Commission has also been active in seeking to liberalize the terms of service within the Community.

On both sides of the Atlantic, regulation has sought to control entry and exit of carriers on routes and to set the prices, frequencies and capacity offered by those carriers. Changing this system has required detailed negotiation among airlines and authorities. The extent to which change is possible depends on the type of market being reformed. It is much harder on international than on domestic services, given the need for agreement between different governments, and the fact that the gains and losses from liberalization may not be evenly distributed between countries.

2.1. The US experience of deregulation

The US civil aviation industry was heavily regulated during the 40 years after 1938, when the Civil Aeronautics Act was passed to reform what was seen as a chaotic and unsafe sector. Experience of the period prior to 1938 had convinced both government and industry that an unregulated air transport market would always be prone to 'destructive competition' (see Morgan, 1981). The Act empowered what was to become the Civil Aeronautics Board to control market entry, pricing behaviour and other aspects of operation. No new trunk airlines were allowed, mergers were tightly controlled, the number of carriers on any one route was closely restricted, and even exit from routes required CAB approval.[2] The Board's role extended in the 1960s and 1970s as the scope of regulation widened (to include a much more sweeping control of fares). But as it did so, it came under increasing criticism. Some critics charged that its regulation was heavy-handed and imposed unreasonable restrictions on carriers, while others thought it offered excessive protection to incumbent operators without giving any incentive to control costs (see Doganis, 1985). The regulated interstate carriers were compared unfavourably with lower cost (and more lightly regulated) intrastate operators in California and Texas (Bailey, Graham and Kaplan, 1985, p. 50). After a series of Congressional hearings in the early

---

[2] A good account of the CAB's powers is given in Caves (1962).

1970s (US Senate, 1975) the pressure for deregulation became over-whelming, and the Aviation Deregulation Act became law in 1978. This legislation dismantled the range of controls which the CAB possessed (as well as preparing for the abolition of the CAB in 1985). There was a steady relaxation of restrictions on route access and on fares. Some changes had already taken place before 1978, especially with regard to the availability of discount fares; indeed, the CAB itself, following the appointment of Alfred Kahn as chairman, had helped to force the pace of change.

2.1.1. Initial effects of deregulation 1978–85. Deregulation had a rapid effect on the industry, though this may have been hastened by the second oil crisis of 1979 and the subsequent recession. This was seen in numerous ways: in the number of companies providing service; in the costs, prices and profits of the industry; in the nature of the industry's operations and in the overall growth of traffic.

The relaxation of entry and exit controls had a dramatic effect on the number of carriers providing scheduled service, which rose from 36 to over 120 by 1984 (there were more than 200 registrations over the period as a whole, indicating a substantial degree of exit as well as entry). With the entry of so many new operators, overall concentration in the industry fell, though not dramatically since the new entrants remained small: while in 1976 the top 12 carriers accounted for 96.5% of overall revenue passenger miles (RPMs), by 1984 they accounted for 90.6%.

The effect of new entry on competition is better assessed by looking at individual routes between city-pairs. Moore (1986) reported that on 22 out of 37 long-haul routes there had been an increase between 1976 and 1983 in the number of carriers offering service, and a decline on only 4. Table 1, reproduced from that study, shows that even on short- and medium-haul routes there was, on balance, a substantial increase in the number of carriers and in the frequency of flights. Where there were increases in concentration, this was mainly on short-haul routes between relatively small cities.

Who were the new operators? In some cases they were drawn from existing intrastate operators, but often they were completely new ventures. They were able to take advantage of their more efficient operating characteristics, both in indirect costs (such as their simplified ticketing services) and direct costs (their more effective aircraft utilization rates). As the industry moved into recession they were also able to buy cheaper aircraft, hire crew at lower wages and avoid some of the overheads of the incumbent carriers. Most entrants offered limited commuter and feeder services, but there were some (like People Express) who sought

Table 1. Changes in US routes 1976–83

Routes (total number in parentheses)	City Pairs (number)				Change in departures (%)
	Carriers		Direct Departures		
	Gaining	Losing	Gaining	Losing	
Long-haul Major (37)	22	4	n.a.	n.a.	n.a.
Large Metropolitan/Big Cities:					
Medium-haul (27)	14	1	16	10	8
Short-haul (25)	13	4	14	11	34
Small Cities/Big Cities:					
Medium-haul (23)	8	6	8	11	15
Short-haul (30)	13	3	17	11	70
California (32)	22	4	23	7	60

Source: Moore (1986).

to compete with the larger carriers, usually by offering a low-cost, no-frills service.[3]

The fact that entrants were able to exploit savings in equipment and labour costs forced incumbents to follow suit, sometimes after lengthy labour disputes. There were substantial savings in costs of operation even against a background of rising fuel bills and general inflation (Button and Morrison, 1988). It is not easy to assess the overall improvements in industry productivity during this period, because of the importance of changes in the quality of service, particularly increases in frequency. But Caves *et al.* (1987) compared a rise of 3.0% per annum in the productivity of US airlines prior to deregulation, with 4.5% in non-US airlines. Since deregulation, US airlines' productivity rose by 3.3% per annum while that of non-US carriers rose by 2.8%. The improvement in relative performance, almost certainly understated by ignoring improvements in quality of service, is attributed to deregulation. Similarly, Forsyth *et al.* (1986) find not only a steady improvement in the efficiency of US carriers between 1979 and 1984, but also that the overall level of efficiency is considerably greater in the US than in other markets.

The effect on fares has been more complex. Standard fares actually increased in real terms on many routes. Discount fares fell by slightly under 10%, with the greatest falls occurring on dense routes[4] (no longer

---

[3] See Utton (1987), p. 68; there is a discussion of the diversity of operators on the New York–Washington route in McGowan and Trengrove (1986), pp. 35–6.

[4] Although some discount fares rose, this was chiefly due to rising fuel costs; Morrison and Winston (1986) estimate that all discount fares were lower than they would have been in the absence of deregulation.

required to cross-subsidize less dense routes). Overall, however, average fares fell by nearly 30%, due to the increased availability of discount fares: more than 80% of passengers in 1984 were travelling on discounted tickets, compared to about 45% in 1978 (Howard, 1988; McGowan and Trengrove, 1986).

Airline profitability fell substantially during this period, with operating losses in 1980–82. But it is hard to separate the effects of competition from those of recession: Morrison and Winston (1986) have claimed that profitability would have been even lower in the absence of deregulation. It has even been estimated that perceived investor risk in the airline industry may have fallen as a consequence of the changes in the market (see Cunningham *et al.*, 1988).

The benefits of deregulation to consumers consisted not just in a reduction in fares to existing travellers. In addition, the fare reductions helped to promote a major increase in traffic. Figure 1 illustrates how, after a period of stagnation during the recession, traffic rose dramatically and by 1985 was nearly 50% higher than in 1978 – a trend that has continued. And a significant extra benefit to consumers consisted in improvements in service frequency. Indeed, by 1985 the benefits of greater frequency significantly exceeded those from lower fares, according to Morrison and Winston (1986). Overall, they claimed, deregulation

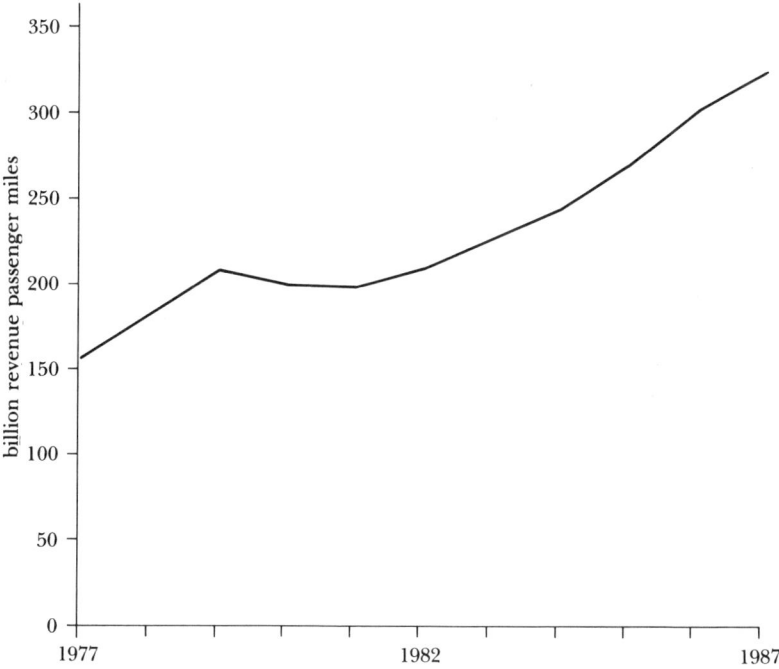

Figure 1. US air traffic 1977–87

appeared to have been an unqualified success, with benefits to travellers estimated at some $5.7 bn. in 1977 dollars, and industry profits likewise estimated to be $2.5 bn. higher than they would have been in the absence of deregulation. The effects gave a boost to proposals for the liberalization of other countries' air transport markets. The air transport industry was widely hailed as demonstrating the relevance of contestability theory to real economic circumstances.

2.1.2. Consolidation 1985–89. From 1985 onwards, the market entered a phase of consolidation. Tough competition pushed a number of carriers into bankruptcy or merger. Many of the incumbent operators, shaken in the early phase of deregulation, had now recovered. They had cut costs, and in many cases had learned to exploit both local monopolies and national system advantages to force out competition and to discourage new entry (Kahn, 1988). Aggressive pricing and scheduling behaviour had proved to be a more effective competitive weapon than some of the advocates of deregulation had foreseen.

Several features of the successful airlines' competitive strategy were now becoming clear. First, deregulation encouraged a move away from direct point-to-point services towards 'hub-and-spoke' route networks. Though by no means peculiar to the deregulation era, these systems came to dominate US air transport with the increased competition of the 1980s. Carriers concentrated their operations at hub airports, to which they flew passengers from surrounding cities to connect with onward flights. This involved linking up with local operators in arrangements which were often the prelude to a take-over. In principle, hub-and-spoke networks allow carriers to increase average traffic levels on all routes. This has been widely interpreted as demonstrating the existence of economies of scope in route networks, and therefore the virtues of large-scale airline operation. We examine this argument in more detail in Section 3.3.2 below.

Other competitive strategies seemed similarly to favour large carriers. The development of computerized reservation systems (CRSs) (which required substantial investments, but were profitable ventures in their own right) yielded significant marketing advantages to carriers with large and complex operations, and were useful competitive weapons for excluding rival operators. Frequent flyer programmes, under which travellers were offered free flights according to how extensively they used the airline's services, became a popular means of ensuring customer loyalty, but one which airlines with fewer routes could not so easily exploit.

One of the greatest pressures for consolidation came from growing congestion at certain major airports, some of it exacerbated by the

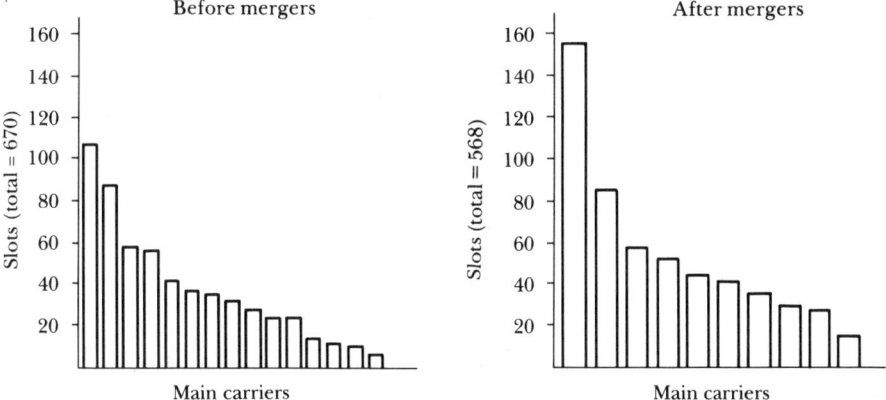

Figure 2. Slot allocations at Washington National Airport before and after 1986 mergers

Source: Aviation Daily.

development of hub-and-spoke systems. While there were no restrictions on entry to individual routes, access to the airport slots necessary to operate these routes profitably was often constrained. A number of mergers were undertaken to obtain additional slots or to consolidate a dominant position at particular airports. Figure 2, for example, illustrates the effect of mergers on slot allocations at Washington's National Airport.

The most dramatic evidence of the consolidation can be seen in the change in the number of carriers after 1984 (when it peaked at 123). In the following three years the number of carriers dropped rapidly as a result of bankruptcies, mergers and take-overs. Of the remaining operators a number were either providing service off the mainland or had feeder arrangements with larger airlines. In effect only 27 truly independent carriers have survived (Howard, 1988, p. 13). Seven of these between them control 89% of the market, and the share of the largest 12 has risen to 97.3%. Table 2 illustrates. However, we emphasized earlier that measures of overall concentration may be an inadequate guide to the nature of concentration on specific routes. On many routes there are still more carriers than there were before deregulation (Kahn, 1988, p. 319).

The overall impact of this consolidation is not immediately clear. Carriers do not appear to have colluded in setting fares. One carrier (Texas Air) has exercised a price leadership role. 1987–88 saw a series of proposals for new fare structures from many carriers, generally involving fewer and less attractive discounts. These fares were subsequently bid down by Texas Air. But throughout 1988 fares have gradually increased, and at the end of the year Texas Air led a price

Table 2. Market share of US domestic airline traffic (% of revenue passenger miles flown)

Carrier	1976	Carrier	1984	Carrier	1988
United	19.1	United	20.3	Texas	19.8
American	14.3	American	15.1	United	16.8
Delta	12.2	Eastern	11.9	American	16.6
Eastern	11.2	Delta	11.3	Delta	13.6
TWA	10.9	TWA	6.6	USAir	9.0
Northwest	5.6	Northwest	4.4	Northwest	7.0
Western	5.1	Continental	4.0	TWA	6.2
PanAm	4.8	Western	3.9	PanAm	2.1
Continental	4.4	Republic	3.9	America West	2.0
Braniff	3.9	USAir	3.8	Southwest	2.0
Republic	2.7	Piedmont	2.8	Braniff	1.1
USAir	2.5	PanAm	2.7	Alaska	1.0
Frontier	1.2	Southwest	2.1	Other	2.7
Other	2.3	Frontier	2.0		
		PSA	1.4		
		Ozark	1.2		
		Other	2.7		
Top 4	56.7	Top 4	58.6	Top 4	66.8
Top 10	91.3	Top 10	85.1	Top 10	95.1

Sources: Bailey, Graham and Kaplan (1985); *Aviation Daily*, various issues.
Note: 1988 figures are for January and February only.

rise on many routes. Preliminary indications are that average fares rose 8% in 1988, the first time since deregulation that they have risen more than inflation, and profitability is recovering. This process of consolidation has taken place within a relatively buoyant market. If the US economy enters a recession, it is not clear whether the airlines' response will be to collude or to intensify competition as occurred in the early 1980s.[5]

Concern has also been expressed about the effect of deregulation on the quality of service. Partly as a result of congestion, there has been a significant increase in the incidence of delays and lost baggage. Threats by the US Congress to introduce legislation to reregulate the industry prompted the Department of Transportation to introduce a report card system. This is a self-regulatory measure to publicize operators' performance by a number of yardsticks, designed to enhance the reputational incentives for maintaining service quality. Preliminary indications

---

[5] At the time of writing Eastern Airlines (a subsidiary of Texas Air) has filed for bankruptcy during a protracted labour dispute. This episode may well be of critical importance in affecting the nature of future competition, but it is too early to tell how it will be resolved.

are that industry performance has substantially improved as a result (*Business Week*, 19.12.88).

A key factor in the rapid concentration of the industry was the role of the Department of Transportation (DoT). The DoT was charged with overseeing the residual regulatory activities of the Civil Aeronautics Board after its abolition, including scrutiny of mergers. Its attitude to mergers was extremely generous: until the end of 1988 (when merger control was taken over by the Department of Justice), it never disallowed a merger or upheld any complaints of predatory behaviour (Shepherd, 1988). These decisions were based largely on the view that the scope for potential competition in airline services was sufficient to discipline incumbent carriers. It is true that this was a period during which antitrust law in general was interpreted in a far more permissive fashion than hitherto. But it is significant that the Department of Justice had been opposed to a number of the mergers that the DoT approved. There are signs that the Department of Justice is taking a more activist line in its new role than the DoT, especially with regard to concentration in CRS ownership (*Financial Times*, 24 March 1989); but it is too early to tell how significant is this change.

The lessons of the US experience for Europe are two-fold. First, the potential overall gains from deregulation, in lower fares and in improved service frequency, are large. A total gain to consumers and producers of around $8 bn. per annum at 1977 prices was a reasonable estimate for the US in 1985; we compare this in Section 2.2 with a range of estimates of the potential gains in Europe. Second, if competition policy is permissive, there is every reason to expect an eventual consolidation of the European industry. There may be a number of new players, but the market could be at least as concentrated as it is today. Whether this would matter depends critically on the strength of *potential* competition from new entrants even in a concentrated market. Unless this were significant, the gains from deregulation might prove to be transitory. We consider this question in Section 3 below. But first we consider the evolution of the regulatory framework in Europe to date.

2.2. Reforming civil aviation in Europe

Reforming European air transport requires both domestic and international measures. Domestic aviation is heavily regulated in most countries, with the principal exception of the UK. Although domestic reforms in the UK have had interesting results, we are here concerned primarily with international services, which comprise around 60% of the total traffic of the major scheduled carriers.

International services in Europe are subject to bilateral regulation, which determines both the procedure for setting fares and the maximum share of capacity that can be offered by airlines of each country. Bilateral agreements also permit carriers to collaborate on scheduling and to pool revenue. In most cases they prevent route entry by any but officially designated airlines. The need for both sides to agree any changes has restricted the scope for reform.

Until recently the European Community has not pressed for change. Despite calls in the 1950s for a Europe-wide aviation system, member states opposed any intervention by the new Economic Community. The Treaty of Rome postponed action on air transport: Article 84 stated the Council would develop a policy on air transport eventually. In the meantime existing bilateral arrangements prevailed. In spite of a 1974 European Court ruling implying that civil aviation was subject to the general rules of the Treaty (including the competition provisions), proposals by the Commission to apply the Treaty's principles were rejected or watered down by the Council. Its most ambitious proposals were enshrined in the Second Memorandum on Air Transport published in 1984. By now proposals for reform of the industry were being made in the context of US deregulation, a pattern resisted by most European governments and by the industry itself. The European Commission (1984, p. 21) also rejected such an option, arguing that reform should proceed by 'introducing more flexibility and competition into the existing system without destroying it'.

The main proposals included removal of the obligation to participate in revenue pooling; relaxation of the rigid capacity split; and greater flexibility in fare setting. In return, the Commission offered to exempt fare setting, capacity sharing and revenue pooling activities from competition rules, subject to certain conditions. Carriers would be allowed to continue in such activities if they wished. But even a whiff of reform proved too much for many parties to the negotiations, who seemed set to resist adoption of the proposals (McGowan and Trengrove, 1986, p. 87 ff.).

While such tactics had worked in the past they were to be less successful in the wake of the Nouvelles Frontieres case. This concerned a French travel agent charged with infringing the French Civil Aviation Code by offering fares below the levels agreed among scheduled carriers. The French Competition Court referred it to European Court on the basis that the Code was potentially in breach of the Treaty of Rome. The Court did not find this to be so directly, but did hold that the sector was subject to competition rules. In the absence of specific enabling measures the Commission could investigate the sector's conduct and make a reasoned decision whether or not it breached the

Competition rules. The prospect that the Commission might find airlines' conduct in breach of the competition rules (not to mention the possible replacement of its proposed reforms with a much tougher package) pushed governments and airlines to agreement at the end of 1987.

The package finally agreed by member states[6] built on the provisions of Memorandum 2. The basis for offering lower air fares according to zones has been codified, allowing discount fares at 65–90% of economy fares for relatively modest ticketing restrictions and at 45–65% for tickets with more restricted conditions. An arbitration process is also established. Capacity sharing must be relaxed to specify 45% minimum and 55% maximum shares on each route, to be extended to 40–60% in 1989. The measure also prevents carriers in one country from trying to enforce a reduction in the other country's capacity merely by reducing their own. Where a member state argues that the share would undermine the financial stability of its airlines, an investigation will be held and the shares reviewed.

The decision also addresses the question of access more generally, allowing multiple designation on country pairs and on city pairs above a minimum size. It opens up combination rights (which allow two destinations for the same flight) and so-called fifth freedom rights (which allow picking up as well as setting down on an onward flight). It also builds on the 1983 regional services directive (which opened up services between regional airports in the Community) by providing access to services between regional and hub airports within certain constraints: it excludes some airports in the Mediterranean and Denmark and leaves existing air traffic distribution constraints in place.

As originally envisaged this set of reforms was granted in exchange for a clarification of the industry's position vis-à-vis the Community's competition rules. First, agreements between airlines on such issues as technical standards, leasing, training and the definition of fare categories have been recognized as exceptions to Article 85(1). Second, and more importantly, the joint planning of capacity, revenue sharing[7] and tariff consultations, while falling in principle under Article 85(1), have been granted a temporary exemption, as have agreements over slot allocation and CRS arrangements. This is at the Commission's discretion and is equivalent to the granting of anti-trust immunity.

It is too soon to assess what effect these measures will have. But to the extent that they increase the scope for independent action, they

---

[6] *Official Journal of the European Communities* L374 of 31/12/87.
[7] Albeit within strict limits. Pooling of revenue is in any case quite rare nowadays.

reinforce the moves by some countries to liberalize services with those that are more reluctant to negotiate. The moves are seen only as a first step: capacity, fares and access provisions are due to be reviewed in 1990, and the exemption lapses in 1991. The Commission is likely to use the possibility of renewing the exemption to persuade member states to agree to further liberalization. It is also attempting to accelerate the pace of developments: the new Transport Commissioner, Karel van Miert, has been pressing for agreement on a second reform package that might take effect in mid-1990 rather than (as currently scheduled) in early 1991. And in April 1989 the European Court of Justice made an important judgment that (*inter alia*) upheld the power of national courts to apply Article 86 to the actions of carriers in domestic and extra-community markets. The judgment will have a significant direct impact on liberalization moves in these markets, and an indirect psychological impact on the liberalization of intra-community bilateral agreements.

The clearest sign of a more ambitious approach by the Commission to air transport regulation has been its reaction to the merger between British Airways and British Caledonian in 1987–88. After the take-over was finally agreed, the Commission's Competition Directorate indicated that it considered the merger a potential abuse of dominant position (and thus a breach of Article 86 of the Treaty). It sought and obtained further concessions from BA, in particular on limiting its operations from Gatwick to European destinations. The conditions it imposed were significantly tighter than the commitments on future route licence applications, given by BA to the UK competition authorities during the merger investigation. Further indications of the Commission's more activist regulatory ambitions have come in its fining of Sabena for restricting access by another carrier to its CRS system, and an action against Italy over fifth freedom flights by Aer Lingus.

In addition the Commission is seeking to integrate civil aviation policy, securing increased access to other markets by negotiating air service agreements en bloc. A measure of the seriousness of this proposal is the fact that many non-EC countries are seeking to coordinate air transport policy with the Community. The Commission is also playing a key role in tackling noise and congestion problems in Europe, problems we consider in Section 3.2 below.

The Commission is helped by the terms of the 1987 package. The block exemption from the Community's competition rules is less of a concession to the interests of incumbent carriers than it appears, since it is only temporary and subject to conditions. When it expires the Commission can take action on any of the hitherto accepted practices in the package. This power effectively establishes that, subject to an exemption, the competition rules apply to the airline industry. And in strategic terms it adds to the bargaining power of the Commission.

In moving towards deregulation, Europe can learn from the perform-ance of the largely competitive charter sector, as well as from the limited experience of liberalization in particular scheduled markets, either domestically or under bilateral agreements between countries. The European charter industry caters to the leisure markets and has developed rapidly over the last 20 years, accounting for roughly half of air transport in Europe. It is subject to a number of controls but within these it is a highly competitive market: entry and exit are largely unrestricted and there are few controls on fares. Carriers operate with load factors, seat pitch and aircraft utilization rates significantly higher than on scheduled services, with the result that operating costs are generally much lower (McGowan and Trengrove, 1986; National Con-sumer Council, 1986). It is not clear how far all these advantages could be replicated in the scheduled sector. There are significant differences in demand in these two markets: charter services are more price-elastic and offer a lower quality of service. Some charter operators (such as Air Europe and Dan-Air) have been permitted to enter scheduled markets, but have found some aspects of their operations difficult to transfer (such as their aircraft utilization rates).

Most such experiments have taken place in those countries which have already liberalized their civil aviation system. The best example is the UK; of the others only the Netherlands has explicitly developed a policy allowing competition on international routes. Most countries do not allow competition with the flag carrier on domestic trunk or inter-national routes, though other airlines may provide services on regional routes that are not operated by the flag carrier. In effect, except in the UK, the Netherlands and the Republic of Ireland, no flag carrier has in the past faced competition on any route. The few reforms in the rest of Europe have tended to focus on ownership: a number of coun-tries have introduced or increased the share of private capital in their flag carriers. Recent reviews of airline policy have involved either reallocations of routes between existing carriers (as in the French decision to encourage cooperation between Air France and Air Inter) or have relaxed licensing procedures only mildly (in a German agree-ment to permit limited direct competition to Lufthansa on domestic routes).

The UK government has been steadily liberalizing internal air services through the 1980s. The 1984 White Paper on Competition in Air Transport effectively lifted all controls on entry and fare setting. In practice there were obstacles to the full implementation of this policy, owing to limited access to Heathrow and Gatwick, and to pressure on the Civil Aviation Authority from small carriers not to allow British Airways to compete unrestrictedly on all routes. But the CAA's licensing policy has since then been generally liberal. Although air transport within Britain is not as developed a means of travel as it is in the US, there are a number of routes where the traffic has been large enough to attract new entrants in competition with existing carriers.

In 1987 the CAA published a comprehensive review of competition on these routes (London to Belfast, Edinburgh, Glasgow and Manchester). The results were a very cautious acceptance that competition had worked. On traffic the results indicate that some of the growth was due to competition. Although the economic recovery and industrial action on the railways also contributed, the study showed that the frequency and quality of service appeared to improve with the entry of another carrier. Competition was also reflected in fares, albeit patchily. Increases in economy fares were more moderate than in other European markets, though falls were not recorded: indeed, between 1980 and 1986, fares rose in real terms. Such fare competition as existed focused on restricted discount tickets (CAA, 1987).

The other strand of the UK government's liberalization programme has been its renegotiation of bilateral agreements. Since 1984 it has revised its agreements with a number of European countries, most notably with the Netherlands. The 1984 agreement, extended the following year, lifted controls on capacity and fare setting and permitted greater access to new entrants in both countries (with the exception of Heathrow where restrictions on new services exist).

Overall the agreement appears to have had a beneficial effect on services, at least initially. The number of airlines operating between the two countries increased from 7 to 14 in the period 1984–87. Though half of these were the only carrier on a particular regional route between the two countries, on some city pairs there was a greater degree of competition, and by 1987 there were seven carriers on the key London–Amsterdam route. But subsequently there has been rapid consolidation: besides the merger between British Airways and British Caledonian, KLM has taken substantial stakes in a number of other carriers, including all the independent Dutch carriers flying London–Amsterdam and in Air UK, which is British-registered but also flies the route. There are now only three independent operators on the route.

The entry of new carriers had beneficial if unspectacular effects on fares. Some airlines offered introductory half price fares while others priced at 90% of existing fares (for the same degree of service as established operators). The latter have generally responded through the introduction of low cost but restricted fares (in one case at 25% of the economy). Abbot and Thompson (1990) in a forthcoming paper

Table 3. Scheduled traffic from London to Dublin and Amsterdam, 1984–88 (thousands of passengers)

Route	1984	1985	1986	1987	1988
London–Dublin	928	993	1,134	1,309	1,558
Luton–Dublin	0	0	75	324	415
Total London/Luton to Dublin	928	993	1,209	1,633	1,973
London–Amsterdam	1,231	1,309	1,417	1,720	1,832

Source: Civil Aviation Authority, *UK Airports*, various issues.

find that most discount fares fell by between 15% and 25% by 1986. There is some indication that these changes resulted in a wider fare mix as yields fell on the London–Amsterdam service (OECD, 1988, pp. 60–62); but the effects of the recent consolidation are not yet clear. Effects on the quality of service are harder to measure: there has been a clear tendency for schedules to 'bunch' towards peak periods, a phenomenon whose significance we discuss in Section 3.3.1 below.

Another indication of the effects of deregulation can be seen on the London – Dublin route, where the Irish authorities have permitted a new carrier (Ryanair) to operate from Luton. It entered offering fares well below the existing economy fare, prompting a price war on the route, compounded with the entry of a further new carrier (Virgin). Three years later, fares are still low and traffic has risen dramatically.[8] Table 3 shows traffic on the London–Dublin and London–Amsterdam routes from 1984 to 1988. Traffic on London–Amsterdam rose by 49%, and that on London–Dublin (including Luton–Dublin) by 117%, over a period in which traffic between the UK and Western Europe as a whole rose by approximately 52%.

London–Dublin is a more convincing case for the value of increased competition than London–Amsterdam. It demonstrates the effect a new entrant can have on a route, even when operating out of a relatively unknown airport. But it has some unusual characteristics as a route: the expansion in traffic has been due partly to the large number of Irish citizens living in the London area, happy to fly in preference to slower surface transport if the price is right (a situation closer to that in the US).

There has been substantial opposition to deregulation within the EC as a whole, especially from countries with commitments to protecting

---

[8] This example was used by the Commission to demonstrate the virtues of liberalization. See European Commission (1988a), p. 98, where a 29% increase in traffic in seven months is attributed to the liberalization.

their flag carriers (whether relatively efficient airlines such as those of France and Germany or relatively inefficient ones as in the case of Greece). Some opposition is to be expected since deregulation will inevitably mean winners and losers within the industry. Nonetheless, changes in the decision making procedures of the Community, backed up by the powers implicit in the expiry of the block exemption, will make it hard to block all further change. It is likely that the Commission will proceed carefully, with at least another series of temporary measures (extending capacity rules and fare zones) before requiring a fully integrated and liberalized European air transport market. Given that the present measures expire in 1990, it is possible that a substantially more liberal framework could be in place before the official completion of the Single Market on January 1st 1993.

How great are the likely benefits, and where will they come from? The European Commission itself held up air transport as an example of what could be achieved by the Single Market, and of what was still needed. If a single market could be achieved, the European Commission (1988a) estimated that liberalization could bring about a 10% reduction in costs and prices. Since passenger revenue of EC airlines from scheduled services within continental Europe totalled $10.8 bn. in 1987, this indicates potential consumer surplus benefits of something over $1 bn. per annum[9] (with producer surplus changes comparatively small).

This estimate is somewhat lower than would have been reached simply by assuming that the European market could achieve benefits equivalent to those estimated by Morrison and Winston for the US in 1985, adjusted for the different size of the two markets. Measured in terms of revenue passenger kilometres flown, the internal European market in 1987 was approximately 25% of the size of the American domestic market 10 years earlier.[10] This would imply total benefits of European deregulation of around $2 bn. per annum at 1977 prices, equivalent to about $3.5 bn. in 1987. Which of these two estimates is to be preferred?

The estimate of $3.5 bn. is undoubtedly unrealistically high. Liberalization in Europe cannot be expected simply to mimic the American experience. First, competition from other forms of transport (such as railways) is much greater than in the US. Second, average journey lengths are shorter, which means that fixed take-off and landing costs represent a larger proportion of total costs. Third, domestic services

---

[9] The Commission estimated a total gain in sea and air transport combined at between 1.4 and 1.7 bn. ECU, which is roughly equal to the same sum in US dollars. See European Commission (1988a), page 186.

[10] US figures are from US Department of Commerce, 1978, and show traffic to have been 156.6 bn. revenue passenger miles in 1977. European figures are from AEA, 1988, showing traffic of 63.7 bn. revenue passenger kilometres in 1987 (approximately 40 bn. revenue passenger miles).

account for a much smaller proportion of the market in Europe than in the US. This explains not just the slow progress towards regulatory reform, but also some of the differences in costs of operation between Europe and the US, such as those arising from utilization of airspace. Political and cultural factors also limit how quickly the market for air transport will develop (a great deal of US domestic traffic falls into the category 'Visiting Friends and Relatives'), and the American single market undoubtedly makes the business traffic potential greater than in Europe.

Europe's potential benefits from deregulation may be lower not just because of differences in costs, culture and geography, but also because of differences in the way regulation has operated. The US never had a significant charter market, for instance. Furthermore, while fares were regulated carriers were free to compete in terms of quality of service, and thus often operated at very low load factors. After deregulation carriers could, therefore, develop markets by providing low-cost service for leisure travellers, and could raise load factors to reduce average costs. In Europe the charter market may serve leisure travellers adequately within its regulatory constraints, and the collusion involved in bilateral agreements appears to have maintained load factors higher than they were in the US. But these features seem less important to us than the potential impact of liberalization on the overall efficiency with which carriers manage their costs, and their ability to provide services of the kind travellers need.

First of all, the regulatory restrictions on charter operations can hardly be stressed enough: flights have conditions on bookings and cancellations, and operate outside peak hours. The geographical overlap between scheduled and charter markets is also quite limited. Of the 51 most significant city-pair routes on which there was charter traffic from the UK in 1987, 23 had no scheduled traffic at all, so travellers had no choice of service. Total scheduled traffic on the remaining 28 routes, at 4.9 mn. passengers, was 21% of all scheduled traffic and much of this consisted of skiers whose demand is highly seasonal. Likewise, on the 35 largest scheduled routes (those with more than 100,000 passengers a year) total charter traffic in 1987, at 4.2 mn. passengers, was only 25% of scheduled traffic, and 65% of this charter traffic was to six Alpine and Mediterranean destinations. Given the differences between these kinds of service there would appear to be scope for developing scheduled services in both business and leisure markets through lower costs and more flexible discount conditions. (It is not just business travellers who value flexibility; cancellation penalties can impose major costs on leisure travellers.) We have already noted the attempts of some charter airlines to enter scheduled operations. In

Table 4. US and European load factors 1976–87 (%)

Year	Europe (local and domestic)	Europe (local)	US
1976	58.4	56.3	55.4
1977	60.9	58.9	56.2
1978	61.5	59.6	61.5
1979	62.0	59.9	63.0
1980	58.7	56.4	59.0
1981	60.7	58.3	58.5
1982	60.0	57.1	59.0
1983	60.3	57.5	60.7
1984	63.0	60.8	59.2
1985	64.0	62.5	61.4
1986	62.6	60.4	60.3
1987	66.0	63.8	62.4

Sources: Association of European Airlines, US Department of Commerce.
Note: US figures include international services (about 15% of revenue passenger miles); these are likely to raise the US average load factors.

addition, in markets where scheduled traffic dominates or co-exists with charter traffic there are signs of more innovative pricing strategies. The best examples are on North Atlantic routes where charter services have been squeezed out by discounting by scheduled carriers; and on routes such as London–Munich and London–Geneva charter fares have been matched by deeper discounts from scheduled carriers.

It is harder to evaluate the likely gains from improvements in load factors. Table 4 shows that average load factors were indeed higher in Europe than in the US prior to deregulation, though not dramatically so. But it also shows that the gains in the US have not been spectacular: the report of the US Senate (1975), which provided the major impetus to US deregulation, hoped for increases in average load factors from 55% to 70%; yet the gains from deregulation have accrued in spite of a failure to improve load factors by even half this margin. And Tables 5 and 6 indicate wide disparities in European load factors between carriers and between routes. As Table 6 reveals, there is no generally discernible impact of liberalization on load factors: carriers may attempt to boost load factors in an attempt to control costs, but it may also be that new entry and competitive scheduling tend to dilute load factors. Load factors are a complex function of market density and carriers' ability to manage service and the mix of passenger types on a given route. While deregulated carriers would attempt to raise load factors if they could, it is more likely to be their management of operational

Table 5. Local European load factors by carrier, 1987 (%)

Carrier	Load factor	Carrier	Load factor
Aer Lingus	66.0	Lufthansa	61.4
Air France	62.2	Sabena	58.1
Alitalia	61.8	SAS	62.0
British Airways	68.5	TAP	71.2
Iberia	72.0	Air Europe	74.5
KLM	59.8	Air UK	48.4
AEA Average	63.8		

Sources: Association of European Airlines, Civil Aviation Authority.

Table 6. Evolution of load factors by route from London, 1984–87 (%)

Destination and carrier	1984	1985	1986	1987
Paris				
Air France	71.0	72.0	67.0	64.0
British Airways	68.0	72.0	63.0	71.0
British Caledonian	63.0	64.0	59.0	67.0
Amsterdam				
British Airways	70.0	67.0	58.0	61.0
KLM	75.0	72.0	66.0	61.0
British Caledonian	64.0	69.0	64.0	67.0
British Midland	—	—	34.0	49.0
Dublin				
British Airways	69.0	67.0	75.0	73.0
Aer Lingus	72.0	72.0	75.0	n.a.
Copenhagen				
British Airways	61.0	61.0	52.0	61.0
SAS	72.0	69.0	67.0	72.0
Frankfurt				
British Airways	59.0	63.0	63.0	71.0
Lufthansa	67.0	69.0	64.0	64.0
British Caledonian	43.0	53.0	50.0	58.0

Source: International Civil Aviation Organization.

costs that will determine their ability to lower fares in a liberalized European market.

Where will the cost savings come from? We provide evidence on the relatively high costs incurred by European airlines in three main areas: rents to labour, poor labour utilization and high indirect and overhead costs. Table 7 shows average labour costs per employee in 1987 for six categories of airline employee, comparing the average for eight major

Table 7. Average labour cost and productivity of airline employees, 1987

Labour cost per employee	Pilots and co-pilots	Other cockpit staff	Cabin crew	Main-tenance staff	Ticket and sales	Other
(US $000s)						
8 US Majors	92	40	28	36	—	36
BA/BCal	65	48	19	25	26	22
BMid/AirUK	34	—	13	20	15	15
Sabena	—	123	39	32	—	28
UTA (France)	164	119	45	46	33	38
Lufthansa	—	130	40	42	37	50
Alitalia	—	93	59	—	—	81
TAP	96	67	26	19	25	16
SAS	—	103	41	29	34	38
Iberia	109	80	37	23	27	26
Adjusted, as % of US level						
BA/BCal	100	173	94	100	100	89
BMid/AirUK	52	—	65	79	58	59
Sabena	—	376	167	108	—	94
UTA	306	516	273	224	152	185
Lufthansa	—	330	141	119	101	141
SAS	—	251	138	78	88	103
Iberia	213	361	232	117	132	130

Productivity	Million revenue passenger kms per employee	Adjusted, as % of US levels
8 US Majors	1.6	
BA/BCal	1.1	65
BMid/AirUK	0.4	—
Sabena	0.6	—
UTA	0.8	—
Lufthansa	0.8	52
Alitalia	0.7	—
TAP	0.4	—
SAS	0.6	46
Iberia	0.7	49

Sources: International Civil Aviation Organization; ILO *Labour Force Statistics*; Forsyth *et al.* (1986); own calculations.
Notes: (i) Pay data not available in each category for all carriers; US figure is weighted average of available figures. (ii) Adjusted pay corrects for relative manufacturing wage rates across countries. (iii) Adjusted productivity based on international output adjustments calculated in Forsyth *et al.* (1986), Table 2, column A, relative to the adjustment factor for American Airlines.

US carriers for whom there exist comparable data (American, Continental, Delta, Eastern, PanAm, TWA, United and USAir) with two groups of UK carriers and seven from other European countries. All the non-UK carriers show remarkably high labour costs compared to the

US (pilots at UTA are paid 78% more, and at Iberia 19% more than in the US; six of the seven carriers pay other cockpit staff more than double, with three paying more than triple US rates). These differentials are hardly reflected in greater labour productivity, with US levels more than double those in Europe. Table 7 also adjusts these figures to reflect the fact that real wages in the US are higher than in Europe: it shows for each European carrier the degree to which the ratio of labour remuneration to average real earnings in manufacturing exceeds the same ratio for US carriers. The rents it reveals are even more striking, and are higher (as might be expected) for pilots, cockpit and cabin staff than for ticketing and sales staff whose skills are less industry-specific (though the comparatively low rents to maintenance staff are surprising in the circumstances). The labour productivity figures are expressed in relation to the average US figure; to some extent such comparisons are difficult because of different circumstances in the two markets, so for four carriers figures are also given adjusted for different stage lengths operated, using adjustments calculated by Forsyth *et al.* (1986). The adjustment makes little difference except in the case of SAS, and even here in no way affects the qualitative results. While the precise nature of such productivity comparisons is very much open to question, it is unquestionable that the very large returns to labour revealed in Table 7 are not reflections of greater productivity; they are basically incumbency rents.

Comparatively poor utilization of capital, particularly aircraft, may be a part of the explanation for high European costs. Pryke (1987, p. 30) cites a study published in 1982 that showed five American carriers used narrow-bodied aircraft for an average 8.33 hours per day on domestic routes, while the corresponding figure for the five leading European carriers was 6.7 hours per day. But there are reasons for caution in making inferences from such figures (apart from the outdatedness of the study). There are wide variations in utilization rates between kinds of aircraft and types of route flown. Table 8 compares average daily hours flown for three kinds of aircraft by different carriers in 1986: in the face of such wide variations between carriers in each region, and variations in fleet composition, it is hard to infer any general tendency for European utilization rates to be systematically lower. This caution is reinforced by Table 9, which breaks down unit operating costs in 1987 into costs of flight operations, maintenance and depreciation costs, and indirect costs. Although some European carriers (notably SAS) have significantly higher depreciation and maintenance costs than others, several have costs that are comfortably in the middle range of the US carriers. The most striking feature of Table 9, however, is the uniformly higher proportion of indirect costs in total European

Table 8. Aircraft utilization rates by carrier and aircraft type, 1986

Carrier	Average daily revenue hours flown by		
	Airbus A300 (* = A310)	Boeing 737	Douglas DC-10
Sabena	9.9*	7.2	12.4
UTA	—	—	10.3
Lufthansa	7.9*	7.1	13.8
Olympic	5.4	6.9	—
Alitalia	8.1	—	—
KLM	5.8*	5.0	11.5
SAS	—	—	11.9
Iberia	5.8	—	11.3
British Airways	—	7.5	—
American	—	—	9.5
USAir	—	8.2	—
Continental	9.1	5.9	11.0
Delta	—	7.8	—
Eastern	8.5	—	10.0
Northwest	—	—	7.8
PanAm	7.5/7.0*	4.6	—
United	—	7.7	9.0

Source: ICAO fleet statistics.

Table 9. Direct and indirect operating costs by carrier, 1987 (US cents per tonne kilometre performed)

Carrier	Flight operations		Depreciation and maintenance		Indirect		Total costs:
	cents	% of total	cents	% of total	cents	% of total	cents
Sabena	30	30.2	11	11.2	58	58.6	99
UTA	18	16.9	18	17.0	71	66.2	107
Alitalia	17	21.5	16	19.9	47	58.7	81
SAS	31	18.6	32	19.2	104	62.2	167
Iberia	20	21.2	13	13.8	61	65.7	94
British Airways	18	22.1	12	14.8	53	63.1	83
American	19	26.4	14	18.7	40	55.1	73
USAir	26	29.1	15	16.4	48	54.5	89
Continental	20	32.4	10	16.0	31	51.6	61
Delta	25	31.6	11	14.5	42	53.9	79
Eastern	20	25.6	16	20.4	40	52.7	76
PanAm	24	28.7	11	13.3	47	57.9	82
TWA	18	27.2	12	18.1	36	54.7	66
United	19	27.5	13	18.9	36	53.6	67

Source: ICAO financial data.

Table 10. Ratios of non-flight to flight staff by carrier, 1987

Carrier	Non-flight/ cockpit staff	Non-flight/ cabin staff	Non-flight/ all flight staff
Air France	9.9	4.1	2.9
Olympic	14.1	5.8	4.1
Alitalia	7.5	3.7	2.5
Lufthansa	8.5	3.2	2.3
TAP	7.8	4.1	2.7
SAS	10.0	5.8	3.7
Iberia	14.2	6.2	4.3
British Airways	9.9	3.4	2.5
Average 8 EC majors	9.9	4.1	2.9
American	4.6	2.9	1.8
USAir	5.4	3.9	2.1
Continental	1.3	1.3	0.9
Delta	4.9	2.8	1.8
Eastern	4.8	3.0	1.8
Northwest	4.2	3.1	1.8
PanAm	5.5	3.5	2.2
TWA	5.9	3.9	2.4
United	4.8	2.5	1.7
Average 9 US majors	4.7	2.7	1.7
UTA	11.9	4.0	3.0
Netherlines	1.5	3.1	1.0
British Midland	5.0	3.7	2.1
Air UK	2.1	2.4	1.1
Air Europe	1.3	0.5	0.3
Dan-Air	1.5	0.7	0.5

Source: ICAO fleet statistics (Personnel)/own calculations.
Notes: (i) Non-flight staff are all staff except cockpit, cabin and maintenance staff. (ii) Air Europe and Dan-Air, being primarily charter flyers, could be expected to have lower overheads than primarily scheduled operators.

costs. These comprise between 52% and 58% of total costs for the US carriers cited, but between 59% and 66% for European carriers for whom comparable data are available. Some of these (especially sales and marketing) may reflect more fragmented national markets, but it would be surprising if there were not also significant inefficiencies involved. One effect is that while the (unweighted) average direct costs of the US carriers were around 15% lower than the Europeans' in 1987, their total costs were around 30% lower.

The impression of inefficiency in indirect costs is strengthened by the figures in Table 10. This compares different airlines' ratios of sales and ticketing staff and of other non-flight staff, both to cabin crew and to pilots and other cockpit staff. On the (conservative) assumption that employment of pilots and cabin crew is determined mostly by service requirements and is less prone to inefficiency than is employment in other categories, the wide variation in these ratios between airlines, and the fact that most European airlines have higher ratios than most US carriers, suggests European overheads may be excessive. The European flag carriers have on average 2.9 times as many ticketing and other non-flight staff as flight staff, compared to an average of 1.7 for the nine major US airlines cited. These differences between Europe and the US are unlikely to be indicative of scale economies, since the differences between European airlines are unrelated to size (the small UK carriers have among the lowest ratios of all, for instance).

Our examination of the sources of potential cost savings suggests that the European Commission's estimate of 10% gains is by no means excessively optimistic (notwithstanding our skepticism about dramatic improvements in load factors). If anything, the Commission's estimates of the overall gains from liberalization may well be too cautious, since they ignore improvements in service frequency. Although frequency improvements may well be less significant than they have been in the US (due partly to shorter journey lengths and the competition from surface transport), the US evidence suggests they are too important to overlook. So a figure of $1.5 bn. to $2 bn. per annum may be a more realistic estimate of the gains from European liberalization.

In moving towards full liberalization, the task for the Commission is not only to ensure that these changes enable greater market access across the Community. Even if freedom of entry is eventually assured, the development of an efficient and competitive industry could be severely restricted by problems of air traffic congestion, and by anti-competitive action (including mergers) on the part of incumbent carriers. As we discuss below, these problems are closely connected: in the absence of an efficient solution to congestion constraints, airlines have additional incentives to engage in anti-competitive practices, and a competition policy has to be correspondingly more robust in order to deal with them. The US experience illustrates the dangers of combining deregulation with a lax anti-trust policy.

The lessons of American deregulation have not been lost on European carriers, and moves to merger have already begun. At times it has even appeared that European airlines may pass from regulation to concentration without bothering to pause for a period of liberalization in between. So far these moves have taken the form of buying minority shareholdings or forming strategic alliances rather than complete take-overs or mergers (with the exception of some acquisitions of small regional carriers, and of course BA–BCal).

There are some encouraging signs in the development of airline competition policy. The UK Civil Aviation Authority is developing a policy focused on detecting and penalizing predatory behaviour. It also denied to British Airways a number of the licences for which it had re-applied under the terms of the merger with British Caledonian. The European Commission has been formulating broader anti-trust powers; in particular, there is a proposal for a regulation for automatic Commission scrutiny of mergers above a certain size (currently between parties with a combined worldwide annual turnover of 5 bn. ECU, falling by 1992 to 2 bn. ECU, equivalent to approximately the same number of US dollars), though similar proposals have encountered considerable political opposition in the past. These proposals are for general application (not just to airlines) – but the Competition Commissioner, Sir Leon Brittan, has identified air transport as a sector which the Competition Directorate will watch particularly closely.

In designing a regulatory regime for the 1990s, how should the Commission proceed? What are the key issues that regulation should address? And in particular, how important is it to avoid a consolidation along American lines? The next section considers some general principles of airline regulation.

3. The purpose of regulation

Why should civil aviation be regulated at all? What are the market failures that regulation seeks to remedy? Economic theory recognizes three broad kinds of reason why unregulated markets may in general fail to allocate resources efficiently.[11] First, there is asymmetric information between the parties to a contract, which means that some potentially beneficial contracts may not be possible, and existing contracts are subject to the problems of moral hazard and adverse selection. Second, there are externalities: equalizing private costs and benefits of economic activity at the margin may not lead to equality of social costs and benefits. Third, there is the presence of market power, when firms may enjoy rents from the ability to maintain prices higher and levels of output lower than the competitive levels. While these sources of market failure are conceptually distinct, measures to remedy them are frequently not so distinct; a common dilemma for regulators is that measures to alleviate market failures of one kind may aggravate those of another.

---

[11] Inefficiency in resource allocation may not be the only feature of market outcomes that causes concern. However, other features, such as inequity in the distribution of welfare, are usually better tackled by means other than direct intervention in industrial markets (means such as the tax and benefit system). Kay and Vickers (1988) provide an illuminating discussion of the general theory of regulation in the context of different sources of market failure.

We discuss the consequences of these three sources of market failure in turn.

3.1. Asymmetric information

Civil aviation is characterized by market failure of all three kinds, but to different degrees. Asymmetric information is the least problematic of the three. There are two reasons for concern about asymmetric information in air transport. The first concerns safety, and the second concerns the availability of information about competing services.

3.1.1. Safety. The safety of air travel is evidently a matter of great concern to the traveller, not least because aircraft accidents are large-scale tragedies attracting a great deal of publicity. There are two main reasons for not leaving the choice of the acceptable level of risk to the market-place. The first is that the risk of accidents depends on a number of factors under the control of the airline but unobservable by the passenger: the frequency and rigour of servicing, the materials used in airframe construction, the training of crew and so on. In some circumstances we might expect firms to overcome such asymmetries by acquiring a reputation for safety. But the second reason for regulation is that the risks of air travel involve very small probabilities of very large accidents. We know enough about the unreliability of human perception of small probabilities to realize that it is difficult for consumers to make informed judgments about the relative riskiness of different airlines on the basis of known accident statistics. And the cost of making uninformed judgments is very large. Given that safety imposes costs on airlines, if consumers were unable to discriminate between safe and risky airlines, there would be adverse selection in which the dangerous carriers drove out the safe. These are all decisive reasons for requiring safety of airline operations to be directly regulated by a licensing system and by rules governing such matters as aircraft servicing, as continues to be the case in the US.

There is no evidence to suggest that the removal of economic regulation has any adverse effects on air safety, a view endorsed by the US Aviation Safety Commission (1988). On the contrary, Morrison and Winston (1988) showed that, after controlling for other factors, deregulation was accompanied by a lower risk of accidents in the US. This risk has declined in proportion to the total volume of air traffic; flying remains, mile for mile, one of the safest of all ways to travel.[12] Even if

---

[12] The rate of passenger fatalities in air transport worldwide was 0.4 per bn. passenger kilometres travelled in 1986. For comparison, the rate in the same year for car travel in the UK (one of the safest countries in Europe) was 5.2 fatalities per b.p.k., with rail travel at 0.4, coach travel at 0.6 and motor cycle travel at 127 per b.p.k. (source: *Financial Times*, 10 January 1989, p. 7).

carriers are operating nearer to the FAA's margins of safety than they did prior to deregulation, this is in no way to be deplored unless the margins are too lax, in which case they should be tightened. Regulation of safety margins can be achieved separately from regulation of entry and exit on economic grounds. For given levels of safety regulation, it is possible that incumbent carriers in a protected market are more solicitous of the safety of passengers than carriers in a more competitive market, but there is no convincing evidence that this is true.

3.1.2. Computerized reservation systems. Asymmetric information about the availability of competing services raises more difficult issues. In recent years a number of carriers in both Europe and the US have made major investments in the development of computerized reservation systems (CRS). These perform the dual function of offering the customer information about alternative means of travel, and undertaking the transactions of sales and reservations (alongside ancillary services such as car hire, hotel reservation and so on). Some 80% of all European airline bookings are now made through travel agents, and 80% of all travel agents' bookings are made through CRSs. Given the relatively few such systems in existence, a number of questions, therefore, arise about the exercise of market power in the provision of CRS services. But there is also the issue of alleged CRS bias in favour of the carriers that own these systems. Between 70% and 90% of all airline bookings on CRSs are made from the first display screen available to the customer. Access to this first screen, therefore, appears to favour carriers' marketing efforts considerably, a fact that has made CRS ownership an important weapon in the competition between airlines in the US. Related questions are raised by the marketing commissions offered by carriers to travel agents; we shall not examine these further here, but Levine (1987) discusses them in some detail.

As in the provision of financial services, there is a conflict of interest between the provision of advice about alternative available services and the sale of those services themselves. The 1986 Financial Services Act in the UK took the view that in some cases the only way to cope with this conflict of interest was the enforcement of 'polarization': firms selling investment services could not simultaneously claim to offer investment advice. The corresponding measure in the case of CRSs would be compulsory divestment. The virtues of divestment depend on the costs of CRS bias and the effectiveness of alternative means of regulation, notably regulation of the conduct of CRS-owning carriers. The US Civil Aeronautics Board issued guidelines in 1984 seeking to eliminate CRS bias. Some dispute has continued since then over the effectiveness of these guidelines, with the Department of Justice

proclaiming itself satisfied in 1985 that bias had been virtually eliminated, but several carriers subsequently filing suits alleging continuing
subtle bias (OECD, 1988, p. 90). In Europe, the Transport Directorate
of the European Commission proposed in 1988 a Council Regulation
requiring that CRS facilities available to any one carrier be available to
all on a non-discriminatory basis, and furthermore that 'the criteria to
be used for ranking information [on CRS screens] not be based on any
factor directly or indirectly relating to carrier identity'. It also proposed
a specific set of default criteria for all flights serving any particular city
pair (European Commission, 1988b). This regulation is likely to be
approved in 1989.

How effective is such regulation of conduct? The possibilities of subtle
CRS bias are considerable, and CRS operators can always keep one step
ahead of regulators in this regard. On the other hand, the more subtle
the bias the smaller the cost – the extra search time required to look
beyond the primary screen is very short, and consumers could always
incur it if the resultant quality of information were significantly
improved. About the costs of CRS divestment it is harder to be sure.
There are undoubtedly economies of scale in establishing databases of
this magnitude. It has been further claimed that only airlines would be
willing to incur the necessary costs, so that divestment would halt further
development. This claim, if true, refers to economies of scope rather
than scale – for example, the benefits of 'yield management' (determining the profit-maximizing mix of full-fare and discount tickets) that
accrue from ownership of a CRS to the controlling carrier via the market
information the CRS can provide. But in principle a CRS that was not
owned by an airline could charge airlines for such market information,
which would have a realizable value. Although there would remain
some problems of cost allocation due to the high level of overheads,
the presence of economies of scope of this nature does not appear a
prohibitive obstacle to divestment.

An intermediate regulatory measure would be the requirement that
participating carriers be granted the right to proportionate ownership
of computer reservation systems. Overall, the threat of divestment is
best reserved as a legislative sanction in the event of flagrant violation
of regulations on CRS conduct, on the principle that it is wise to require
an onus of proof on any proposal for restrictions on entry into markets,
including the market for CRS services. It is also likely that changing
technology will allow consumers to make direct reservations without
the intervention of travel agents, making market entry very much easier
for providers of unbiased travel information.

Different questions are raised by the possibility that, even if the direct
consumer welfare losses of CRS bias due to asymmetric information

are small, CRS ownership may be used by incumbent carriers as a barrier to entry in the transport market. In such a case, new entrants might need to incur substantial sunk costs of advertising in order to overcome even mild CRS bias. Without such advertising, consumers would rarely bother to look beyond the first page of a CRS screen, because in equilibrium there would very rarely be any bargains from so doing – but the reason there would be no bargains is that firms would not think it worth while to offer any, since consumers rarely looked beyond the first page! The need to overcome CRS bias will be especially crucial in the presence of economies of scale, since these raise the costs of failure to attract adequate traffic on a route. We argue in Section 3.3.3 below that the presence of such sunk costs may, through restricting new entry, lead to potentially large losses to consumers. This makes it particularly important that rules of conduct are rigorously enforced, and that the authorities be willing to impose divestment if such a sanction becomes necessary to ensure compliance.

Overall, then, the problems posed by asymmetric information alone in the airline industry are not great: safety can be regulated independently, and given the service products on offer, the costs of biased information may not be large. But asymmetric information in combination with market power may be very costly, as Levine (1987) in particular has emphasized – because it will affect the costs of entry and, therefore, the service products that carriers will be willing to offer in the first place.

3.2. Externalities

Market failure due to externalities arises in air transport in two main ways: through noise pollution and through congestion.[13] We argue below that the regulation of noise pollution, like safety, is quite distinct from the regulation of competition in the industry. The regulation of congestion, however, is quite a different matter, and has important implications for competition policy.

3.2.1. Noise and the community. Noise externalities can be of major importance. There is an important question whether solutions involving direct quantitative constraints on airline activity, such as present regulations

---

[13] Although air transport is sometimes misleadingly called a 'network industry', it is not significantly affected in a third way, by network externalities. It is true that the opening of a new airport offers improvements in the facilities available not just to passengers who live in the catchment area of the airport, but also to others who wish to travel to it – but charges are levied on passengers travelling in both directions. There are no significant uncharged benefits that accrue merely from belonging to a larger network (unlike in the case of telecommunications, for example).

governing aircraft noise emissions and curfews on night-time flying, are preferable to solutions involving the price mechanism, such as taxes on noisy aircraft or on departures at certain times. Existing regulatory procedures involve a combination of the two kinds of solution: noisy aircraft are charged higher landing fees by some authorities (though the basis on which these are determined is somewhat arbitrary), and certification becomes harder to obtain as a particular generation of aircraft grows older. The European Commission is currently involved in negotiation of common measures for member states.

The advantages in principle of pricing solutions involve their greater sensitivity to changing circumstances, such as changes in people's preferences between a quieter environment and enhanced travel opportunities. Appropriate levels of prices can nevertheless be difficult to set. One possibility would be to use levels of house prices as an indicator of the damage suffered by individuals living close to airports. Airport authorities could be required to compensate householders for developments like extra runways in areas where house prices had fallen relative to the regional average, and to recover the sum from airlines in landing charges. While a number of difficulties suggest themselves, it should not be forgotten how arbitrary and unsatisfactory in many ways are some of the existing solutions to the problem of noise externalities; the undoubted deficiencies of pricing solutions may come in time to seem small by comparison.

Different methods of dealing with noise externalities have no general tendency to favour incumbent carriers over entrants to a market (nor vice versa) and, therefore, raise no particular issues of competition policy. The same cannot be said for the regulation of congestion, whose important implications for competition policy we now discuss.

3.2.2. Congestion. The inadequacy of existing solutions to congestion externalities is of much greater urgency. We argued in Section 2 that failure to deal properly with congestion problems had exacerbated the consolidation of the US industry; we shall now discuss why this is so. Congestion externalities arise in two ways: at airports and in airspace under air traffic control. Provided appropriate measures are taken to ease the immediate airspace problem, in the medium to long-term congestion at airports is undoubtedly the greater problem.

Problems of access to landing slots (especially at peak hours and in peak seasons) arise already at a number of European airports, particularly Frankfurt, Gatwick and Heathrow. The present system of slot allocation is by scheduling committees of incumbent carriers, and is based on the 'grandfather principle', whereby carriers who have previously had slots have a presumption of continued access. A degree of informal trading of slots takes place, allowing some reallocation in response to changing market conditions. Though not subject to detailed regulation, slot allocation is affected by regulatory constraints: most generally at Heathrow, where there is a blanket prohibition of access by new carriers; but also in more particular cases, as when the Monopolies and Mergers Commission (1987) made it a condition of approval of British Airways' merger with British Caledonian that British Airways agree to surrender some of British Caledonian's slots at Gatwick, a condition subsequently tightened by the European Commission (1988c).

In the presence of capacity constraints, allocation by committees on the grandfather principle has a number of disadvantages. It does not allocate slots to those airlines that can most economically use them. In particular, it gives a significant advantage to incumbents, constituting in some circumstances a serious barrier to entry, whose implications for competition policy will be discussed below. (*Ad hoc* regulatory measures to ensure access to particular new entrants cannot except fortuitously avoid systematically disadvantaging entrants versus incumbents or vice versa.) It creates incentives for merger activity motivated purely by considerations of slot access.[14] Overall, it does not ensure that airport landing charges, besides covering direct costs of provision of airport facilities, reflect the congestion externalities that carriers impose on each other. Existing landing charges tend to be lower for small than for large aircraft, for instance, despite the fact that small aircraft take up similar amounts of terminal space and greater amounts of time on runways[15] (the latter being the binding constraint in most cases). There are, therefore, insufficient incentives for carriers to use larger aircraft, the most likely way in the long term for capacity constraints to be overcome. And in the absence of an effective peak-load pricing system, landing charges also provide inadequate incentives for airlines to carry passengers in off-peak periods. Perhaps most important of all, the absence of congestion pricing means that the development of route networks does not accurately reflect the social costs of connecting flights in hub-and-spoke systems relative to those of direct flights, a point of considerable importance for the development of European route structures after deregulation.

---

[14] The take-over of Connectair by Air Europe in 1988 appears to have been mainly to gain slots at Gatwick, in spite of Air Europe's having already been allocated slots for its operations by the scheduling committee. As discussed in Section 2, a number of US mergers have been similarly motivated, such as those between Texas Air and Eastern, and between USAir and Piedmont (OECD, 1988, p. 124).

[15] This is due to the fact that small aircraft are more vulnerable to turbulence and have, therefore, to remain further behind large aircraft in front of them.

It would be possible either to modify the existing system to reflect more accurately the costs of congestion, or to move towards a more competitive system. Modifying the existing system might involve setting aside a certain proportion of slots to meet the needs of new carriers (though the proportion chosen would have an element of arbitrariness), ensuring that charges to small aircraft more accurately reflected their pressure on runway capacity, and explicitly introducing some form of peak-load pricing. Besides not rocking the boat too much, it is doubtful whether a partial reform of this nature has much to recommend it (though even such mild proposals have faced considerable opposition from carriers). Indeed, since partial reform would leave significant distortionary incentives for merger, it might require a more interventionist regulation of merger activity than would otherwise be necessary, to the detriment of some of the incumbents themselves.

More fundamental measures could take the form of instituting an explicit market for slots while retaining the committee mechanism for initial allocations (a system introduced at the end of 1985 for domestic services at four congested airports in the US[16]); or allocation by auction.

3.2.3. Slot markets: the arguments. Compared to an auction system, one that makes initial allocations on a grandfather basis and then allows carriers to trade has one significant feature: it allows incumbent carriers rather than airport authorities to enjoy the rents from scarcity. It thereby preserves an advantage for incumbents over entrants (though sometimes a lesser one than might otherwise obtain, especially under an exclusion rule such as that operating at Heathrow). And to the extent that it restricts trading between categories (between small and large aircraft, say) it perpetuates some of the disadvantages of the full committee system.

Slot auctions have, however, come under heavy criticism, much of it from incumbent carriers. The main grounds are that slot auctions would lead to an overall rise in landing charges; that they would be inconsistent with existing international obligations of the European countries; that they would 'discriminate' against various classes of carriers, including small carriers, short-haul carriers, charter airlines and carriers of the countries whose airports were most congested; and that the auctions

---

[16] These were La Guardia and Kennedy airports in New York, and Washington's National and Chicago's O'Hare airports. Separate categories of slots are provided for 'air carriers' and 'commuter airlines' as defined by size of aircraft, with trading possible within but not between categories. Entitlement to slots is only partial, with a priority system in case the authorities require extra slots (say for international flights or those designated Essential Air Services) and a 'use it or lose it' rule.

themselves would be dominated by predatory bidding on the part of carriers with market power (CAA, 1988a, Annex F).

The only one of these objections that need be examined in detail is the last. An overall rise in landing charges consequent upon the introduction of slot auctions would not be creating the rents to scarcity that the airport authorities would subsequently enjoy (but which could in any case be taxed). These rents already exist, and are enjoyed by incumbent carriers, especially by carriers with the good fortune to be allocated slots at peak hours. Because they already exist they enable airline operations to be carried on in forms that might not otherwise be profitable and may, therefore, be to the detriment of operations that could be profitable but do not currently have access to slots. And because these rents already exist there is no reason to fear that a rise in landing charges would lead to a rise in fares.

It has, however, been claimed (including by the UK government) that if airport charges were to exceed cost of provision this would violate international obligations under the 1944 Chicago Convention, and also under the UK/US bilateral agreement Bermuda II. Much seems to turn on the precise interpretation of 'cost of provision': the International Civil Aviation Organisation's statement on airport charges suggests this is 'the full economic cost to the community', but the UK government's statement interprets this as precluding 'the operation of pricing mechanisms to ration scarce capacity' (CAA, 1986). This makes little economic sense: the phrase 'cost to the community' seems designed to include externalities. If airport capacity is scarce due to the desire of communities not to endure more of the external costs of having airports, then the price established in an auction market for that capacity will represent in a precise sense the 'full economic cost to the community' of providing it. It is in any case doubtful whether international obligations can reasonably be represented as constraining indefinitely the establishment of reasonable charges for assets of such economic import-ance as airports – though it may suit incumbent carriers to put forward this argument.

The complaint about discrimination between classes of carriers is based either on the view that certain classes (such as long-haul scheduled carriers) have more market power than others – and is, therefore, a variant of the fourth objection; or on the view that an increase in price for one class of carrier is intrinsically a bad thing. However, if slot auctions merely correct unrealistically low charges faced by certain carriers under the existing system, that is to be welcomed: the greater the bias in favour of short-haul multi-stage flights in small aircraft, the more capacity constraints will restrict the overall growth of the European industry and thus its ability to offer a low-cost service to the consumer.

The more liberal European governments have made a point of seeking to enhance opportunities for small carriers, on the grounds that many potential new entrants are small carriers. Though a more competitive charging system would tend to raise charges for carriers flying small aircraft, these carriers need not only be small carriers, nor need small carriers be the only entrants. The solution is to improve access for new entrants as such, not to bias the decisions of both entrants and incumbents towards smaller firm size or aircraft size than profitable operation would otherwise require. Likewise the possibility that an auction mechanism would raise charges for airlines of the countries with the most congested airports (for whom flights to these airports represent a greater proportion of overall services) reflects merely the fact that current undercharging for congestion systematically favours these airlines.[17] Although governments often have a preference for hidden over visible subsidies, there is no reason why economists should not call their bluff. Finally, it remains true that if, for whatever reason, it is wished to protect certain categories of services against others, auctions can be carried out separately by category.

The claim that the auction market would not be competitive, but would be vulnerable to manipulation by carriers with market power in the air transport market itself, is altogether a more serious objection, though not in the end a decisive one. There are two main sources of anxiety. One is that carriers with greater market power than others might bid in the slot market in such a way as to force out competitors for similar services (thus if British Airways were threatened by new entrants on its London–Paris route it might bid artificially high prices for slots around the time its competitors required them). It may be harder, on this view, for the regulatory authorities to identify and control predatory behaviour in the slot market than in the transport market itself. Now although it is true that predatory behaviour is a possibility, there are convincing reasons for thinking it will not be sufficiently serious to outweigh the reduction in rents to incumbents that an auction system would bring about. These are that predatory bidding is less effective in forcing out competitors than predatory pricing of services, and that it is actually easier for competition authorities to identify.

The reason why a predator will find a given investment in predation in the auction market less effective than one in the market for the service is that slots are transferrable between services; slots used on

---

[17] Very substantial rents are enjoyed in this way by many flag carriers; British Airways' privileged position at Heathrow, notably its access to Terminal 4, is one of the most striking examples.

different services are, therefore, closer substitutes than the services themselves. At an airport of any size, there are many hundreds of slots per day: the slot market, though far from perfectly competitive, would nevertheless be more competitive than the market for any particular service. In order to force out a competitor on a particular service, a predator would need to 'overbid' on a very large number of slots indeed, so as to force up the price of all slots that were substitutes for the slot the competitor desired. The cost to the predator of inflicting a given reduction in the competitor's profits would be greater than if the predation could be achieved directly in the market for the service.

The reason why predation in the slot market has been feared is probably due to a misleading analogy with another market for monopoly rents, namely investment in acquiring patents. It is a well established principle that incumbents have greater incentives than their rivals to acquire patents, *even patents for inferior technologies than those they own already* (Gilbert and Newbery, 1982). This is because the rent to a monopolist exceeds the sum of the rents to two duopolists. Hence, the incumbent monopolist's incentive to win the patent is always greater than any potential rival's.

However, while bidding in the slot market has some features in common with competing for patents, it differs in that there may be many slots that are more or less suitable for the entrant to use in starting up a new service on a particular route. Suppose there are N such slots, with values which may differ, reflecting the different suitability of different slot times. To enter the rival need bid for only one, but to keep the rival out the incumbent must bid for all N of them, and must, therefore, pay for each slot more than the rival would pay for any one. Thus, the incumbent's benefit from keeping out the rival must exceed the *sum* of the benefits to the rival over all the N possible slots.[18] Such conditions could be fulfilled – perhaps in the case of a very large airline that could use slots on other services, and anticipated very significant reputation benefits from its predation. But this clearly becomes less and less likely as the number of slots becomes large.

Predation in the slot market is also somewhat easier to identify than predation in the market for the service. This is because the value of a slot to the carrier is the rent to operating the most profitable service from that slot. The entry of a new carrier on that service must reduce

---

[18] This condition corresponds to an extreme form of condition (5.15) in Dasgupta's (1986) model of patent investments. The rival's payoffs are subadditive in that, after one slot has been bought, no others are of value. An important difference between slot auctions and Dasgupta's model is that bids for slots are not forfeit unless successful: the condition holds irrespective of the bidding order, for example.

the rent to the original carrier. If the carrier then bids more for that slot than it did previously, the bidding is clearly predatory (this differs from pricing of the service itself, where a reduction in price after new entry may be predatory but is not necessarily so). It might be wise also to implement additional safeguards against across-the-board overbidding by carriers large enough to dominate the auction market as a whole. So, for example, there could be limits on the total proportion of slots owned by a single carrier, both overall and in any period of, say, one hour during the day. And a 'use-it-or-lose-it' rule would be a useful supplement. At all events, if predation in the slot market is less effective and easier to identify than in the air service market, the risk of such predation is a small cost to set against the clear benefit of reducing the rents to incumbents implicit in the existing system.

The fear of market power in slot markets has also been expressed in a second form (CAA, 1986, para 3.31): as the fear that relatively uncompetitive kinds of service (long-haul scheduled, for example) would tend to drive out more competitive kinds (such as charter, and those short-haul scheduled services that already face significant competition from surface transport). The extent to which this might occur is not easy to evaluate, particularly in the case of charter services, since the charter market is effectively a creation of the current regulatory system. But more important is the fact that, contrary to the implication of the objection, transfers of slots from more competitive to less competitive services tend to increase, not reduce overall welfare. A change in output in a relatively uncompetitive market will affect its price by more than it would in a relatively competitive market. If so, a transfer of output from a more to a less competitive market brings about an unambiguous reduction in distortions.

On balance, therefore, we believe that objections to the auctioning of space at congested airports do not outweigh the real benefits that would accrue from a reduction in the rents afforded to incumbents by the current system. The competition authorities could significantly reduce the risks of predatory action in slot markets. Perpetuation of the current system would constitute a significant obstacle to the establishment of a more competitive European market.

3.2.4. Air traffic control. There has been growing public awareness of the problems of airspace congestion, due partly to media interest in air-misses and disruptive industrial action at the height of the charter holiday season. Yet there appears little reason to fear that airspace congestion in the medium term will be a binding constraint. European airspace capacity can be increased at least to the level of airport capacity, and the solution to the airport problem – the use of larger aircraft – will also relax the airspace constraint. Nonetheless, there are short-run problems of capacity management, and the ability to solve these problems is likely to depend on a coordinated international policy.

Even at peak hours there are still empty airspace slots, due to problems of coordination between different control centres in Europe. Some of these problems are technical (the compatibility of information systems); others simply require centralization of the flow management process. The European Commission (1988d) has made a proposal for a Council decision establishing, *inter alia*, a common European flow management centre under the direction of the European Organization for the Safety of Air Navigation (EUROCONTROL). This measure, coupled with technical advances in data processing equipment, will make possible significant capacity increases in the medium term. It will also be necessary to train larger numbers of air traffic controllers, and there is a strong case for reducing the considerable proportion of European airspace devoted to military use. Most of these measures raise no questions of particular economic significance. However, as in the case of airport congestion, there is an issue about whether charging for capacity provides the appropriate incentives for carriers, especially with regard to optimum aircraft size. It is striking that, after a period of increase in average aircraft size during the 1970s (chiefly due to the introduction of wide-bodied aircraft), average size of European scheduled operations has declined slightly during the 1980s, in spite of a major increase in total traffic. Figure 3 illustrates.

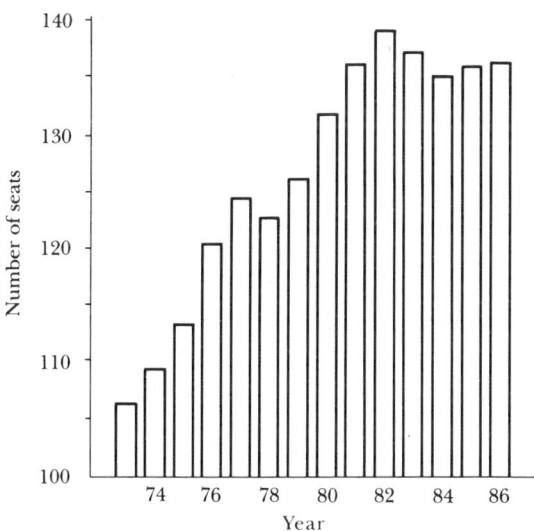

Figure 3. Average aircraft size, local Europe and domestic

Source: European Commission (1988d).

This has been due to new entry by carriers flying small aircraft (especially on regional routes). By contrast, the average size of charter operations has continued to increase during the 1980s. In spite of the widespread public perception that the 1988 air traffic control problems were due to the increase in charter traffic, the number of charter flights in 1988 was slightly down on the 1987 figure despite a 20% increase in passenger kilometres (European Commission, 1988d, p. 5). At present air traffic control charges are lower for small aircraft than for larger aircraft, and as in the case of airport charges there is a strong case for rectifying this anomalous situation; the common European airspace proposal may make this easier to achieve.

This completes our discussion of externalities: the third and most significant cause of market failure in air transport is due to the exercise of market power. It is the potential exercise of market power that provides the main ground for concern at the consolidation of the US industry that we described in Section 2, and the probable consolidation that we foresee for the European industry.

3.3. Market power

Air transport is a service product differentiated in both space and time (and also in certain other dimensions such as comfort). As with nearly all differentiated products there are economies of scale in production (if not, there would be as many different products as there were consumers). There are also economies of scope: when an increase in output of service A reduces the cost of service B. The question then arises: to what kinds of market failure do these phenomena give rise? For the purposes of this discussion we shall treat the spatial differentiation of products as given. We shall consider the nature of competition on routes between pairs of cities, given that carriers can differentiate their products by travel time.

3.3.1. Economies of scale. How do economies of scale affect competition on a city-pair route? It is important to distinguish economies of *density* in operating a given route (the degree to which average costs fall as overall traffic rises on that route) from economies of route length and economies of overall route network size. The principal source of economies of density lies in the use of different kinds of aircraft. As Table 11 reveals, there is a steep decline in average operating costs per seat mile as aircraft size rises from below 100 seats to around 130, and a milder but still significant decline in costs thereafter. Some of this decline is due to the fact that smaller aircraft tend to be used on shorter routes, where fixed costs are higher. But there is also a clear tendency for costs to decline with aircraft size for given route length.

Table 11. Direct operating costs by aircraft type, 1988

Aircraft	No. of seats	Average cost per available seat mile (US cents)
BAC-111	91	7.71
Douglas DC-9-10	92	5.92
BAe-146	100	8.38
Boeing 737–200	133	3.92
Boeing 727-100	134	4.31
Boeing 737-300	149	2.94
Boeing 727-200	192	3.60
Airbus A310	218	3.69
Boeing 767-200	292	2.95
Airbus A300	300	3.48
Douglas DC-10	385	2.81
Lockheed Tristar	413	2.87
Boeing 747-100B	505	2.59

Sources: Avmark (1988); Lloyd's aircraft types.

Given current technology, the decline in average costs is exhausted at the size of aircraft represented by the Boeing 747. But the temporal differentiation of the product means one cannot conclude that economies of density have been exhausted once 747s can be operated on a route. An increase in traffic may make possible, not a further increase in aircraft size, but a greater frequency of scheduling and, therefore, an improvement in average product quality. Economies of density, therefore, continue until services are sufficiently frequent to render negligible the costs to consumers of waiting for flights. This does not, of course, make each route a natural monopoly, since different services on the same route can be operated by different carriers as efficiently as by one.

There are still unavoidable market failures: the actions of one carrier on a route (its pricing and scheduling decisions) affect both the quality of service provided by another and the cost of providing it, a set of production externalities that can be internalized by a single carrier on a route but not by multiple carriers. These externalities affect service *quality* in two main ways. The provision of an extra service on a given route has a beneficial effect on the quality of output (i.e. the frequency of service) consumed by existing purchasers. But quality is a function not just of frequency but also of average load factors, since these affect the probability that a passenger will be able to find spare seats on a given flight. A price reduction on one flight, by attracting travellers away from neighbouring flights, reduces their load factors and thus improves their seat availability. The combined effect of these two phenomena is ambiguous. On very dense routes, where services are already so frequent that the social benefits of extra frequency are negligible, unregulated competition will lead to more frequent services and lower load factors than the social optimum.[19] However, on less dense routes the frequency benefits are greater and may outweigh the effects on load factors.

The effects of one carrier's actions on the *costs* of another may lead to market failure in two ways. First, even where a profitable multiple-carrier outcome exists it may be infeasible under competition, since the scheduling of existing flights may make entry unprofitable, although it would be profitable were schedules to be re-adjusted after entry. (This scheduling barrier to entry may be called the crowded bus problem: there is room for another passenger only if everyone moves further down the bus, but everyone would rather keep the extra passenger off by refusing to do so.) In effect, an incumbent enjoys a form of first-mover advantage in scheduling. More generally, this highlights the fact that scheduling strategies may be affected by the possibility of inducing exit by competitors, so that scheduling may be as much a form of predation as is pricing behaviour. Second, even when competitive entry is feasible it may be undesirable, since it may consist of 'cream-skimming'. This involves entry targeted to carrying peak period traffic that had previously been carried jointly in large aircraft with off-peak traffic, and in the absence of which the carriage of off-peak traffic becomes unprofitable, with an overall cost in social welfare terms. The Appendix provides stylized examples of the scheduling barrier and of cream-skimming (the latter is of less importance in practice).

These arguments all tend to imply that competitive entry has a tendency to lead to overprovision of services on very dense routes and at peak periods, and to underprovision of services on less dense routes and at off-peak periods. They should not be confused with the argument that off-peak provision is desirable on 'social grounds', like bus services in rural areas (this implicitly appeals to considerations of equity, which would hardly be appropriate in the case of airline passengers). Nor are they equivalent to the invalid argument that air transport is a natural monopoly because the marginal cost of extra passengers on a given

------

[19] Panzar (1979). In equilibrium, the carrier does not appropriate the beneficial effects of a marginal price reduction on one flight upon the quality of service of neighbouring flights, so prices will be above the optimum. Panzar's model makes a number of special assumptions, including uniform demand distribution, absence of locational advantages and of scheduling barriers to entry, which mean that it cannot be used to infer a general tendency to over-provision of service under competition.

flight is below average cost.[20] Nevertheless, they do constitute strong grounds for expecting market failure in an unregulated industry. This does not imply that any particular regime of economic regulation will improve matters: Morrison and Winston (1985) found that by far the greatest consumer benefit from US deregulation consisted in increased service frequency. In practice, regulation has tended to make few concessions to patterns of peak demand. Figure 4 compares the temporal distribution of departure times on the London Heathrow – Amsterdam Schipol route in 1980 and in 1988. It is notable that there were more flights at peak times in 1988: the only periods in which there was less frequent provision in 1988 than in 1980 were around 11 a.m. and after 7 p.m. This does not, of course, tell us whether there was excessive peak traffic under competition or insufficient peak traffic under regulation (possibly both are true) – but it underlines the significance of the regulatory regime for service provision as well as for costs. On balance, the US evidence in Table 1 (Section 2.1.1) suggests that deregulation provides such improvements in service frequencies for all except the least dense short-haul routes, that the under-provision of off-peak services may not be a very high price to pay. This conclusion is strengthened by the consideration that surface transport provides a more effective substitute for such services in Europe than in the US.

3.3.2. Economies of scope; hub-and-spoke systems. As we discussed in Section 2, one of the most striking features of the evolution of the US industry since deregulation has been the development of hub-and-spoke route network systems. These are often held to imply that carriers need to be large to compete effectively, since they reflect economies of scope in route operation. It is not easy to evaluate this claim, for two reasons. First, the alleged economies of scope may reflect simply the way in which networks enable carriers to engage in certain predatory practices (such as predatory scheduling, or frequent-flyer programmes). Second, even if there appear to be private cost advantages to operating networks these may not reflect true social cost, because (for example) they do not incorporate the extra congestion costs of connecting as compared to direct flights.

---

[20] See Pryke, (1987), pp. 69–73, which convincingly refutes this argument. If some availability of empty seats on the average flight is a planned phenomenon, there is no temptation for airlines to cut fares to fill these seats (except for very last-minute bookings on a standby basis). In exactly the same way, a vendor of perishable commodities such as fruit will tend to have unsold stock at the end of the average period, to meet unforeseen fluctuations in demand.

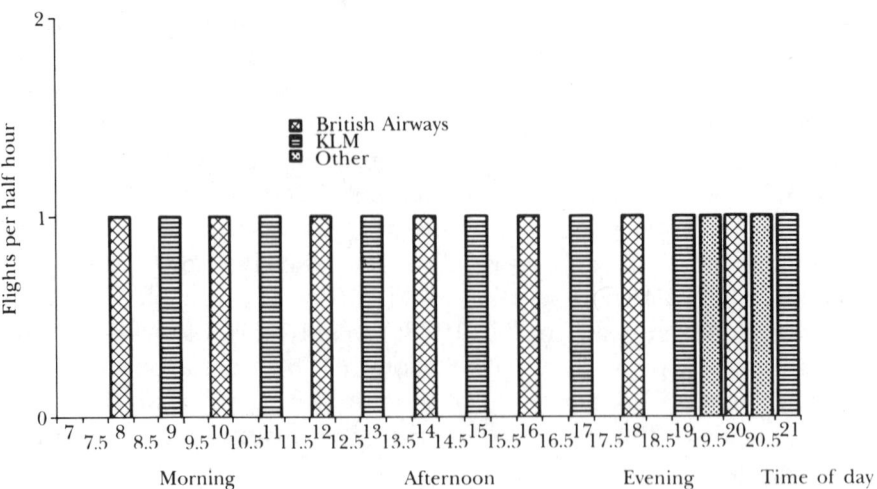

Figure 4a. Distribution of departures by time, Heathrow to Schipol, 1980

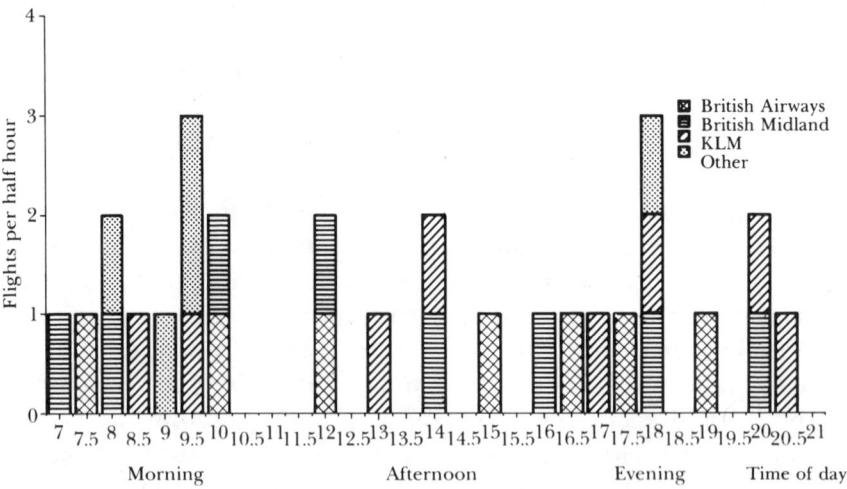

Figure 4b. Distribution of departures by time, Heathrow to Schipol, 1988

The possibility of economies of scope arises *because* of economies of density on individual routes. Traffic on a direct flight from A to B may not be so heavy as when the carrier operates via a hub at C: traffic from A to C is heavier because it incorporates traffic from A to *all* destinations, while traffic from B to C is heavier because it incorporates traffic to C from all destinations. This increase of traffic on each leg may reduce costs or improve service frequency. Against these benefits must be set certain higher costs: a traveller from A to B takes off and lands twice instead of once, takes longer to reach the destination, travels further in total and may have to suffer the inconvenience of changing aircraft and an increased risk of baggage loss or missed connections.

It is misleading to describe all the cost savings from hubbing as economies of scope. True economies of scope describe only the cost savings accruing to an airline in operating a service from A to C if it operates the connecting service from C to B *itself*, as opposed to another carrier's doing so. Mere complementarity of services on one route with those on another is not sufficient, unless the complementarity is carrier-specific. There are undoubtedly some true economies of scope in hubbing: 'intralining' can help with coordination of travel and reduce the risks of baggage loss, though this is not of major significance.[21] But what looks most like an economy of scope turns out on closer examination not to be so at all. The complementarity of connecting services is time-specific; given the *de facto* differentiation of carriers' services by time, this looks like a complementarity that only a single carrier can exploit, thus ensuring more rapid connecting flights. However, the latter benefits can in principle be achieved as efficiently by agreements between carriers, like those between a firm and its suppliers in any vertical chain of production. To the extent that these are difficult to achieve it is because many firms that operate complementary services are also direct competitors, and would, therefore, prefer to schedule in a predatory[22] rather than a symbiotic fashion. We have an instance of the familiar problem that firms may have an incentive to integrate vertically, not because of true economies of scope, but because of a shortage of suppliers who are not already vertically integrated with the firm's competitors. In addition, since hubs are spatially differentiated, vertical integration allows a carrier to exploit a local monopoly in the vicinity of the hub.[23] In short, one of the main benefits of hubbing is to increase a carrier's market power, and to enable it to resist the market power of competitors.

This is particularly true in respect of predatory scheduling. Possession of a hub and spokes network can allow a carrier to exploit economies

---

[21] Bending over backwards to find some virtue in the argument that the benefits of intralining can offset the threats to competition in hubbing, the Civil Aviation Authority (1988b) suggests that 'identification of the agency who lost one's baggage is of some advantage even if it does not yet get the baggage back'!

[22] Predatory scheduling can take two forms: on a given route, one carrier may schedule services close to those of another so as to 'squeeze out' the competitor: the battle between People Express and USAir is an example (see Sawer, 1987, p. 35). Predation may also involve scheduling flights *away* from times when they would connect with those of a competitor. The latter is the issue here.

[23] Bailey, Graham and Kaplan (1985) estimated that an airline with 50% of the departures from a hub could charge fares 7% higher than one with only 25% of the departures. Borenstein (1988) finds a strong effect of airport dominance on the share of departures on a particular route.

of density on individual routes without facing the risks of predatory scheduling involved in services connecting with those of other carriers. Once established, it also provides incentives for predatory scheduling by the carrier itself, should another carrier attempt to provide services connecting with its own (since any service connecting with one of its own is also competing with another service of its own). And the more routes an airline operates, the more its strategy on one route can act as a signal of its intentions on others. Route operation is a repeated game, so the value of networks in establishing competitive reputations is an important component of their attractiveness.

Carriers with large networks can also employ an increasingly popular form of predation: the frequent flyer programme. In effect this imposes a switching cost on the consumer who wishes to change to another carrier, and is, therefore, clearly a form of predation against new entrants. Why do travellers allow this form of switching cost to be imposed on them, taking frequent flyer bonuses rather than demanding a price reduction on each flight? The answer may lie partly in a tax-induced distortion: most frequent flyers are business travellers, whose employers buy their tickets, but whose frequent flyer bonuses are a form of untaxed income. Removing the tax distortion may not prevent this form of predation altogether, however (see Klemperer, 1987; Banerjee and Summers, 1987; Bulkley, 1989). The fact that switching costs are an entry barrier makes it evident why incumbents as a group benefit from them. But it might be thought that one incumbent willing to offer flight-by-flight benefits would attract business at the expense of another incumbent offering indivisible benefits that required saving over time, so that competition between incumbents would drive out frequent flyer programmes.

The main reason for expecting such predation to persist is that switching costs, by effectively segmenting the market between incumbents, allow them to exploit monopoly power; they are, in effect, a form of multi-period tacit collusion. Frequent flyer programmes may also act to diminish carrier risk: in particular, once such programmes exist, incumbents operating them may be able (by exploiting economies of density from existing customers) to offer lower prices than entrants as well as offering frequent flyer benefits. So entrants may need to offer frequent flyer benefits (which become a cost only after some time and only if entry is successful) in order to obtain economies of density themselves. In order for them to do so, large route networks may be indispensable.

Hub-and-spokes networks constitute, in effect, a form of vertical integration that becomes indispensable for one carrier if enough others are also vertically integrated, and if the density benefits of indirect over direct flights are sufficiently great. Given the consequences for market power, it is important, therefore, that the true social costs of making indirect rather than direct flights should be borne by carriers. This adds a degree of urgency to the issue of congestion: perhaps the strongest argument in favour of charging adequately for congestion externalities is that failure to do so may bias networks towards more hubbing-and-spoking (and, therefore, to the creation of greater market power) than is optimal.

To what extent do the density benefits of indirect flights offset the other costs? Estimated cost equations tend to suggest that 'there are substantial economies with respect to load factors, aircraft size and stage length' but that 'there are diseconomies when an airline serves more ports and when it operates more flights from a given port', the former being substantially greater than the latter.[24] Such estimates ignore changes in service quality, as measured by improvements in scheduling frequency and deteriorations in journey time and convenience. Morrison and Winston (1986) estimated that the frequency benefits of deregulation, at an average of $8 per trip, were approximately double those from lower fares, and compared with costs of only $0.96 from longer journeys due to hubbing.

Two issues arise: first, whether market power may lead to hidden costs of hubbing, in the form of smaller fare decreases than would otherwise occur; and second, whether these results would change substantially if carriers bore the full costs of congestion. On balance it seems unlikely that these factors would alter the judgment that consumer benefits of deregulation even under hub-and-spoke systems are significantly greater than those of the old regulated regime. But they may still be inferior to those of an alternative outcome in which congestion externalities are fully charged and tighter restrictions on predation reduce the incentives for carriers to resort to hubbing. Whether and to what extent such an alternative is feasible will be the concern of our discussion of competition policy below.

3.3.3. Sunk costs and contestability. Our discussion of economies of scale and scope has revealed a number of predatory strategies available to incumbent airlines besides the familiar strategies of predatory pricing. We have not yet discussed whether these significantly affect the degree of contestability of the market. In the early days of US deregulation, civil

---

[24] Kirby (1986), pp. 344–45. The cost elasticity with respect to the number of ports is 1.041, and to the departures per port is 1.084. Both are significantly different from unity at the 1% level, but compare with elasticities of 0.911, 0.314 and 0.495 for load factor, stage length and aircraft size, respectively.

aviation was thought to be very close to the textbook ideal of contestable markets: the mere threat of entry was enough to ensure that, for example, 'local service monopolists have been pricing more or less competitively on their long-haul routes' (Bailey and Panzar, 1981). More recent empirical work has cast doubt on this conclusion, particularly since it has often been observed to require actual rather than merely potential entry to reduce fares on routes to which entry had previously been restricted (Call and Keeler, 1985). Moore (1986) found that 'price competition becomes significant only when there are five or more carriers'. The emerging consensus appears to be that airline markets are 'imperfectly' contestable; potential competition has a significant effect on incumbent behaviour, but not as strong an effect as the presence of actual competitors. For example, Morrison and Winston (1987) estimate that the number of actual carriers on a route has a highly significant effect on passenger welfare. The number of potential carriers (those serving at least one airport on the route) has a significant effect provided there are at least four.

The reason why airline markets were believed to be highly contestable was that sunk costs were considered negligible: aircraft were 'capital on wings' (Baumol, Panzar and Willig, 1988). It has become evident, first, that costs may be sunk in a number of ways that were not previously evident; second, that sunk costs do not have to be large to allow incumbents to enjoy significant rents; and third, that there are other barriers to entry than those that consist in the presence of sunk costs (scheduling barriers and congestion problems, for example).

Sunk costs in air transport consist partly of advertising expenditure, which may need to be fairly high to persuade travellers to switch to a new airline (especially in the presence of frequent flyer programmes and CRS bias; see Levine, 1987); this may be less necessary in the case of an established airline entering a new route. Given that it takes time to determine whether a new service will attract sufficient traffic to be profitable, there is also a sunk cost implicit in the need to operate a service at below-profitable traffic levels in the meantime. This is partly a switching cost, but partly the intrinsic cost of uncertainty: the greater the uncertainty about market conditions, the longer a carrier may have to operate at below profitable levels in order to discover whether entry will ultimately be profitable or not. Price and schedule wars, besides being directly predatory, can also serve to increase the uncertainty faced by an entrant and, therefore, raise the sunk cost of uncertainty.

While sunk costs may be greater in air transport than was once thought, they are, nevertheless, low by the standards of many industries. But it is not necessarily the case that low sunk costs imply low rents to incumbents. 'Hit-and-run' entry – the means by which incumbents are

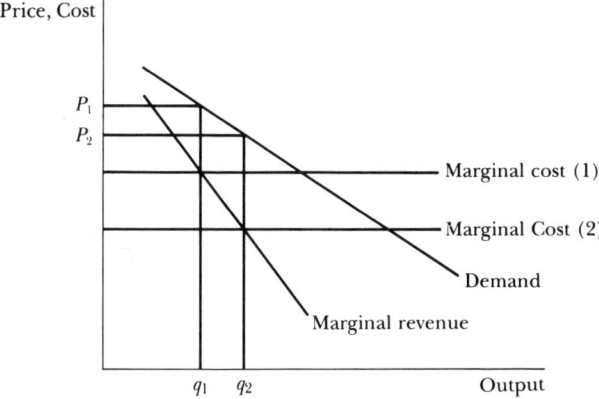

Figure 5. The effects of cost reduction on the price and output decisions of a monopolist

Note: In this example, marginal costs are assumed for simplicity to be constant and equal to average costs.

disciplined in contestable markets – is difficult when incumbents can lower prices very quickly, and when rents to operating a service may take some time to be realized. Entries to the US air transport market have not tended to be of the hit-and-run variety, in which firms leaving the market have made positive profits as a result of entry. Entry has more often been either 'hit-and-stay' (Texas Air) or 'get-hit-and-run' (People Express). However, the possibility of 'hit-and-stay' entry has undoubtedly helped to reduce the extent to which incumbents enjoy monopoly rents in the form of high costs ('the quiet life') – though Levine (1987) emphasizes that the successful US carriers since deregulation have by no means been those with the lowest costs.

This suggests that it may be quite misleading to describe airline markets as even imperfectly contestable. 'Almost contestable' may mean 'not contestable at all': if incumbents are able to lower prices faster than entrants can set up profitable operation, then even if sunk costs are very low an incumbent can enjoy full incumbency rents without fear of hit-and-run entry.[25] By contrast, potential competition undoubtedly can curb X-inefficiency (high costs) on the part of incumbents, since costs (unlike prices) cannot be quickly lowered in the event of entry. But, as Figure 5 shows, potential competition that reduces these inefficiency rents can lead to a reduction in prices without in any way reducing the profit rents that the incumbent enjoys. This is because a

[25] See Schwartz and Reynolds (1983). A good account of these issues is given in Vickers and Yarrow (1988), pp. 53–77.

lowering of the incumbent's costs makes it profitable to increase output (and lower price) even if the slope of the incumbent's demand curve is undiminished and, therefore, his market power in the traditional sense is preserved.

This makes it natural to distinguish between markets that are *cost-contestable* and those that are *profit-contestable*. Both the empirical evidence and a common-sense view of the speed of incumbents' reactions, are consistent with the claim that airline markets may display a degree of cost-contestability, without being profit-contestable to any degree at all.

Furthermore, Figure 5 makes clear that if deregulation increases cost-contestability without increasing profit-contestability, total profits of incumbents can be expected to increase. This is exactly what the US evidence suggests, as we discussed in Section 2.1.1. Morrison and Winston (1986) estimated that industry profits had risen as a result of deregulation: at 1977 prices the (counterfactually deregulated) profits were equivalent to a pretax rate of return of 14%, compared to an average for US manufacturing corporations during 1977 of 12.8%. They suggest this difference may be due to higher mean rates of return being required in air transport to compensate for greater riskiness of profits. Even if this is true, the view of air transport as imperfectly contestable would imply that profitability should be *significantly lower* than the average for other industries, many of which are by any standards hardly contestable at all.

We have argued in addition that, even without economic regulation, there exist other significant barriers to entry than the presence of sunk costs. In particular these include scheduling barriers (the crowded bus problem), and the shortage of slots at congested airports. These have important implications for the regulation of market power.

4. Conclusions: can regulation diminish market power?

Although there are reasons to expect market failure in unregulated airline markets, there is nothing to recommend a comprehensive economic regulation of the kind in force in Europe today. A removal of artificial entry barriers, as in the US deregulation, would bring undoubted benefits to Europe; an annual gain of $1.5 bn. to $2 bn. (mainly to consumers) is a reasonable estimate. But opportunities would remain for incumbent carriers to exercise market power. Over a period of years this exercise of market power might erode many of the benefits of liberalization. It is true that air transport could be expected to retain a degree of cost-contestability, so incumbents would enjoy rents in the form of profits rather than high costs. This may well be preferable to the current situation, where consumers are disadvantaged by regulation and there are not even any monopoly profits to show for it. But high costs in the past have been a reflection not just of inefficiency but also of rents to labour and other inputs, which will tend to be reduced by liberalization. At all events, it is important to avoid a liberalization that pays insufficient attention to the need to prevent the abuse of market power.

Some forms of market power are relatively easy to control more effectively than the US authorities have done; others will remain hard for regulation to alleviate. Regulation should differ from the US system in two main ways. First, it should reduce the rents to incumbents due to congestion. The best way to cope with congestion is to auction slots at airports. There is no real case for separate auctions by categories of carrier, except as a transitional measure. (Another way to cope with the transition might be to return some of the proceeds of auction to carriers on a lump-sum basis, provided this could be achieved in a way that did not systematically favour incumbents.)

The second way in which European policy should differ from that in the US is by adopting a much tougher stance towards mergers. The economies of scale in airline operation consist almost entirely of economies of aircraft size (and derivatively, of route density) and of route length. So the defence that mergers enable carriers to achieve benefits of large size that outweigh any diminution of competition is nearly always spurious. To the extent that a number of US mergers have been motivated by considerations of access to congested airports, a more competitive system of congestion management would in itself reduce the incentives for anti-competitive mergers. But there are other anti-competitive motives for mergers: the claim that two carriers could integrate their existing routes into a hub-and-spoke network, for instance, is not a strong justification for a merger unless there are convincing reasons why the necessary coordinated scheduling could not be achieved by agreements between independent airlines. It has also been claimed (Levine, 1987; Howard, 1988; OECD, 1988) that CRS bias makes it difficult for small carriers, especially feeder airlines, to receive fair treatment unless they agree to code-sharing, and ultimately to merger. This makes it especially important that abuse of CRS dominance be policed effectively, with the presumption that resulting mergers be regarded as anti-competitive.[26] And the importance of potential as well

---

[26] Mergers of this kind could naturally be regarded as an abuse of dominant position under the terms of Article 86 of the Treaty of Rome, with ownership of the CRS constituting prima facie evidence of dominance.

as actual competition means that it would be unwise to limit merger scrutiny solely to mergers that increase concentration on a given route or at a given hub.

It is harder for the competition authorities to control predation, particularly predatory scheduling, though it could be contained more effectively than has been the case in the US. Even where predation itself cannot be prevented, a hostility to mergers that appeared to be a partial consequence of predatory behaviour by one of the carriers concerned might help to reduce the incentives for predation in the first place. In particular, since entry on a route should lead to scheduling of existing services *away* from the new service, the competition authorities could regard an incumbent response that scheduled flights *towards* the new service as presumptively predatory. Predatory pricing itself is almost impossible to prevent, not least because predation in the US has tended to involve, not any reduction in fares as such, but a relaxation of the conditions attached to discount fares. But it can be made less likely by a requirement that a carrier that has reduced its fares or relaxed discount conditions should maintain the change for a certain length of time after any exit of a competitor on the relevant route. We suggested above that the dangers of predation in the form of frequent flyer programmes may be significantly contained, not by direct regulatory prohibition but by international agreement that the benefits of such programmes be fully taxable: the threat of prohibition may be an incentive to reach such agreements. But there is certainly a case for an outright prohibition.

The tendency for competition to provide sub-optimal levels of service at off-peak periods and on less dense routes is difficult to regulate effectively. In principle, there could be subsidies to off-peak services, but there would always be imperfect information about the precise subsidies that were needed. It is hard to see how a programme of subsidies could operate without becoming a covert means for national governments to underwrite anti-competitive behaviour by their own airlines. But on balance we believe the costs of this form of market failure would not be high. This is particularly true in Europe, where surface transport provides an important substitute.

It is sometimes argued that the entrenched interests involved in the European airline industry make it unrealistic to hope for significant reforms. But the speed of recent change has been dramatic by historical standards, and the initiatives of the European Commission have given reason to be guardedly sanguine. There are two considerations which regulators may use to soften the opposition of existing carriers to long-overdue reform. One is that some reforms (such as slot auctions) may diminish the intrusiveness of others (such as merger policy). The second consideration, of which both airlines and their patron governments ought to be more aware, is that both economic principles and the available evidence suggest that reform is good for the profitability of the industry. Even with a more vigorous competition policy than that adopted in the US, most European carriers could expect to make higher profits under a more liberal system than they do now.

To sum up, the dangers of market failure in an unregulated air transport market are very real. The best long-term future for Europe lies in a removal of artificial barriers to entry, supplemented by a more competitive approach to congestion, and a rigorous policing of anti-competitive behaviour in the areas of predation by incumbent carriers and of mergers.

Discussion

Stephen Breyer
US Court of Appeals

In this paper, Francis McGowan and Paul Seabright present an excellent analysis of airline deregulation in Europe. I have no serious disagreement. In what follows, I shall point out three differences between American and European circumstances, which I would recommend the authors to take into account. I will also take issue with the authors on a couple of subsidiary points. Finally, I will reemphasize the need for policymakers to pay attention to potential roadblocks to free competition in air transport.

There are three important differences between the regulated (i.e. pre-1976) American marketplace and Europe. These differences counsel some caution before Europeans generalize too far, too fast, from the American experience. First, it seems that the American industry prior to deregulation was very different from the European industry today. Before deregulation, America's domestic airline industry was regulated in terms of price and entry conditions. The firms were, however, privately owned and the industry was an oligopoly. The result of this regulation was in accordance with what economic theory would predict when firms cannot compete in price; there was a substitution of service for price competition and accordingly the fares were high, the service was frequent and the planes were empty. For example, load factors in California's unregulated intra-state markets where carriers could freely compete with respect to price were some 10.6 to 15% higher than in all other domestic markets, where they could not.

By contrast, European airlines are often both regulated and owned by national governments. As McGowan and Seabright point out,

European agreements mean that their airlines may 'collaborate on scheduling ..., pool revenue', and, through agreement, 'determine both fare levels and the maximum share of capacity' that each airline can offer. The result is that European 'regulation' permits far more complete cartelization than American regulation ever allowed. At the same time, the national governments might, in principle, use the power they derive from ownership to prevent the cartel from earning supra-normal profits. Still, given the higher degree of coordination achieved by European carriers, the extent of excess capacity ('overscheduling') may not be as large in Europe as it was in America before deregulation. Potential efficiency gains may thus be smaller than those achieved in America.

Second, it seems the pricing policy of American carriers prior to deregulation was very different from what is observed in Europe today. In particular, it is useful to distinguish between two types of traveller: on the one hand, business travellers are willing to pay more for frequently scheduled service and last-minute seat availability; on the other hand, vacation travellers are keen and able to reserve in advance, they will fly at less convenient times and are anxious to pay lower prices. European air services apparently offer both types of customer extensive service. The business traveller uses regularly scheduled services while the vacation traveller flies at a discounted, restricted fare or takes a charter flight. American 'regulated' services, however, in the early 1970s did *not* provide much special, low fare service for vacation travellers. The Civil Aeronautics Board had begun to phase out discount fares, and it had virtually eliminated charter travel. As a result, deregulation promised American vacation travellers extensive price reduction.

The widespread availability of low fare charter and discount services in Europe, however, makes it harder to say, in advance, that increased competition will bring travellers large benefits. Of course, benefits will still presumably accrue. Indeed, it is unlikely that regulators, national governments, or the airlines devising cartel agreements have designed a pattern of fares and service frequency which mimics the outcome of market forces. A competitive marketplace is still likely to operate adjustments and to come closer to offering the combination of prices and services that consumers want. Still, it would be helpful to identify empirically the areas where the major misallocations currently occur.

Third, it is clear that deregulation in America has led to significantly lower fares and a large increase in air travel. Indeed, according to the Air Transport Association, the number of passengers flying per year increased from 173 mn. in 1971 to 475 mn. in 1987. As a result, airports became congested, which, in turn, gave rise to a demand for building additional airports. Assume for the sake of argument that deregulation in Europe also leads to a significant increase in air travel. The external costs of providing necessary additional airport space might be significantly higher in Europe, for the land near major cities may, at present, serve arguably more valuable purposes than in the US. At the same time, the alternatives to increased air travel, namely the use of trains, are, as McGowan and Seabright point out, more readily available in Europe than in the US.

On the whole, the high degree of coordination achieved by European carriers and the widespread availability of discount fares in Europe suggest that the potential for major efficiency gains is likely to be lower in Europe now than it was in the US in 1976. In addition, if deregulation leads to significantly greater use of air service, the social cost of providing that service may be somewhat greater in Europe than in the US.

Next, I wish to express some minor disagreements with the authors' analysis. First, it seems to me that McGowan and Seabright overstate the degree to which mergers have led to a 'concentrated' American industry. Prior to 1976 (and since 1938) 10 domestic carriers provided intra-regional air service. In addition, there were several local service carriers (admitted just after World War II) and a handful of charter carriers. Pan American did not offer significant *domestic* service. The industry Herfindahl–Hirschman Index (HHI) for 1972 was about 1205 and the top four carriers accounted for 60% of all revenue passenger miles; the top eight accounted for 85%. McGowan and Seabright's data for 1988 reveals an HHI of about 1120. The top four carriers then account for about 58% of all revenue passenger miles while the top eight account for about 88%.[27]

On the whole, one is thus led to conclude that the industry is not significantly more concentrated now than it was when regulated. At that time, there was a consensus that the industry was structurally competitive. Accordingly, it does not seem that the current concentration has yet reached the point where one would say the industry is not workably competitive.

Second, the importance of market failures in the provision of city air services can be questioned. McGowan and Seabright refer to a 'quality externality' which stems from the fact that additional flights, by attracting passengers away from existing ones, will make those less crowded and more comfortable. Still, the overall impact of competition in the US was to make virtually all flights more crowded. The other market failures listed by the authors stem from the fact that the provision of

---

[27] This assumes Eastern and Texas Air are separated; in fact, the sale of the Eastern shuttle means that the concentration figures presented here should be somewhat lower, but uncertainty as to Eastern's future must cast doubt on all recent figures.

air service is a discrete, and not continuous process. I simply wonder whether these market failures are important. The policy question with respect to 'regulation' or 'deregulation' is not whether either will achieve *precisely* the efficiency gains of a theoretically perfect world. The question is rather to determine on efficiency grounds which regime is on the whole preferable.

Finally, I wish to reemphasize the obstacles to competition described by McGowan and Seabright. There are five prominent obstacles. First, I agree that mergers must be watched carefully. To discriminate between mergers on efficiency grounds is, however, a difficult task, which is left primarily to anti-trust authorities; whether or not they have been sufficiently vigilant is, of course, currently a subject of considerable debate. Second, computerized reservation systems may, indeed, impede competition and within a hub-spoke system, they may build the dominant carrier's market power. The problem may, however, be less serious in Europe because of the widespread availability of the minitel. Third, it seems that airlines have built market power with travel agents by using commissions which increase with the volume of sales. This should be watched. Fourth, the problem of slot availability at airports is indeed serious. The solution proposed by McGowan and Seabright is the correct one. Finally, I agree completely with McGowan and Seabright about the non-competitive effect of frequent flyer programmes. Given the popularity of frequent flyer rewards, however, I suspect that their solution based on taxation will be hard to implement, from a political perspective.

Overall, it seems to me that the American experience is so far surprisingly similar to what the advocates of deregulation predicted in the early 1970s. Fares are down; travel is up; congestion is a problem; safety has not been affected. Problems exist, particularly with respect to the development of pockets of market power, even though the restructuring of Eastern may help in this respect. Whether European markets offer sufficient promise of benefits through deregulation to warrant the costs of major institutional change is, of course, a matter that will be left to the Europeans, well informed by papers like McGowan and Seabright's.

David Encaoua
University of Paris I

This paper describes very well the current state of scheduled air transport in Europe. The problems that the industry faces on the eve of the internal market are well presented. Indeed, the question of airline deregulation in Europe gives rise to ambivalent feelings.

Following US deregulation, there is something of a consensus that the regime of bilateral agreements between airlines should be disposed of within the short to medium term. At the same time, there is considerable scepticism about the merits of deregulation along the lines of the American experience. Complete liberalization is certainly regarded as inappropriate by the European Commission and by many European governments. Despite the pressure that international carriers put on them, government officials have often preferred to shy away from substantive liberalization. The attitude of the French government regarding competition between domestic carriers is a good case in point. In this context of considerable indecisiveness, the paper by Francis McGowan and Paul Seabright is very welcome. The authors provide a careful assessment of the American experience. They accurately present the gradual reforms adopted by the European Commission. Finally, they identify the most important market failures in the industry and propose adequate solutions. In these comments, I wish to explore further the issues of whether the American experience is directly applicable to the European environment. Subsequently, I will also expand somewhat on the authors' discussion of market failures and their proposed solutions.

At the outset, I wish to emphasize that the average distance between cities, either within or across countries, is much smaller in Europe than in the US. This has two consequences; first, the economies of scope which can accrue by organizing networks around hubs will be more limited. Second, competition with alternative modes of transportation, railways in particular, should be taken into account. Another difference between the US and the European environment stems from the diversity of interests across European countries. Roughly, one may divide Europe into three zones, namely the South (Spain, Portugal and Greece), the Centre (The UK, France, Germany, Italy and Benelux) and the North (Scandinavian countries). Countries in the South are mainly concerned with charter flights for leisure trips, which fall outside the bilateral agreements. Flag carriers in those countries tend to be opposed to deregulation, because their residual traffic is low and their costs are high. Countries in the North wish to make sure that their main carrier (SAS) will not become a feeder to some large hubs in the Centre. This, they fear, would be the result of deregulation. The countries in the Centre are thus the only ones to favour more competition. Still, the various European carriers do not start from equally desirable competitive positions. For example, my own estimates suggest that total factor productivity (measured in the European network by the Tornquist input and output indices) can vary by as much as 20% across the five largest European carriers. As indicated by the authors, there are also large differences in labour costs. Interestingly, the ranking that the authors obtain on the basis of labour costs does not match the ranking that I obtain from estimates of total factor productivity.

The market for air passenger transport has traditionally been considered as a textbook example of a contestable market. Appreciations of this matter are currently more sober for several reasons. First, competition occurs at the level of the network and not on a route-by-route basis. Accordingly, airlines try to obtain some market power by acquiring a dominant position in specific hubs. Second, efficient management of the network is greatly enhanced by the availability of computerized reservation systems which contain information on load factors. Such reservation systems can effectively act as a barrier to entry. An appropriate solution to this problem might be to regulate the reservation systems. In particular, the management of reservations could be set as a prerogative of travel agents. Third, in the presence of network externalities, efficient operation will entail some level of coordination. The question arises of how, if at all, to organize the coordination of the various networks. On the one hand, one could let the airlines freely coordinate their schedules and frequencies. The problem is that they might be tempted to coordinate prices at the same time. At the opposite extreme, one could let the market operate, ruling out coordination between carriers. As indicated by US experience, substantial consolidation might then occur, thereby increasing the risk of tacit collusion.

The shortage of airport facilities might also lead to a significant market failure. The prime objective of some mergers in the US has actually been to obtain take-off and landing slots at specific airports. The mechanism which is used to allocate these slots is rather arbitrary. It is often criticized as favouring incumbent airlines. As advocated by the authors, the auctioning of airport slots could be an appealing alternative. Still, there is no guarantee that such a system will allocate airport slots efficiently, given that there might very well be a divergence between private profitability and efficiency. In particular, an allocation of slots driven by the market might not provide the optimal mix of flights on high and low density routes. Indeed we know that monopolistic competition will not in general lead to socially optimal product diversity.

General discussion

Some panel members were concerned about comparing airline productivity across countries. In particular, Richard Portes was sceptical about David Encaoua's claim that productivity is higher in France than in the UK and wondered about the exact measure of productivity that was used. Encaoua replied that his measure referred to total factor productivity. He added that his estimates also suggest that labour productivity is significantly lower in France than in the UK. Still, one should exercise great care in using those estimates. Portes insisted that extensive rent sharing with labour could lead to high wages and inflate output. Productivity measures would, thus, be distorted by the presence of some monopoly in labour and product markets. Paul Seabright added that productivity measures also crucially depend on a proper valuation of the quality of the services and on a proper decomposition of output. The estimates that he puts forward consider only aggregate output and do not make adjustments for the quality of services. These estimates should, thus, not be taken too seriously.

Jacques Melitz was worried about safety. In particular, he was not convinced by the authors' proposal of auctioning off airport slots. To price congestion is fine as long as there are no significant externalities on the way. As far as airport and airspace congestion was concerned, he thought that safety was a major externality at stake, which would justify a degree of formal cooperation between airlines. Stephen Breyer and Paul Seabright concurred to claim that safety in the US had not been impaired by deregulation. As a result, they thought that the issue of safety was orthogonal to the problem of deregulation. John Black argued that in principle externalities in terms of safety could not be ruled out. Yet, he suggested that the appropriate market to internalize this problem is the insurance market. Large compensation should be awarded to passengers in case of casualties. The associated insurance premiums will then provide airlines with the appropriate incentives to run safe operations.

Michael Emerson indicated that he was optimistic about the prospect of deregulation. Indeed, a recent decision by the European Court of Justice has ruled bilateral price fixing agreements illegal. At the same time, the ruling has empowered the European Commission to determine the circumstances under which pricing agreements could be allowed. Even though it is not clear at this point what will emerge, it seems that the present institutional and legal environment is adequate for deregulation to take place.

Appendix. The crowded bus problem and cream-skimming

To give a simple (if unrealistic) example, suppose that on a particular route there are three kinds of aircraft, as follows:

Type A (a 350-seater) costs £11,000 to operate per trip.
Type B (a 180-seater) costs £10,000 to operate per trip.
Type C (a 120-seater) costs £9,000 to operate per trip.

Each consumer has a preferred hour of departure during the day, and places a maximum value £x on a flight if it departs at her preferred time. A flight that leaves y hours before or after her preferred time has a maximum value of £$(x - 10\ y)$. A consumer chooses the available flight (if any) that maximizes her value minus cost. Carriers cannot discriminate between classes of passenger.

Example 1. There are 300 consumers per day, with preferred times distributed evenly over the 24 hours of the day. Each consumer places a maximum value of £160 on a flight at her preferred time. There is a single incumbent. It is easy to check that the most profitable schedule for the incumbent is to fly two flights per day at 12-hour intervals, using aircraft of type B. Each flight carries 150 passengers at a profit-maximizing fare of £100, yielding total profits per trip of £5,000. Suppose the flights depart at 12 noon and 12 midnight. A new entrant would need to schedule a flight at 6 a.m. or 6 p.m. to gain maximum traffic, using an aircraft of type C. But at a fare of £100 it would capture a daily traffic of only 75, thus making a loss and leaving the incumbent with reduced but still positive profits. Even at the entrant's profit-maximizing fare of £80 it would still make a loss and the incumbent just make a profit. Of course, if the incumbent were to reschedule so that departures were at eight-hour intervals, both entrant and incumbent would make positive profits, but the incumbent would have no incentive to do so if by maintaining the original schedule it could force the entrant to withdraw. So profitable entry is impossible even though the market could support a positive-profit multiple-carrier equilibrium.

Example 2. In this example consumer demand is not distributed evenly over 24 hours but concentrated at two points: there are 150 travellers daily with a preferred departure time of 9 a.m. and a maximum value of £160; and 50 travellers daily with a preferred departure time of 11 a.m. and a maximum value of £130. Assume that prices can be changed instantly in the event of entry (so limit pricing is unnecessary) but that schedules can be changed only with a lag (due to slot constraints). A monopoly incumbent would schedule a single flight at 11 a.m. with a fare of £130, and an aircraft of type A. Profits would be £15,000 and consumer surplus £1,500. However, the incumbent would be vulnerable to 'cream-skimming' entry by an entrant scheduling a flight at 9 a.m. with a fare of just under £150 (say £145) and operating a type B aircraft. Profits to the entrant would be £11,750 and consumer surplus £2,250; but it would become unprofitable for the incumbent to continue to carry passengers at 11 a.m., so total social welfare would be reduced. To deter this the incumbent would fly at 9 a.m. but at a price of £160 which would leave the 11 a.m. traffic without any service at all. The optimum would be to require the incumbent to fly at 9 a.m. at a fare of £110 or less. But if price control is infeasible free entry could have undesirable effects.

References

Abbot, K. and D. Thompson (1990). 'Deregulating European Aviation – The Impact of Bilateral Liberalisation', Working paper, Centre for Business Strategy, London Business School.

Association of European Airlines (1988). *Yearbook 1987*, Statistical Appendices.

Aviation Safety Commission (1988). *Final Report and Recommendations*, U.S. Government Printing Office, Washington, D.C.

Avmark (1988). *Quarterly Aircraft Operating Costs and Statistics*, London.

Bailey, E., D. Graham and D. Kaplan (1985). *Deregulating the Airlines*, MIT Press, Cambridge, MA.

Bailey, E. and J. Panzar (1981). 'The Contestability of Airline Markets During the Transition to Deregulation', *Law and Contemporary Problems*.

Banerjee, A. and L. Summers (1987). 'On Frequent Flyer Programs and Other Loyalty-Inducing Economic Arrangements', Discussion Paper no. 1337, Harvard Institute of Economic Research.

Baumol, W., J. Panzar and R. Willig (1988). *Contestable Markets and the Theory of Industry Structure*, 2nd edn., Harcourt Brace Jovanovitch, New York.

Borenstein, S. (1988). 'The Competitive Advantage of a Dominant Airline', Discussion Paper no. 280, Institute of Public Policy Studies, University of Michigan.

Bulkley, G. (1989). 'Loyalty Discounts as Options in a Market with Price Uncertainty', mimeo, University of Exeter.

Button, K. and S. Morrison (1988). 'The Effects of Reforming the Regulation of US Domestic Civil Aviation', *The Royal Bank of Scotland Review*.

Call, G. and T. Keeler (1985). 'Airline Deregulation, Fares and Market Behavior; some empirical evidence', in Daughety (ed.) *Analytical Studies in Transport Economics*, CUP, Cambridge.

Caves, R. (1962). *Air Transport and its Regulators*, Harvard University Press, Cambridge, MA.

Caves, D., L. Christensen, M. Trethewey and R. Windle (1987). 'An Assessment of the Efficiency of U.S. Airline Deregulation via an International Comparison', in E. Bailey (ed.) *Public Regulation*, MIT Press, Cambridge, MA.

Civil Aviation Authority (1986). *Air Traffic Distribution in the London Area*, CAP 522, London.

—— (1987). *Competition on the Main Domestic Routes*, London.

—— (1988a). *Air Traffic Management in the United Kingdom*, CAP 537, London.

—— (1988b). 'Decisions on Air Transport Licence Applications', 7/88, London.

Cunningham, L., B. Slovin, W. Wood and J. Zaima (1988). 'Systematic Risk in the Airline Industry', *Journal of Transport Economics and Policy*.

Dasgupta, P. (1986). 'The Theory of Technological Competition', in K. Binmore and P. Dasgupta (eds.) *Economic Organisations as Games*, Blackwell, Oxford.

Doganis, R. (1985). *Flying Off Course*, George Allen and Unwin, London.

European Commission (1984). 'Second Memorandum on Air Transport', COM (84) 72, Brussels.

—— (1988a). *The European Economy*, March 1988.

—— (1988b). 'Proposal for a Council Regulation on Computerised Reservation Systems', COM (88) 447, Brussels.

—— (1988c). 'Green Light to BA/BCal Merger', Press Release ISEC/7/88, 10 March, London.

—— (1988d). 'Communication from the Commission on the Air Traffic System Capacity Problems', COM (88) 557, Brussels.

Forsyth, P., R. Hill and C. Trengrove (1986). 'Measuring Airline Efficiency', *Fiscal Studies*.

Gilbert, R. and D. Newbery (1982). 'Pre-Emptive Patenting and the Persistence of Monopoly', *American Economic Review*.

Howard, L. (1988). 'The Changing US Airline Picture in Transport Research', Washington, The Future of Aviation, circular no. 329.

Kahn, A. (1988). 'Surprises of Airline Deregulation', *American Economic Review*.

Kay, J. and J. Vickers (1988). 'Regulatory Reform in Britain', *Economic Policy*.

Kirby, M. (1986). 'Airline Economies of "Scale" and Australian Domestic Air Transport Policy', *Journal of Transport Economics and Policy*.

Klemperer, P. (1987). 'Markets with Consumer Switching Costs', *Quarterly Journal of Economics*.

Levine, M. (1987). 'Airline Competition in Deregulated Markets: Theory, Firm Strategy and Public Policy', *Yale Journal on Regulation.*

McGowan, F. and C. Trengrove (1986). *European Aviation – A Common Market?*, London, Institute for Fiscal Studies.

Monopolies & Mergers Commission (1987). *British Airways PLC and British Caledonian Group PLC: a Report on the Proposed Merger*, Cm. 247, HMSO, London.

Moore, T. (1986). 'U.S. Airline Deregulation: Its Effects on Passengers, Capital and Labour', *Journal of Law and Economics.*

Morgan, I. (1981). 'Government and the Industry's Early Development', in J. Meyer and C. Oster (eds.) *Airline Deregulation: the Early Experience*, Auburn House.

Morrison, S. and C. Winston (1985). 'Intercity Transportation Route Structures under Deregulation', *American Economic Review*, papers and proceedings.

—— (1986). *The Economic Effects of Airline Deregulation*, Washington, Brookings Institution.

—— (1987). 'Empirical Implications and Tests of the Contestability Hypothesis', *Journal of Law and Economics.*

—— (1988). 'Air Safety, Deregulation and Public Policy', *The Brookings Review.*

National Consumers Council (1986). *Air Transport and the Consumer*, HMSO, London.

OECD (1988). *Deregulation and Airline Competition*, Paris, Organisation for Economic Co–Operation and Development.

Panzar, J. (1979). 'Equilibrium and Welfare in Unregulated Airline Markets', *American Economic Review*, papers and proceedings.

Pryke, R. (1987). *Competition among International Airlines*, Thames Essay no. 46, Trade Policy Research Centre, London.

Sawer, D. (1987). *Competition in the Air*, Research Monograph 41, Institute of Economic Affairs, London.

Schwartz, M. and R. Reynolds (1983). 'Contestable Markets: an Uprising in the Theory of Industry Structure: Comment', *American Economic Review.*

Shepherd, W. (1988). 'Competition, Contestability and Transport Mergers', *International Journal of Transport Economics.*

Smith, A. and A. Venables (1988). 'Completing the Internal Market in the European Community: Some Industry Simulations', *European Economic Review.*

US Senate (1975). *Civil Aeronautics Board Practices and Procedures*, Report of the Subcommittee on Administrative Practice and Procedure of the Committee on the Judiciary, U.S. Government Printing Office, Washington.

Utton, M. (1987). *The Likely Impact of Deregulation on Industrial Structures and Competition in the Community*, Office for Official Publications of the European Communities, Luxembourg.

Vickers, J. and G. Yarrow (1988). *Privatization*, MIT Press, Cambridge, MA.

Economic Policy   October 1989   Printed in Great Britain

Capital taxation

Alberto Giovannini

Summary

The current structure of taxes on capital income across EC countries can be exploited by corporations to reduce tax burdens. Skilled individuals can indulge in tax avoidance too. The liberalization of capital movements stands to turn tax avoidance into a cottage industry. This article provides a primer on capital income taxes and describes strategies which reduce the tax burden. From a policy perspective, the question is how to avoid massive tax evasion after 1992. There is no need to harmonize if the right taxation principle is adopted. Two principles are contrasted: the territorial principle, according to which taxes are levied on domestic investment irrespective of the country of residence of the beneficiary, and the worldwide principle, according to which taxes are levied on domestic savings irrespective of where they are invested. It is shown that the worldwide principle involves much fewer distortions than the territorial principle. A strict application of this principle would effectively solve the problem of tax evasion in Europe, without requiring full harmonization of the tax systems. Its full implementation would require the abolition of withholding taxes, the elimination of tax deferrals which are quite pervasive throughout Europe, and an in-depth review of blocking and secrecy laws.

National tax systems versus the European capital market

Alberto Giovannini

Graduate School of Business, Columbia University, CEPR and NBER.

1. Introduction

Extreme political instability during the interwar years and World War II led to very high levels of taxation, and prompted investors to transfer their wealth to stable countries, mainly Switzerland and the US. The current political climate in Europe is of course very different, but this fairly recent experience still influences some of the individual countries' laws, the attitude of investors, and the nature of controls on international capital flows. For example, Italian controls on international capital movements date from the interwar years. They were established at the time to permit heavy taxation of domestic wealth (see Giovannini, 1988a). At the opposite extreme, Switzerland has traditionally attracted foreign capital and shunned capital controls; she established her reputation in the 1930s, when she invented bank secrecy laws to protect foreign investors' anonymity. Today, both capital controls and secrecy laws represent serious obstacles to the development of an efficient European capital market.

The link between international capital flows and tax avoidance is returning to centre stage as European countries plan to integrate further. Capital markets have indeed been strongly segmented by a series of regulatory constraints on financial intermediation and international transactions. One can wonder whether the liberalization of capital markets which is envisaged will have disruptive effects on the economies and public finances of European countries. *The Economist* (11 February,

I am grateful to Daniel Frisch and Douglas Holtz-Eakin for discussions, and to the Economic Policy panelists for useful comments. Edmond Malinvaud's remarks gave me an opportunity to rethink several of the issues here discussed: these further thoughts are hopefully reflected in the final version of the paper. Peter Brooks provided outstanding research assistance: most of the material on tax strategies in Europe was collected and organized with his help, through interviews with bankers, accountants and lawyers. Of course, I am solely responsible for any errors or inaccuracies.

1989) recently stressed that the issue of capital income taxation 'is a diplomatic bomb that could blow up the progressive, financial parts of project 1992 by reversing a present commitment to remove remaining EEC exchange controls next year'. Indeed, it may well be that national tax systems are ill-suited to an integrated Europe-wide capital market.

The purpose of this paper is to identify and assess the distortions that the current tax systems can induce in an integrated European capital market. In order to highlight the main areas of policy concern I first study in Sections 2 and 3 the incentives for tax avoidance that the present patchwork of tax systems generates. Then in Sections 4 and 5, I explore the interplay between capital mobility and the distortions induced by the interactions of different tax systems. Finally, I apply this analysis in Section 6 to evaluate policy options, with particular reference to the current drive to 'harmonize' tax systems. The main conclusion of the paper is that, indeed, many features of the current system of capital income taxation are obsolete and ill-suited to an integrated capital market. However, Member States should not be forced to harmonize their tax rates: I will argue that individual countries can keep the freedom to tax, without jeopardizing the integration of capital markets. The distortions generated by the coexistence of independent tax authorities can be effectively minimized.

2. Capital income taxes in Europe

2.1. Corporate tax rates

It is well known that the corporate income tax is not exactly a tax on income from capital (Stiglitz, 1986): first, depreciation allowances are not equal to the actual decrease in the market value of plant and equipment and, conversely, assets are sometimes not valued according to market price. Second, interest income, unlike profits, is exempted from the corporate income tax. Still, corporate income taxes have a sizeable effect on the profitability of capital – and investment strategies. Table 1 reports the rates of corporate income taxes applied by European countries. Although tax bases are not directly comparable (given that there is a variety of accounting rules), the table suggests that capital income taxation varies a great deal. Still, corporate tax rates tend to converge somewhat towards low levels, as indicated by the recent fall in the rates in the UK (1983) and the firm prospect of a fall in West Germany, Ireland and Luxembourg[1] which follow the trend set by the

---

[1] In Germany the corporate tax rate for retained earnings will be lowered to 46.50% by January 1990, in Luxembourg to 34%, in Ireland it has been 43% since April 1989.

Table 1. Corporate tax rates

Country	Top corporate tax rate %
Belgium	43.0
Denmark	50.0
France	42.0
Germany	56.0
Greece	49.0
Ireland	50.0
Italy	52.2
Luxembourg	36.0
Netherlands	42.0(a)
Portugal	35.0
Spain	35.0
UK	35.0

Source: *Managing International Bank Taxation*, Arthur Young International, Euromoney Publications, 1988.
Note: (a) Rate to be lowered to 35%.

US Tax Reform Act 1986. As of 1988, profit taxes range from 56% in West Germany to 35% in the UK, 36% in Luxembourg and 10% (for some manufacturing activities) in Ireland.

The profitability of an incorporated investment is also affected by the tax treatment of dividend payments to shareholders. This tax treatment differs depending on whether the shareholder is an individual or a corporation, but also depending on whether the shareholder is a resident of the country where the company is incorporated or a foreign resident. Differences in the tax treatment of capital income of individuals and corporations are important because, with international capital mobility, they create tax arbitrage opportunities for the corporations. These problems are discussed in Section 6.2. The tax treatment of dividend payments when shareholders are foreign residents are described in Section 2.3.

2.2. Individual tax rates

Table 2 reports the rates of individual income taxes. The comparison of individual income taxes is complicated by progression in the rates, which of course differs from country to country. Hence, the table offers no clue as to the average or marginal individual tax rates prevailing in the different European countries. Nevertheless, the differences are worth noticing. Personal tax rates will influence international investment decisions of individuals (see Sections 2.3. and 3.4.). They might

Table 2. Taxation of resident individuals

Country	Top individual tax rate %
Belgium	67.5
Denmark	70.0
France	65.0
Germany	56.0
Greece	63.0
Ireland	65.0
Italy	62.0
Luxembourg	57.0
Netherlands	72.0
Portugal	60.0
Spain	46.0
UK	60.0

Source: Price Waterhouse.
Note: The basic rates reported may be supplemented by state and municipal taxes as well as by other surcharges such as for unemployment or social security.

also influence the location of managers, thereby affecting the location of corporate headquarters across European countries.

Wealth taxes represent another form of individual taxation which can have an important effect on international portfolio diversification. Wealth taxes can be applied to net wealth, inheritance and capital gains. In many countries these taxes date back from a time when tax administrations were less sophisticated, and the assessment of income was too costly. By contrast, assessing the base for a tax on net wealth was relatively easier, especially when net wealth consisted of real estate. Individuals have an opportunity to *evade* wealth taxes by concealing their assets abroad given that international portfolio diversification, *per se*, cannot in general change the tax base. (See Section 2.6 for a description of the institutions that facilitate the evasion of wealth taxes.) The revenue from wealth taxes in Europe amounts to a very small percentage of total revenue: in 1985 it represented 0.58% of total revenue in Belgium 0.92% in Denmark, 0.85% in France, 0.42% in Germany, 0.23% in Italy, 0.51% in Luxembourg, 0.94% in the Netherlands and 0.64% in the UK (OECD, 1988b).

2.3. Foreign source income taxes

International investment strategies are affected by domestic tax systems in two ways; first, through differences in the statutory rates of tax on different sources of *domestic* income, and, second, through the different treatment of foreign source income by tax authorities. Broadly speaking, alternative systems of foreign source income taxation can be characterized by using the distinction between savings and investment which, in an open economy can diverge *ex post*. On the one hand, according to the *source principle*, or *territorial principle*, income of domestic residents is taxed at different rates depending on its source. A strict application of the source principle requires the taxation of income from domestic investment only, but exempts income from foreign sources. On the other hand, according to the *residence principle*, or *worldwide principle*, domestic residents are taxed on all their investment income, irrespective of the country where the investments are located. Hence, the territorial system can be considered as a system which taxes domestic investment income, while taxation under the worldwide principle is applied to income from all savings. When income from both foreign and domestic investments is taxable, governments' jurisdictions end up overlapping: foreign source income is taxable both by the authorities of the host country (where the income is produced), and by the authorities of the country of residence of the parent company (or the individual owner). To avoid double taxation, taxes paid to foreign authorities are credited against domestic taxes by most countries following the residence principle. (In practice, foreign taxes are credited by first computing domestic taxes owed on foreign source income grossed up by foreign taxes. Net domestic taxes are then computed by subtracting foreign taxes. In some countries, like West Germany and Ireland investors have the option of deducting from taxable income the taxes paid abroad.)

Table 3 reports the method of taxation of foreign personal and corporate income in Europe. Almost all countries, except France, and, to some extent, the Netherlands, follow the worldwide (or residence) principle. This is in accordance with the OECD *Model Double Taxation Convention* (1977), which aims at achieving a sort of 'capital export neutrality', whose theoretical justification and normative implications are discussed in Section 4. Some of the countries that tax worldwide income allow exemptions for special kinds of foreign source income. In Belgium, if a foreign corporation is a 'permanent investment' of a domestic corporation, 95% of its dividend income (90% if the Belgian parent company is a holding company) is exempted from Belgian taxes. In the Netherlands, dividends of companies that qualify for the 'participation exemption' are exempted from Dutch taxes.

The application of the worldwide principle is, however, subject to a couple of major exceptions. First of all, countries impose a limitation on foreign tax credits, which is usually equal to the domestic tax rate

Table 3. Taxation of foreign-source income

	Individual	Corporate	
Country	Taxation principle	Taxation principle	Credit/deduction
Belgium	W	W	Deduction
Denmark	W	W	Credit
France	W	T(d)	Both (a)(d)
Germany	W	W	Both (a)
Greece	W	W	Credit
Ireland	W	W	Credit
Italy	W	W	Credit (b)
Luxembourg	W	W	Both (a)
Netherlands	W	W(c)	Exemption
Portugal	W	W	Credit
Spain	W	W	Credit
UK	W	W	Either

Source: Price Waterhouse.
Note: W stands for 'worldwide' and T stands for 'territorial'. (a) Taxes paid abroad in excess of the allowable credit are deductible as expenses. (b) Taxpayer is entitled to a refund of the excess foreign tax credit. (c) Resident corporations often receive proportionate relief for taxable income in other countries granted by way of unilateral relief (see discussion of the 'participation exemption'). (d) In general France does not allow any tax credits against foreign income taxes paid on the business income of foreign permanent establishments. However, the territorial principle applies only to the income of foreign permanent establishments. It does not apply to foreign-sourced dividends or interest, which are subject to French corporate tax when realized, and for which a foreign tax credit may offset French taxes.

applied to foreign source income. This ceiling has two effects. First, whenever investors accumulate excess tax credits (foreign taxes paid exceed the credit limitation) and these credits cannot be offset against future or current taxes, income from domestic and foreign investments is taxed at the domestic and foreign tax rates, respectively.[2] Second, whenever excess credits in some countries can be offset against excess limitations in other countries, the allocation of foreign investments among high and low income tax countries can also be distorted. The

---

[2] The calculation of tax credit limitations varies significantly across European countries. In Belgium, the foreign tax credit for 'nonpermanent' investments is 15%. In Denmark, the limit is either 50% of the Danish income tax attributable to the net income of the foreign affiliate (in the case where the parent is jointly taxed with the subsidiary) or the equivalent of the Danish tax rate applied to foreign income (in the case where the parent is not jointly taxed with the subsidiary). In Germany the tax credit is 36% of the foreign income. In Greece and Spain the limitation is based on the domestic corporate tax rate. In Luxembourg, any foreign taxes in excess of the domestic rate are deductible as expenses.

second exception to the worldwide principle relates to the timing of the determination of the domestic tax liabilities on foreign source income. In general, when foreign source income is in the form of dividends, most countries require that domestic taxes be levied when the dividends are paid by the foreign subsidiary to the parent company, and not when the dividend income is produced. The deferral of dividend payments amounts to a deferral of the payment of domestic taxes, while foreign taxes are regularly paid as income is produced. Deferral thus defeats the main purpose of the worldwide principle: foreign subsidiaries pay only the foreign tax as long as dividends are not repatriated. The incentive to defer the payment of dividend is equal to the difference in the tax rates times the time value of money. In addition, the tax deferral can become permanent if the timing of the dividend distribution can be matched with the occurrence of excess tax credits from elsewhere or if the host country tax rate falls in the future. Legislation against the systematic use of deferral is well developed only in the US, and, to some extent, in West Germany (where special rules were introduced in 1972 on the attribution of passive income) and the UK (where tax authorities may allocate a proportion of the undistributed profits of foreign subsidiaries of UK companies). In France, the exemption of foreign source income does not apply to income produced in tax havens. There is no such legislation in Belgium, the Netherlands or Italy.

2.4. Withholding taxes

Withholding taxes represent perhaps the most significant exception to the worldwide principle. They are levied at source on interest and dividend payments to foreigners. They are justified by the concern that certain forms of income (like portfolio investment income abroad) can easily escape taxation by both host and home country authorities. Withholding rates are reported in Tables 4 and 5. The rates differ depending both on the origin and the destination of dividend and interest income. Those differences are determined by particular bilateral tax treaties. As Table 5 shows, tax treaties have in many cases brought withholding taxes on interest payments down to zero, while withholding tax rates on dividend payments still differ substantially.

2.5. Capital gains taxes, and the taxation of foreign-exchange gains or losses

In many countries, capital gains are taxed when they are realized. In addition, some countries tax capital gains at lower rates than ordinary income. A further distinction applies to short-term versus long-term gains. Differences in the treatment of capital gains stem both from the

Table 4. Withholding taxes on dividend income (%)

Paying country:	Bel	Den	Fra	Ger	Gre	Ire	Ita	Lux	Neth	Por	Spa	UK
						Recipient country:						
Belgium	—	15	10-15	15	15	15	15	10-15	5-15	15	15	15
Denmark	15	—	0	15	30	0	15	15	15	10	10	15
France	15	0	—	0	25	10-15	15	15-25	15	15	10	15
Germany	10-25	10-25	10-25	—	25	10-20	25	10-25	10-25	15	15	10-25
Greece	25	42-53	42-53	25	—	42-53	25	42-53	35	42-53	42-53	42-53
Ireland	0	0	0	0	0	—	0	0	0	0	0	0
Italy	15	15	15	30	25	15	—	15	0-30	15	15	5-15
Luxembourg	10-15	5-15	5-15	10-15	15	5-15	15	—	2.5-15	15	15	5-15
Netherlands	5-15	0-15	5-15	10-15	5-15	0-15	0	2.5-15	—	25	5	5-15
Portugal	12	10-12	12	12	12	12	12	12	12	—	10-12	10-12
Spain	15	10	10	10	18	18	15	18	10	10	—	10
UK	*	*	*	*	*	*	*	*	*	*	*	*

Source: Price Waterhouse, 1987.
Note: For the UK, tax treaties have been renegotiated. No withholding taxes are normally levied on dividends. The exact treatment can vary depending on the type of treaty.

Table 5. Withholding taxes on interest income (%)

Paying country:	Bel	Den	Fra	Ger	Gre	Ire	Ita	Lux	Neth	Por	Spa	UK
Belgium (a)	—	15	15	0–15	10	15	15	0–15	0–10	15	15	15
Denmark	0	—	0	0	0	0	0	0	0	0	0	0
France (b)	10–15	0	—	0	0–10	0	15	10–45	0–10	10–12	10	10
Germany (c)	0–15	0	0	—	10	0	25–50	0	15–50	0–15	10	0
Greece	15	25	10	10	—	25	10	25	10	25	25	0
Ireland	15	0	0	0	35	—	10	0	0	35	35	0
Italy	12.5–25	12.5–25	12.5–25	0–25	10	10	—	0–10	12.5–25	12.5–25	12	12.5–18.2
Luxembourg	0	0	0	0	0	0	0	—	0	0	0	0
Netherlands	0	0	0	0	0	0	0	0	—	0	0	0
Portugal	15	15	10–12	10–12	30	30	15	30	30	—	30	10
Spain	15	10	10	10	18	18	12	18	10	15	—	12
UK	15	0	10	0	0	0	27	0	0	10	12	—

Recipient country:

Source: Price Waterhouse, 1987.

Notes: (a) No withholding tax on interest is due on commercial debts and interest paid by banks established in Belgium to foreign banks or to certain non-residents. (b) The lower rates generally apply to income from bonds and other negotiable securities. No tax withheld on interest on foreign currency deposits with French Banks. The rate may also be reduced to 10% for interest paid on loans granted to French companies by foreign banks. Luxembourg Holding Companies are not entitled to any of the benefits of the France–Luxembourg treaty. (c) Interest payments on normal loans and publicly issued bonds are not subject to withholding tax.

practical difficulty of determining the market values of assets when they are not actually being sold, and from policy objective of providing incentives for investment and risk taking. Table 6 shows corporate and individual capital gains taxes. Capital gains of corporations are taxed at lower rates in Belgium and France, while elsewhere they are taxed at the same rate as ordinary income. For individuals, the tax treatment of capital gains depends on the maturity and the nature of the investments. For example, in Belgium, Germany, the Netherlands and Italy, capital gains are in general not taxable if they arise from a long-term investment, which is not undertaken for speculative reasons.

A specific form of capital gains, which assumes special importance in Europe, is foreign-exchange gains and losses, arising both from commercial and financial transactions. It is only in Denmark, France and, to some extent, Italy that the gains and losses from foreign-exchange transactions are explicitly covered by tax legislation. Two main questions arise in connection with such taxation. First, are capital gains/losses recognized on an accrual basis or at the time of realization; second, are foreign-exchange gains taxed as ordinary income or capital gains? Most countries tax foreign-exchange gains when realized, using the ordinary income rate. In some countries, however, gains and losses are not treated symmetrically. For example, in Belgium and Germany, and in the Netherlands for long-term assets and liabilities, foreign-exchange gains are taxed upon realization, while losses are taxed upon accrual. Finally, there are circumstances where foreign-exchange gains and losses are not recognized. Britain, for example, does not recognize long-term foreign-exchange gains and losses if they are not on equity, cash or bank deposits (Alworth, 1988; OECD, 1988).

2.6. Bank secrecy laws and blocking laws

The laws protecting the privacy of investors are an important feature of European capital markets. These laws are also unfortunate since they provide an opportunity to evade capital income taxes and regulations affecting financial intermediaries. The privacy of investors is protected in Europe by two types of laws: secrecy laws and blocking laws. The former prevent third parties from accessing information regarding investments placed with domestic financial intermediaries. The latter prohibit the general disclosure of evidence related to domestic economic and business interests, for the purpose of complying with foreign authorities.[3] The protection of bank secrecy originates, in part, from

----

[3] General surveys on secrecy and blocking laws are in Salminen (1988) and *Crime and Secrecy: The Use of Offshore Banks and Companies, a report of the Permanent Subcommittee on Investigations of the Senate Committee on Governmental Affairs* (August 1985). See also Nadelmann (1985, 1986).

Table 6. Taxation of capital gains

Country	Preferential individual capital gains tax	Corporate capital gains tax %
Belgium	Yes (a)	21.5
Denmark	Yes (b)	50.0
France	Yes (c)	12–25.0
Germany	Yes (d)	NA
Greece	No	30.0
Ireland	Yes (e)	40–60
Italy	Yes (f)	52.2
Luxembourg	Yes (g)	36.0
Netherlands	Yes (h)	42.0
Portugal	Yes	12–24
Spain	Yes	35.0
UK	Yes (i)	35.0

Source: Price Waterhouse.

Notes: (a) In general there are no capital gains taxes. A special lower tax of 33% is, however, imposed on individuals for gains resulting from the sale of land in certain circumstances; a special tax is also due at the rate of 16.5% on capital gains made by holders of more than 25% of Belgian corporations shares in certain circumstances. (b) Certain gains and losses on sales of shares, fixed assets and intangibles are taxed as special income. (c) The sale of a principal residence is tax exempt. The gains from the sale of other real property are taxable but the base may be reduced based on the holding period. There is also a special tax rate of 16% on gains arising from the sale of securities in certain circumstances. (d) Long-term capital gains are free of tax while short-term gains of more than DM 1,000 are added to an individual's taxable income. The time limits for long-term gains are: land and buildings, two years; and securities and other assets, six months. Other special rules apply to sales of controlled businesses and investment income. (e) The same basic rules that apply to companies apply to individuals. Rates range between 40% and 60%. (f) Capital gains are not normally taxable unless arising from speculative intent such as real estate development or by way of a business. No special exceptions are made for the profit on sale of a personal residence. (g) A reduced rate of 28.5% is assessed on real estate that is sold between two and 10 years after purchase or construction. The same rate applies to privately owned land more than 10 years after acquisition in certain circumstances. Profits from speculation are taxable at the normal tax rate up to a maximum of 57% plus the unemployment surcharge of 7.5%. (h) In general, capital gains not arising from the exercise of a business or a profession are not taxable. (i) In principle, all gains accruing on the disposal of all forms of property and rights are subject to a capital gains tax of 30%. Exceptions to the principle include gains on the sale of a principal private residence, moveable property sold for less than £3,000, in certain government securities, qualifying corporate bonds and business assets on retirement up to a maximum of £125,000.

World War II and the interwar period. It is also part of the general philosophy underlying the civil law of some European countries which extend the protection of individual privacy. The country most involved in disputes on bank secrecy is Switzerland, not a EEC member. The Swiss system of bank secrecy was established in November 1934 by the *Federal Law relating to Banks and Savings Banks* (last updated in 1971); at the time, the objective of Swiss authorities was to protect the assets of German Jews from attempts by Nazi agents to seize them. Providing information on the holders of individual bank accounts, or any other information about deals carried out by the banks' clients is liable to a fine and imprisonment for up to six months. What makes the protection of bank secrecy from foreign authorities especially effective in Switzerland is, among other things, the use of *penal* sanctions against infractions. Violations of bank secrecy are also subject to criminal penalties in Luxembourg (where a law was passed in 1981) and in France (where a law passed in 1984 confirmed the early extension of the rule on professional secrecy to the banking profession). In France, however, information can be released either with the consent of the client, or to legal and banking supervising authorities. In the UK, Germany, Denmark, Belgium, the Netherlands and Italy, violations of bank secrecy laws are subject to civil sanctions. In Denmark, tax authorities have access to information about individual taxpayers, while in Germany a 1986 law discontinued the requirement that banks provide information to tax authorities on interest earnings. Bank secrecy and blocking laws are against the spirit of the *OECD Model Double Taxation Convention*, Article 26, which stresses the importance of the exchange of information among tax authorities.

In addition to providing protection to tax evaders, secrecy and blocking laws can also be exploited by financial intermediaries like commercial banks to bypass domestic prudential regulations. As a case in point, the 1981 secrecy law in Luxembourg was used by German banks to escape domestic prudential regulations (including exposure limits *vis-à-vis* any borrower): most of the Euro-Deutschemark market is located in Luxembourg and is carried out by branches of German banks (Dale, 1984; *Crime and Secrecy*, 1985, p. 52).

The general tightening of secrecy and blocking laws in recent years might very well result from better awareness on the part of legislators with regard to their powerful effects on international capital flows. It might also result from a defensive reaction to each other and to US pressures. The requests of business information from US Courts in connection with anti-trust cases were received with the suspicion that they might damage the competitiveness of European companies. Such legal actions prompted the erection of blocking laws by a number of countries.

3. Investment strategies for tax avoidance

In this section, I review the most basic techniques that can be followed
to minimize the tax burden on European investments. Many of the tax
avoidance strategies described here are already feasible. (For excellent
surveys of international tax avoidance schemes, see OECD, 1987; Adler,
1979; and Alsworth, 1988.) These strategies are indeed followed by
multinational corporations. My presumption is that, with the completion
of the internal market, and in the absence of significant reforms of
national tax systems, a much larger number of individuals or corporations will be in a position to pursue these strategies. This will happen
because the removal of physical, technical and fiscal barriers will probably multiply the number of Europe-wide corporations, which, by their
very nature, are best suited to undertake tax arbitrage. In addition, as
the liberalization of capital flows will prompt a demand for Europe-wide
financial services, financial intermediaries will have to take into account
tax asymmetries. The tax laws surveyed above provide a number of
incentives to select specific countries for sourcing funds or locating
investments.

3.1. Conduit Companies

Conduit companies, also called intermediary holding companies, are
set up to minimize withholding taxes by taking advantage of tax treaties.
Figure 1 shows the standard case. Consider a French company interested
in setting up a subsidiary in Italy: given the bilateral tax treaty between
Italy and France, dividend payments from the Italian subsidiary would
be subject to a 15% withholding tax. In an alternative structure, a Dutch

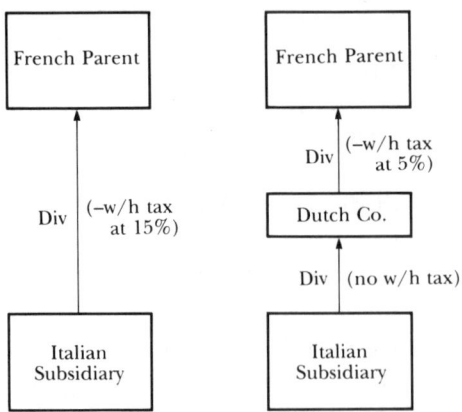

Figure 1. Conduit companies

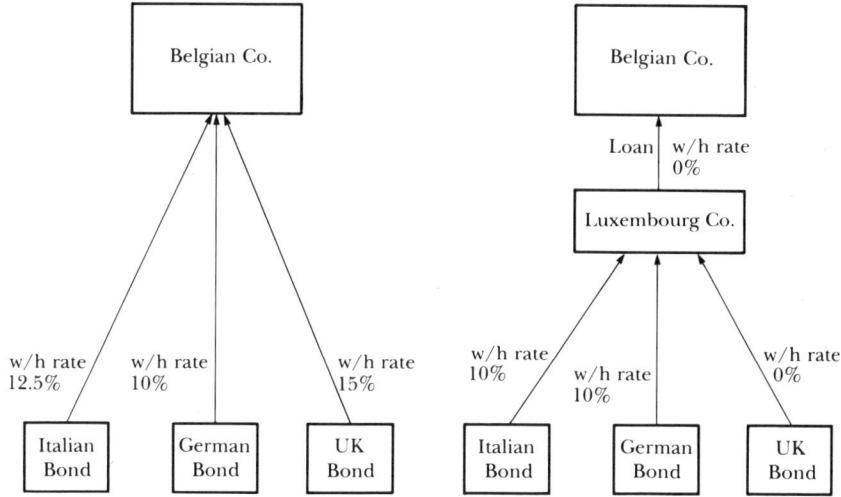

Figure 2. Intermediary holding companies

company is positioned between the French parent and the Italian subsidiary. The withholding tax rate on dividend payments from Italy to the Netherlands is 0%, and 5% from the Netherlands to France: the amount paid in withholding taxes is reduced by two-thirds.

Conduit companies are also often used in the international management of interest income. In this case, the intermediary holding company manages a portfolio of foreign investments on behalf of a foreign parent corporation. By locating in a country with an extended network of tax treaties, the intermediary holding company can substantially reduce the total tax bill. Figure 2 illustrates the point. A Belgian company holds a portfolio of Italian, German and UK bonds. Given the bilateral tax treaties with these four countries, interest income to Belgium are subject to withholding rates of 12.5, 10 and 15%, respectively. An alternative structure places a conduit company in Luxembourg. Tax treaties involving Luxembourg impose much lower withholding taxes on interest income produced in Italy and the UK (10% and 0%, respectively). Moreover, interest payments from Luxembourg to Belgium are subject to a 0% withholding tax. On the whole, the tax saving represents as much as 15% of gross interest income from the British investments and 2.5% of gross interest income from the Italian investments (the tax paid on German bonds is unaffected).

3.2. Foreign base companies

Even though most countries apply the worldwide principle of taxation, differences in corporate tax rates provide a powerful incentive to locate companies in low-tax countries. Such incentives exist because most European countries recognize foreign income only at the time it is paid to the parent company, not at the time when it is produced. The strategy implied by the option of deferring domestic corporate income taxes is to accumulate lowly taxed income. The companies set up for this purpose in countries with low corporate income are called base companies. Generally, base companies are used to defer taxes, to allocate income away from countries with high tax rates, and to minimize excess tax credits. Base companies can take different forms. The simplest form is a holding company in a tax haven, collecting income from foreign subsidiaries and deferring the payment to the parent company.

For example, in the Netherlands, 'participation exemption' (a feature of Dutch law which attempts to treat domestic and foreign subsidiaries in a similar fashion) allows companies that hold a majority stake in foreign corporations not to pay taxes on the dividends received from their foreign subsidiaries.[4] An additional advantage of the Netherlands stems from its bilateral tax treaties specifying low withholding tax rates on dividend income and zero withholding taxes on interest income. Finally, the Dutch holding company qualifying for the participation exemption is not charged taxes on any capital gains realized on the sale of its foreign holdings. To illustrate, a French corporation could thus set up a base company in the Netherlands to collect dividend income from subsidiaries in third countries, and receive this income as interest payments on intra-company loans. A thinly capitalized holding company in the Netherlands makes use of both deferrals and withholding tax advantages.

Another example of base companies is the Belgian coordination centre. Coordination centres have to meet the following requirements; they have to carry out specific activities (resale, financing, leasing, factoring, headquarters operations, research and development, or foreign-exchange management), they need to have at least 10 employees and they are prohibited from holding stock in foreign companies. Their taxes will be based on their costs, with financing and personnel expenses excluded from the computation (see Price Waterhouse, *Doing Business in Belgium*, 1983). Moreover, they do not pay withholding taxes on interest or dividends. Figure 3 illustrates the use of a Belgian coordination centre. The parent company in France has subsidiaries in Germany

---

[4] Through the 'participation exemption' – *deelnemingsvrijstelling* – qualifying companies can claim tax exemption of the income from domestic and foreign subsidiaries alike. These subsidiaries must be held for at least 5% of their paid-up capital, and must, broadly speaking, represent an investment effectively linked with the business of the parent company, not just a portfolio investment.

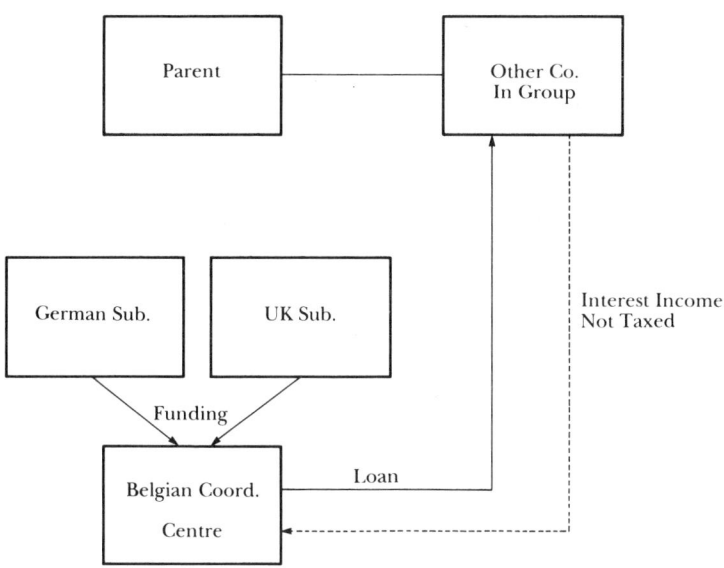

Figure 3. A Belgian coordination centre

Note: Upstreaming of income from German and UK subsidiaries is subject to withholding taxes.

and the UK. These companies, rather than paying dividends to the parent which are subject to withholding taxes, fund a Belgian coordination centre. The Belgian company then uses these funds to finance other companies in the group, and pays no tax on its interest income.

3.3. Transforming interest costs into foreign-exchange gains

Since the inception of the European Monetary System, inflation rates across Europe have not completely converged and exchange-rate realignments have, to some extent, accommodated inflation differentials (see Giavazzi and Giovannini, 1989). The special treatment of foreign-exchange gains provides an opportunity for tax arbitrage, as long as inflation rates continue to diverge. The strategy consists of borrowing in currencies which depreciate because of higher trend inflation rates, and lending in low inflation, low interest rate currencies. Interest rate differentials tend to reflect projected changes in the exchange rate. The (negative) net interest costs are taxed at the corporate income tax rate, while the foreign-exchange gain is either not taxed, or taxed when realized. If the foreign-exchange gain is taxed at the same rate as interest income but only when it is realized, profits from deferrals are still available. To illustrate, consider a German company issuing a five-year French franc bond, covering the franc liability with a five-year currency swap, and using the proceeds to buy a Deutschemark bond. At the end of 1983, a plausible value for the interest rate payable on a five-year French franc bond was 13% and the equivalent Deutschemark interest rate was 7.75%. If the cost of the currency swap is determined by interest rate parity, and if the difference in the Deutschemark value of the principal of the French franc bond at the beginning and at the end of the loan is not taxed, the profit, net of tax, from this operation is as high as 10.25%.[5] This is the difference between the principal value of the Deutschemark bond and the present discounted value of after-tax cash flows to service the French franc bond. By contrast, if the gain on the principal repayment is fully taxed at the 56% rate, the net gain from this strategy reduces to 50 basis points.

3.4. Mutual funds: the uses of UCITS

To protect savers who venture their wealth across borders, the Commission has proposed a set of standards that intermediaries have to meet in order to be allowed to sell investment products throughout the EEC (previously, investment funds had to be listed in individual countries' stock markets to carry out their business locally). Such chartered investment funds are called Undertakings for Collective Investments in Transferable Securities or UCITS.[6] Significantly, Luxembourg was the first EC country to pass legislation to comply with UCITS rules. The tax system in fact gives Luxembourg a comparative advantage in hosting UCITS since investment funds are granted tax-exempt status, are exempt from withholding taxes, and double-tax treaties do not apply to them (see *Doing Business in Luxembourg*, Price Waterhouse, 1986). Luxembourg UCITS are an effective instrument to minimize taxes on capital income. By investing in a Luxembourg UCITS, a resident of any country applying the worldwide principle of taxation is able to defer the payment of domestic taxes indefinitely, by capitalizing tax free the mutual fund investment income in Luxembourg. Furthermore, residents of the majority of European countries can use income from UCITS to absorb excess tax credits generated elsewhere.

---

[5] This number is obtained as follows. Using the forward rates of the currency swap, I convert all French franc cash flows into Deutschemarks, I subtract taxes, and compute the present discounted value of the resulting stream of net payments, using the after tax Deutschemark interest rate. The 56% tax rate is applied in all calculations.

[6] UCITS must be open-ended, and cannot be property, venture capital, commodity, or cash funds. They must be administered in the country of registration, they cannot hold more than 5% of their portfolio in any one security, and cannot engage in short selling and other speculative strategies.

4. Economic effects of the current tax system

4.1. Evidence on the use of tax loopholes

The description of tax avoidance strategies and even a rough assessment of their profitability do not provide a proof that these strategies are actually carried out. Transactions costs, informational barriers and other impediments to capital flows, could more than offset the benefits from tax arbitrage. Direct evidence on the use of base companies to defer domestic income taxes in the US is offered by Hines and Hubbard (1989). As the provisions against deferral in the US are perceived to be among the tightest in the world, these results raise doubts about the effective implementation of the residence principle in Europe, where anti-deferral laws are in general less stringent than in the US. An intriguing set of calculations on the impact of tax changes on inter-national capital flows, based on a highly stylized model, is presented by Sinn (1985, 1987 and 1988). He finds that, even when the worldwide principle is applied, accounting rules like depreciation allowances may give rise to large wedges between gross rates of return on capital in different countries. Using simulations, Sinn concludes that the equi-librium inflow of capital to the US triggered by the Accelerated Cost Recovery System (ACRS) could have been as large as 1.1 trillion dollars. By contrast, he suggests that the recent 1986 Tax Reform Act might cause substantial capital outflows from the US.

Two examples of the responsiveness of international capital flows to changes in withholding taxes come from the US and Germany. Before 1984, the US levied a 30% withholding tax on interest payments to non-residents. However, a number of tax treaties would reduce that rate substantially: residents of 16 countries (Austria, Denmark, Finland, Germany, Greece, Hungary, Iceland, Ireland, Luxembourg, the Netherlands, the Netherlands Antilles, Norway, Poland, Sweden, the UK and the USSR) faced zero rates, while other countries enjoyed substantial reductions. A foreign investor wishing to take advantage of her tax-treaty status, would have to provide information about her country of residence and address. In the case of bearer bonds, this information would have to be provided at every interest payment. This provision was apparently enough to discourage many investors from lending to US corporations directly in the US. Throughout the 1960s and 1970s, however, investors' anonymity and zero withholding tax could be achieved through conduit companies in the Netherlands Antilles because of the tax treaty between the two countries, which prompted the remark that the treaty with the Netherlands Antilles was a 'one way treaty with the world'. As a result, interest payments to the Netherlands Antilles accounted (in 1983) for more than 33% of all interest payments by US residents to the rest of the world. The Deficit Reduction Act of July 1984, which exempted from the withholding tax most interest payments to foreigners, had two effects. First, the sales of domestic assets to non-residents mushroomed: sales of corporate bond to foreigners jumped from (practically) zero to $8.8 bn. in just one quarter (1984Q4), and kept a quarterly average of about $7.5 bn. in the ensuing years; sales of government bonds tripled in 1984 relative to the previous year (Papke, 1988). Second, corporate bonds issued through the Netherlands Antilles collapsed after 1984Q3, from an average of about $2 bn. per quarter in the preceding two years.

The second example is provided by Germany's decision in early 1989 to impose a 10% withholding tax on interest payments from Deutschemark bonds. Less than 20% of the bonds sold to German residents in 1988Q4 were Deutschemark bonds (subject to the withholding tax), just one-fourth of the comparable figure for 1988Q3.[7] These sudden and dramatic capital outflows from Germany prompted the new finance minister Theo Waigl to announce his intention to abolish the tax or at least to suspend it.

4.2. The nature of current tax distortions and their effects

Even granting that the response of international capital flows to tax asymmetries is large and fast, the effects of these flows remain to be determined. The main (first-order) distortions associated with the strategies described above are, however, easy to identify.

4.2.1. Conduit companies.
The systematic use of conduit companies located in countries with low withholding tax distorts the location of financial intermediaries. With the liberalization of European financial markets under way, most European savers will find it advantageous to use the services of intermediaries in low tax countries. As a result, financial intermediaries in high tax countries will face a significant fall in profitability. Substantial geographical concentration of some financial services might also follow, significant relocation costs being incurred in the process. Moreover, as new financial markets emerge in response to the removal of capital controls, the exploitation of secrecy and blocking laws to escape domestic regulations (prudential and otherwise) might

---

[7] The February 1989 issue of the *Monthly Report of the Deutsche Bundesbank* claimed that the behaviour of yields of Deutschemark bonds relative to foreign and Euro-Deutschemark bonds reflected the investors' anticipation of the withholding tax: 'It therefore seems reasonable to conclude that the prime motive for many domestic buyers was the fact that these bonds (foreign and Eurobonds) are not subject to withholding tax on interest income.'

come back into fashion. Prudential regulations, such as capital requirements, reserve requirements, or exposure limits, in general increase the cost of financial intermediation and, therefore, can be seen as a form of taxation. Firms set up branches in countries where their own regulatory authorities cannot gain access, so that they can avoid complying with regulations and maintain their profits.

4.2.2. Base companies. The systematic use of base companies allows corporations to take advantage of foreign countries with low taxes, by deferring the payment of dividends to the parent, or re-routing within the group the financial resources generated by profits in low-tax-rate countries. These strategies are accomplished not only through the use of shell financial subsidiaries, but also through judicious location of sourcing, manufacturing and distribution. In fact, the use of base companies defeats the worldwide principle, effectively allowing for different taxation of domestic and foreign investments. As a result, the pre-tax rates of return of domestic and foreign investments will not be equalized. The pre-tax rate of return in countries with high tax rates will be higher than the rate of return in countries with low tax rates. Hence, given the current features of tax systems in Europe, low-tax-rate countries, other things being equal, tend to attract more investment than high-tax-rate countries.

4.2.3. Foreign-exchange gains and losses. Finally, the special treatment of foreign-exchange gains and losses introduces a distortion that causes permanent inflation differentials across countries to have real effects. Indeed, if foreign-exchange rate gains and losses are taxed at a lower rate than interest income, the real rate of interest must be higher in countries with high inflation in order to discourage tax arbitrage. This obviously distorts savings and capital allocation decisions.[8]

On the whole, this survey of the effects of tax avoidance schemes suggests an important observation: from the perspective of any European resident, taxes owed on income from capital can differ substantially, depending on where capital is located. This is a glaring

---

[8] In the absence of risk aversion after-tax returns denominated in the same currency are equalized: $i_t(1-\tau) = i_t^*(1-\tau) + ({}_te_{t+1} - e_t)(1-\tau^*)$ where τ^* is the effective tax on foreign exchange gains and losses, with $\tau^* \leq \tau$, i_t and i_t^* are the domestic and foreign nominal interest rates, respectively, and e_t and ${}_te_{t+1}$ are the log of the exchange rate, and its expectation at time $t+1$ held as of time t. If we assume, to simplify, that purchasing power parity holds, so that: ${}_te_{t+1} - e_t = {}_t\pi_{t+1} - {}_t\pi^*_{t+1}$ where π_{t+1} and π^*_{t+1} are the domestic and foreign rates of inflation, from time t to time $t+1$, respectively, then: $r_t = r_t^* + (\tau - \tau^*)/(1-\tau) ({}_t\pi_{t+1} - {}_t\pi^*_{t+1})$ where $r_t = i_t - {}_t\pi_{t+1}$ is the domestic real rate of interest. For a discussion of these effects in a closed economy, see Feldstein (1976) and Tanzi (1974). For the open economy, see Gordon (1987), Alworth (1988) and Wahl (1987).

violation of the worldwide principle, formally adopted – as shown in Table 3 – by almost all European countries. A preliminary idea of the actual size of the tax wedges across countries comes from the comparison of the tax rates reported in Tables 1 to 6. A more accurate estimate should take into account the interaction of all tax effects, accounting rules and so on. Intercountry comparisons of capital taxation have been pioneered by King and Fullerton (1984), and performed by many other researchers. Their methodology, however, relies crucially on the assumption that investment is *ex post* identically equal to saving, which is true only in the absence of international capital mobility. Bovenberg (1988) offers some preliminary discussions regarding the estimate of effective tax rates in the presence of international capital mobility. Given that these wedges are quite likely to be significant, the next issue to address is the welfare consequences of deviating from the worldwide principle.

5. Welfare analysis of the worldwide and territorial principles

This section identifies the welfare effects of a regime where investment income is taxed at different rates in different countries, and capital is internationally mobile. A regime where investors face different rates of taxation of domestic and foreign investment income is a combination of a worldwide system of taxation (whereby each country taxes all capital income at the same rate), and a territorial system (whereby each country taxes only domestic investment income). The taxation of domestic and foreign investment income at different rates is thus a combination of savings taxes and investment taxes. In a closed economy, of course, savings or investment taxes have identical effects, since savings is identically equal to investment. In an open economy, the distinction between the two becomes essential. To highlight the welfare effects of the current regime, I show the effects of the two extremes.

5.1. Comparing savings and investment distortions

The formal framework underlying the analysis is fully laid out in the Appendix. To simplify the discussion, I assume that there is no tax at all on capital income abroad. When the worldwide principle is applied, domestic residents face the domestic tax rate wherever they invest. In order to attract domestic savings, the rate of return on domestic investment (say on physical capital) must, therefore, equal the world real rate of interest. At the same time, the decision to save instead of consuming will be driven by the after-tax world real interest rate. Hence, the tax drives a wedge between the marginal rate of intertemporal substitution and the world real interest rate, i.e. it produces a distortion in the decision between consumption and savings. By contrast, portfolio allocation, and hence production, are undistorted: international portfolio allocation maximizes the present discounted value of GNP at the given world interest rate. The situation is summarized as follows:

marginal rate of intertemporal substitution

$$= \text{world real interest rate net of taxes} \tag{1}$$

marginal productivity of domestic capital

$$= \text{world real interest rate} \tag{2}$$

When the territorial principle is applied, foreign income is not taxed. Physical capital must now offer a return which offers, *after tax*, the world real rate of interest. The situation becomes:

marginal rate of intertemporal substitution

$$= \text{world real interest rate} \tag{3}$$

marginal productivity of domestic capital net of taxes

$$= \text{world real interest rate} \tag{4}$$

Territorial taxation leaves the intertemporal terms of trade to consumers unaffected, but distorts domestic production.

The welfare evaluation of the territorial and worldwide principle will thus depend on the relative importance of the distortions induced respectively in production and consumption. In turn, the relative importance of these distortions is determined by the relative substitutability between present and future consumption on the one hand, and between domestic and foreign assets on the other hand. If intertemporal substitution in consumption is low (see Hall, 1988, for empirical evidence supporting this hypothesis) and if international asset substitutability is high, raising a given amount of revenue by taxing savings is less damaging to society's welfare than raising the same amount of revenue by taxing domestic investment only.

The worldwide principle would *always* be superior to the territorial principle in the presence of another factor of production, say labour, whose income accounts for all remaining value added and can be taxed, and whose supply decreases with higher income taxes, or when pure profits are taxable. Under these conditions, production efficiency requires that the marginal product of capital equals its opportunity cost, represented by the world rate of interest. (Diamond and Mirrlees, 1971, have established the production efficiency result.) On the other hand, when governments cannot raise the optimal amount of revenue from all sources, the 'relative substitutability' criterion provided here is the correct one.

5.2. International tax policy interactions

When individual fiscal authorities set capital taxes independently, they do not take into account the fact that resulting outflow of capital may benefit other countries. The flip side of this remark is, of course, that a fall in domestic tax rates, which will attract capital from the rest of the world, is a beggar-thy-neighbour policy. In principle, it would be optimal for all countries to recognize this effect and accordingly to set taxes in full coordination. Unlike most of the literature on macroeconomic policy coordination, I shall, however, assume that the optimum coordinated agreement is not achievable, and I discuss which of the alternative regimes minimizes the damage from non-cooperative interactions. This approach is justified by the practical difficulties that would be encountered in making the parties agree on a cooperative solution. Imperfect information, together with imperfections in the bargaining process, make it difficult to achieve a cooperative solution.

If countries set taxes independently, they take the policies of their neighbours as given, and hence end up misestimating the effects of their own policies. Lack of coordination leads to suboptimal taxation. Following Gordon (1983) I assess the effects of the distortions induced by lack of coordination by comparing the rules for choosing taxes followed by individual countries and those followed in the ideal (and unattainable) coordinated optimum under the two regimes: territorial taxation and worldwide taxation. A formal analysis is presented in the Appendix. In what follows, we restrict ourselves to an exposition of the results.

Consider first the case where the *territorial* principle is applied. Then, from (3) and (4) above, a tax on capital will be perceived by a country acting in isolation as leading to a capital outflow with no effect on savings. With high international capital mobility, countries would set the tax rate at an artificially low level, for fear of a massive capital outflow to the rest of the world (this is the phenomenon of tax competition). If all countries were to cooperate and choose the same rate of taxation, there would be no capital movement, but the choice between savings and consumption would be affected everywhere (as the 'world' rate of interest would be reduced). Since with high capital mobility the difference between the perceived and the actual response can be arbitrarily large, the cost of tax competition can be very significant.

Consider now the case where countries apply the *worldwide* principle. From (1) and (2), each country acting in isolation believes that the tax will have no effect on investment since its domestic capital must yield the world real interest rate, perceived to be unchanged. The only response that each country perceives is that of savings, *via* a change in the accumulation of foreign assets. By contrast, if all countries jointly agree on the same tax rate, they know that total investment decreases and this raises the gross rate of return to capital. The nature and the size of the distortions arising from non-cooperative tax policies depend, in this case, on the response of savings to the real rate of interest. When the responsiveness is zero or negative, tax authorities in each country expect savings to be higher through larger foreign asset accumulation, and accordingly, there is an incentive to tax more than under coordination: uncoordinated tax setting would give rise to excessive revenue from capital income taxation. Only when the responsiveness of savings is positive and implausibly large can the distortions produced by uncoordinated tax setting lead to undertaxation of capital.

In conclusion, for plausible responsiveness of savings to real interest rates and in the presence of high capital mobility, the worldwide principle of taxation is superior to the territorial principle, for two reasons. First, the welfare cost of raising a given amount of tax revenue is lower when domestic and foreign investments are subject to the same treatment, and second, high capital mobility would lead to disruptive tax competition: countries impose taxes on capital income which are too low (suboptimal) whenever investors can escape taxes by investing abroad. The losses from uncoordinated tax setting can thus be large in the presence of territorial tax discrimination, but are likely to be negligible when capital export neutrality is preserved.

6. The policy options

According to popular perceptions, the best way to eliminate the existing distortions is to 'harmonize' tax systems, i.e. to bring tax rates and tax bases to the same level. This view underlies an early proposal for an EC Council directive to bring withholding tax rates to a uniform level of 15%. The purpose of this proposal was to discourage tax evasion through failure to report interest payments from low withholding tax countries. The drive towards harmonization clashes with countries' right to choose the form of taxation of their citizens. In addition, it cannot possibly solve another major issue raised by the liberalization of capital markets. Europe is not a closed economy, and taxing capital income at the same rate within the EEC, given the current structure of tax systems, will not avoid an outflow of capital to tax havens. This outflow could occur through countries which are presently imposing few or no capital controls, giving rise to a boom of financial intermediaries in those countries, unless strict controls *vis-à-vis* the rest of the world are imposed. This would be undesirable because it would implement at the scale of Europe a problem that the completion of the internal market was meant to eliminate. It might also prompt resistance, or even some form of retaliation, from the rest of the world. In addition, this measure would not be acceptable to member countries like Luxembourg and the UK. The crucial question is to what extent it is possible to reconcile the freedom of individual countries to tax their residents with the international mobility of capital. The answer is to eliminate, as much as possible, distortions to the international allocation of investment arising exclusively from taxes, and incentives to pursue beggar-thy-neighbour policies.

6.1. An alternative to harmonization

The paper has strongly argued that a stricter application of the world-wide principle, already formally adopted by almost all EC countries, is likely to be less distortionary than the current system. Two other reasons can be added. First, under the worldwide principle, there is no need to force individual member countries to adopt the same tax rates and tax rules as the other partners. Under this principle, the right of every government to choose how to tax its residents is preserved because incentives to invest internationally for the purpose of avoiding taxes are eliminated, no matter what tax rates are being applied in the rest of the world. Yet, a gradual convergence of tax rates and tax rules might eventually be useful to eliminate residual loopholes and make it easier to conduct a Europe-wide business. Second, the worldwide principle implies equal treatment of all international income, whether or not it is produced inside the EEC: it does not discriminate against countries outside the EEC, and it does not require the imposition of capital controls *vis-a-vis* the rest of the world.[9] A number of institutions currently prevent a full application of the worldwide principle. The priority should be to remove them, as far as possible.

6.1.1. Deferrals. In most European countries, income from foreign source is treated differently from domestic income: the rules to eliminate

---

[9] In practice, however, there might be some difficulties in discouraging tax evasion through the use of offshore (outside of Europe) tax havens. This problem and others are discussed in the following section.

double taxation of group profits do not apply to profits from foreign sources and corporations can (often indefinitely) delay profits repatriation. An outright elimination of deferral would represent a big step towards full application of the worldwide principle. This would entail a requirement that taxes on foreign investment income be paid when the income is produced (and not just when it is repatriated), coupled with an extension of the provisions to eliminate double taxation of group profits to foreign (or just European) subsidiaries.

6.1.2. Withholding taxes. They are in clear contradiction with the worldwide principle. They are inherited from a time when financial markets and fiscal jurisdictions were isolated enough to make tax collection on foreign investments a very difficult task. Withholding taxes (on both interest and dividend payments) could be eliminated when recipients are residents of the EC and replaced by a rule requiring investors to declare their tax residence. Financial intermediaries would simply collect records of investment income produced by EC residents and make it available to tax authorities.[10] The administrative costs of implementing this system are likely to be just a fraction of the resources being spent on avoiding withholding taxes. The dismantling of withholding taxes in Europe would eliminate all incentives to locate financial intermediaries in low withholding tax countries.

6.1.3. Bank secrecy and blocking laws. The problem with the application of a Community-wide system of keeping records for tax purposes is that secrecy and blocking laws in several countries would currently not allow it. Secrecy and blocking laws have three functions. The first, a desirable one, is to protect political refugees from their own governments: presumably, this service is not going to be needed by EC citizens. The second, also desirable, is to provide a last resort defence against confiscatory wealth taxes, which – as is well known – are an easy device to eliminate large fiscal deficits. Since the incentive to raise taxes without warning is always present, it would be appropriate to institutionalize the protection of European savers by law. The third, undesirable, function is to attract tax evaders from foreign countries by offering anonymity, and to shelter foreign financial firms from the reach of their own regulators. In this sense, bank secrecy and blocking laws can be used by countries as beggar-thy-neighbour policies. Ideally, these policies should be prohibited in an integrated European capital market.

---

[10] The Dutch authorities have apparently been suggesting this solution is an alternative to withholding tax harmonization: see *The Economist*, February 11, 1989.

6.2. Objections to the worldwide principle and problems of implementation

A number of objections have been raised against the worldwide principle (see the comments by Edmond Malinvaud and the Panel discussion). The following comments are not meant to prove that the worldwide principle is indisputable. They are simply meant to hint that appropriate solutions to these practical issues are possibly not out of reach.

6.2.1. Optimal taxation. The first objection is that according to the theory of optimal taxation, capital income from all countries should not necessarily be taxed at the same rate, since countries are not necessarily identical, and taxes can be used to correct distortions affecting investment. The current system of territorial discrimination of capital income might be a reflection of the need to accommodate these differences by appropriate taxes.

The evidence presented above suggests that in most relevant cases differences in capital income taxation do not reflect optimal tax considerations. The most glaring tax breaks are in tax havens, where there are no obvious distortions which would discourage investment. The worldwide principle is not meant to be the optimum regime of coordination among tax authorities, but simply aims at minimizing the losses from non-cooperation.

6.2.2. Citizens' avoidance strategies. It is argued that the full application of the worldwide principle does not prevent individuals from acquiring residence or citizenship in countries with low taxes. This phenomenon would not be new but is likely to remain quantitatively insignificant. The costs for individuals of changing residence or citizenship are very high. Only very big difference in tax rates would justify migration in large proportions and this would be resisted by the host countries' governments.

6.2.3. Corporations' avoidance strategies. There is an additional risk that companies will incorporate in low tax countries, and will carry out tax arbitrage instead of their shareholders. In fact, the elimination of deferral would substantially decrease incentives for tax arbitrage by corporations, by integrating further the taxation of income produced by parents and subsidiaries. On the other hand, if corporate income taxes are levied independently of personal income taxes, companies would be able to increase after-tax returns to their shareholders by locating in countries with low income tax. Hence, corporations would end up carrying out tax arbitrage for their shareholders. This can happen only in the absence of integration between corporate and personal income taxation (for a discussion of these problems see McLure, 1983). The integration of corporate and individual income taxation differs across Europe[11] and further integration could eliminate any potential for tax arbitrage. These incentives could also be neutralized by requiring that companies choose as countries of incorporation those where they carry out most of their activities.

6.2.4. Administrative complexity. The administration of a residence-based tax system is complicated. For example, if withholding taxes are preserved, the same withholding agent should levy different taxes, depending on the country of residence of its payees. The clearing of these payments could be a bureaucratic nightmare. The answer is, as proposed above, to eliminate withholding taxes on European residents. The declaration of foreign source income should be voluntary, and the sources and amounts of income produced in Europe should be made available, upon request, to all EC tax authorities. This system of free exchange of tax information, coupled with stiff penalties against transgressors, should effectively discourage evasion. Anyway, the alternative territorial system is even worse since it requires determining how much income multinational corporations produce in each country. Even theoretically, this problem does not have clear-cut solutions, as shown by Hines (1989). Multinationals can easily allocate income towards low tax countries using transfer pricing strategies. The distortions produced by 'formula apportionment' methods in the US are a good example of the difficulties of administering a source-based system (see Gordon and Wilson, 1986).

6.2.5. A non-distortionary system. It is sometimes argued that the current system of withholding taxes is not distortionary as it only encourages roundtripping. As a result, worthwhile investment projects would still be financed (Gros, 1989). The answer is that it does not matter whether or not the funds channelled through offshore centres come back to the country of origin if the countries involved are part of an integrated area, characterized by well functioning capital markets. What is relevant is, first, that roundtripping or treaty shopping decrease tax revenue (and can completely eliminate it when the arbitrage operations are costless), and, second, that the location of financial intermediaries is in fact distorted. The elimination of revenue from capital income taxes requires increased revenue elsewhere, and, of course, raises questions of equity.

---

[11] Countries like Luxembourg and Spain keep corporate and individual income completely separated: hence the income produced by the corporation is 'taxed twice' in these countries. Belgium, Denmark, France, Ireland and Italy adopt an 'imputation system' whereby shareholders pay taxes on dividend payments grossed up by the corporate income tax, and can obtain credit for at least part of the taxes paid by the corporation. Germany has a mixture of an imputation system and a 'split rate' system, whereby distributed profits are taxed at a lower rate than undistributed profits.

6.2.6. Secrecy. One might object that the countries which best protect investors' privacy have penal laws defending bank secrecy and that these laws are very difficult to change. In fact, changes in bank secrecy laws are in any case likely to be the most serious legal hurdle against the full application of the residence principle. There are, however, a number of legal solutions to this problem that might give tax authorities access to information regarding foreign bank accounts without actually changing the laws. A particularly interesting device to bypass Swiss bank secrecy has been developed by the US. Each taxpayer is now required to declare any interest, signature or authority in any foreign bank account. Failure to reveal this information, according to US law, may amount to tax fraud. Countries like Switzerland, which do not permit the release of information to foreign authorities pursuing tax evasion, allow it in the cases when tax fraud is suspected (Abrams, 1978).

7. Concluding remark

The creation of a single market requires substantial revision of the existing economic institutions, and, possibly, the creation of new ones. This represents a rare opportunity for a thorough rationalization and improvement of the laws and regulations affecting capital markets. The taxation of capital income, perhaps more than any other institution, would benefit tremendously from this process of rationalization and improvement. The payoffs from rationalization are also likely to develop outside Europe. For example, reforms aimed at a more effective application of the worldwide principle, and at eliminating tax evasion through foreign investment, would most likely be welcomed by the US government. Indeed, the US government, perhaps more than any other industrial country's government, has waged lonely and sometimes unsuccessful battles in the effort of chasing tax evaders who make use of foreign tax havens.

Discussion

Edmond Malinvaud
College de France

This is a paper about a tragedy in the spirit of Corneille, namely 'achieving European unification while maintaining national autonomy'; in the background there is a second tragedy in the same spirit, 'cherishing a free worldwide capital market but longing for macroeconomic stability'. Alberto Giovannini considers a particular aspect of both tragedies, namely the taxation of capital. This issue stands high in present concerns and we should be particularly thankful to Giovannini for bringing it to our attention.

The 'primer' on European capital markets, which makes by far the longest part of the paper, states very well the terms of the dilemma. Tax avoidance strategies are already present in the European capital market. They will certainly become very common after the full liberalization of this market unless something is done to suppress incentives for them. Present incentives would entail damaging consequences. The main point of the dilemma is well understood by national authorities. The liberalization of capital markets will force them to lower the taxation of capital, otherwise financial and productive capital would move abroad. This consideration also applies to all countries that want to be included in the free worldwide capital market. As a result, given that some countries already have hardly any taxation of capital, the final outcome will be a world in which capital will be exempt from tax.

There are two reasons for objecting to such an outcome. First, a low level of overall taxation may result in an inadequate provision of public goods. Second, the objectives of redistribution, to which European tax systems pay so much attention, will be jeopardized. One may even wonder whether these objections will not be so serious as to prevent, or delay, the removal of remaining EEC exchange controls. Confronted with the various aspects of taxation, the European Commission has so far aimed at harmonization within the Community. In particular a Council Directive of June 24, 1988 has instructed the Commission to make proposals for the harmonization of taxes on personal savings. Giovannini argues that this is not the correct solution and he proposes a wholly different alternative.

Two objections can be raised against the harmonization proposal. First, unless harmonization is accompanied by strict controls *vis-a-vis* the rest of the world, it will not avoid an outflow of capital to tax havens. Giovannini argues that such controls will result in a protected European capital market. This is not desirable, in principle. It is also contrary to the intention of the Single Act and unacceptable to some members of the Community. The argument can be acknowledged, except in one respect about which the author should have provided a fuller discussion. Is a free worldwide capital market without any powerful central authority the optimal solution? Is it the best solution from the European point of view? From the world point of view? Perhaps one day the question will be very seriously raised. The second objection stems from the assertion that national governments have a fundamental right to choose their tax systems. Such a right is stated without any qualification or justification. Yet I wonder whether countries living more and more together and slowly moving towards a federation can long recognize such an unqualified fundamental right of their respective governments.

Instead of harmonization, Giovannini recommends a strict application of the worldwide principle of taxation and lists in the last part of his paper the dispositions that have to be taken to this effect. Before discussing the positive arguments given in the paper in favour of this solution, its feasibility can be questioned. First, it seems that applying the worldwide principle to the taxation of goods and services would lead to the present VAT system. Yet, governments have apparently agreed to change this system in favour of an alternative that will combine partial harmonization of tax rates with the use of the territorial principle; this change is intended to eliminate border formalities within Europe. In order to persuade European authorities, the author should thus convincingly argue that capital taxation is essentially different from indirect taxation with respect to this aspect of European integration. Still, the main difficulty with the worldwide principle has the same nature as the one raised by the author against the harmonization solution: in order to avoid an outflow of capital outside of Europe for tax evasion, in particular to tax havens, cooperation of all non-European governments would be required. There is a good deal of optimism in the idea, put forward at the end of the paper, that the solution could be enforced by joint action of the US and EEC.

The attraction of the worldwide principle of taxation should, however, not be denied. The author makes a good case for it, both in the paper and in the Appendix. He works with a small open two-period economy. This country can use only proportional taxation of the second period gross returns in order to finance its public goods, consumed in the second period. There is a choice between investing in production at home or investing abroad at an exogenously given rate of return. The question is then raised as to which taxation principle, territorial or worldwide, is preferable. With respect to the first-best solution, the territorial principle generates a distortion by driving too much investment abroad; the worldwide principle generates a different distortion by inducing too little saving. But since intertemporal substitution in consumption is low and international asset substitutability is high, this second distortion reduces welfare by less than the first one. Accordingly, the worldwide principle of taxation must be preferred. Then, Giovannini considers several independent countries, each of them being similar to the small open economy discussed above. The non-cooperative equilibrium that arises when all countries apply either the territorial or the worldwide principle is analysed. As a benchmark, the cooperative equilibrium is also considered. This equilibrium should still be seen as a second-best optimum, since in equilibrium public consumption has to be financed by distorting taxes.

I have two remarks about this analysis. First, considering the main point made in the paper, it would have been interesting to compare the harmonization solution with non-cooperation outcome under the worldwide principle. Yet, this cannot be achieved because the author assumes that all countries are identical. As a result, the harmonization solution is also the cooperative equilibrium. The model is thus biased in favour of harmonization since 'the right to tax differently' can only be interesting when there are differences in economic or social structures. At this point, one may, however, wonder whether these structures really differ much across European countries. Second, it seems that the non-cooperative equilibrium is not fully solved. This is apparent in the Appendix where individual country behaviour is considered, with a given world rate of return r^*, resulting in some value for the flow of capital (A) to or from abroad. Still, equilibrium requires that r^* has a value such that $A = 0$. Taking this requirement into account might be interesting. In particular it may lead to comparing the non-cooperative equilibrium under the worldwide principle with the cooperative equilibrium, a comparison that would nicely complete the argument.

To conclude, let me stress that the territorial principle combined with non-cooperative behaviour appears to be particularly damaging to tax revenue from capital. This is well shown by the Appendix and is really at the heart of the problem discussed in the whole paper.

Colin Mayer
City University, London

I want to illustrate the questions raised by Alberto Giovannini's paper in a simple model of international taxation. I will focus on two issues, namely the incentives for authorities to deviate from optimal rates of taxation and to leave taxable income undisclosed. This analysis will suggest a particular form of worldwide taxation which clarifies the relation of worldwide to territorial based taxation and suggests circumstances in which territorial based arrangements are appropriate. Consider a unit investment that yields $(1 + r^d)$ domestically and $(1 + r^f)$ overseas before tax (see Table 7). Tax is levied at a rate t^d domestically and t^f overseas. G^d is the revenue raised by the domestic government on the proportion, λ^d, of the unit that is invested domestically. G^f is the revenue raised by the foreign government.

Consider two systems of taxation: territorial (source-based) and worldwide taxation. Assuming free capital flows, $r^d = r^f(1 - t^f)/(1 - t^d)$ in the presence of a territorial system. Thus, location decisions are distorted with $t^f = 0$ but not with equal rates of overseas and domestic taxation (see Table 8). In the case of the worldwide system, location decisions are not distorted irrespective of the rate of overseas taxation. *Pre-tax* rates of return are equated in all cases under a worldwide system. However, total savings are distorted since domestic taxes are levied

Table 7. Returns to domestic and foreign source income

	Domestic	Overseas	Interest rate parity
No taxation	$(1+r^d)$	$(1+r^f)$	
Territorial taxation	$1+r^d(1-t^d)$	$1+r^f(1-t^f)$	$r^d = \dfrac{r^f(1-t^f)}{(1-t^d)}$
	$G^d = t^d r^d \lambda^d$	$G^f = t^f r^f (1-\lambda^d)$	
Worldwide taxation	$1+r^d(1-t^d)$	$1+r^f(1-t^d)$	$r^d = r^f$
	$G^d = [t^d r^d \lambda^d + (t^d-t^f)r^f(1-\lambda^d)]$	$G^f = t^f r^f (1-\lambda^d)$	

even when overseas tax rates are zero. In contrast, there is no distortion to total saving in the presence of a territorial system of taxation where the overseas tax rate (t^f) is zero. The marginal rate of return will then be the *pre-tax* rate of return on overseas income.

In summary, location decisions are never distorted under worldwide taxation. This arises only with harmonization under a territorial system. If overseas income is untaxed, total savings are not distorted under a territorial system but are always distorted with worldwide taxation. Since location decisions are more sensitive to tax wedges than savings, Alberto Giovannini favours the worldwide system.

However, the argument ignores the incentives on governments to change tax rates. With a territorial system, the effect of a rise in t^f on G^f depends on the mobility of capital since higher tax rates reduce taxable income by encouraging a capital outflow. In contrast, the effect of a rise in t^f on G^f is unequivocally positive in the presence of a worldwide system. There is no influence of t^f on location or total savings under the worldwide system, so that overseas governments can only benefit from raising taxes. Essentially, by raising t^f, foreign governments are earning revenue at the expense of domestic governments which have to pay larger tax credits to domestic firms (see the last line of Table 7). In other words, there is an externality which encourages too high a level of taxation under the worldwide system. In addition, the analysis has so far assumed that income is observable by tax authorities irrespective of its source. Now, suppose foreign source income is unobservable by domestic authorities (see the last section of Table 8). There is then always a distortion to location decisions under the worldwide system. An increase in the proportion of undisclosed foreign income under a worldwide system is equivalent to a reduction in the foreign tax rate under the territorial system. It has uncertain effects on foreign country tax revenue but encourages a capital flow into the foreign country.

Table 8. Domestic rates of return and government income

	$t^f = 0$	$t^f = t^d$
Territorial taxation	$r^d = \dfrac{r^f}{1-t^d}$	$r^d = r^f$
	$G^d = t^d r^d \lambda^d$	$G^d = t^d r^d \lambda^d$
Worldwide taxation	$r^d = r^f$	$r^d = r^f$
	$G^d = t^d r^d$	$G^d = t^d r^d \lambda^d$
Worldwide taxation (foreign source income unobservable)	$r^d = \dfrac{r^f}{1-t^d}$	$r^d = \dfrac{r^f}{1-t^d}$
	$G^d = t^d r^d \lambda^d$	$G^d = t^d r^d \lambda^d$

Given these problems of overtaxation and underdisclosure, some thought has to be given to the design of a worldwide system of taxation. The most straightforward system that avoids overtaxation is an extension of a tax credit system. Taxes are collected at source in the overseas country and a tax credit given for overseas taxes paid. The incentive to overtax is avoided by allowing the domestic country to claim tax credits from the overseas tax authority. The overseas tax authority is then merely acting as a tax collecting agent and deriving no tax revenue. This is exactly analogous to a local office of a national tax system. Thinking about the tax credit scheme clarifies two problems that can arise. First, a country may refuse to pass on the tax revenue that it has collected. That is the withholding tax problem. As bilateral negotiations over withholding tax illustrate, that difficulty is diminished where reductions are seen to be in the mutual interest of the countries concerned. The second problem is that a country may refuse to act as a tax collecting agent. That is the tax haven or undisclosed income problem. This is improved by not passing on tax credits that are collected on overseas income. This has the effect of making a country like a shareholder who is unable to claim a tax credit on income collected at source in an imputation system of taxation. Provided that all major financial markets participate, the threat of withholding tax credits can be used to discourage countries from failing to disclose income. There is no implication that the operation of a tax credit system means loss of autonomy in setting tax policy. It has already been noted that imposition of common tax rates is not necessary. Furthermore, in principle, it is possible to accommodate differences in tax bases. For example, taxes may be levied on different definitions of profits. It is the destination not the source tax rate and base that will affect the investor.

But what happens if it is desirable to deviate from neutrality on the basis of the source and not the destination of income? One can think of circumstances in which deviations should be destination based, for example, where investors in particular locations are unduly myopic. However, for the most part, deviations from neutrality are considered in relation to the source of income: for example, externalities of production in particular locations and capital market imperfections. In that case, the tax system should appropriately move away from a worldwide to a territorial-based income scheme. It should not become the hybrid that is currently in existence where source-based taxation is distorted by the application of worldwide principles by destination countries. Instead, it should be a true source-based tax where tax bases are dependent on sources of income irrespective of their destination.

It is actually easier to operate a true source-based tax under a worldwide system than existing systems. By setting tax credits at different levels from taxes paid, it is possible to encourage or discourage activities in certain locations. For example, credits in excess of taxes are equivalent to tax havens that encourage capital inflows. They reduce the final tax burdens of investing in particular locations. Conversely, taxes without corresponding credits are equivalent to withholding taxes and discourage capital investments. The extremes are a zero tax credit in which case the tax system is equivalent to double taxation at source and destination and a tax credit which exceeds taxes paid by the destination tax and leaves income completely untaxed. However, we have seen that individual nations' incentives to withhold tax or undertax are not the same as is socially desirable. It is at this stage that the autonomy of nations to set their own tax bases should be curtailed. To avoid countries unilaterally setting tax credits at levels different from taxes levied, incentives to invest in particular locations will have to be perceived to be both fair and desirable. Otherwise, worldwide systems of taxation will degenerate to territorial as countries attempt to reestablish source-based incentives. It is thus entirely appropriate that a worldwide system of taxation should be introduced in the context of the emergence of a single European market.

General discussion

Some panel members commented on the model that Alberto Giovannini used to show that taxation under the worldwide principle would be desirable. Jacques Melitz indicated that the model underscores the benefits of the worldwide principle, by assuming that countries are identical. A significant advantage of this principle is also that the extent to which tax laws have to be harmonized is well defined and limited. This principle does not require a full harmonization of the tax systems and this advantage would presumably appear in a model allowing for a diversity of countries. Charles Wyplosz was worried about the robustness of the results; in particular, he pointed to the assumptions that there is no tax distortion in the rest of the world, that inputs other than capital are not subject to distortive taxation and that returns are (for the main part) exogenous. He wondered whether under different assumptions the territorial principle might not become attractive. Giovannini acknowledged this. At the same time, he warned about the difficulty of comparing taxation under the worldwide principle with an optimal set of taxes under the territorial principle; indeed, tax rates in Europe set under the territorial principle do not correspond to any optimal scheme. Rather, the current pattern seems to be the result of a systematic beggar-thy-neighbour policy, which would be the appropriate benchmark against which the worldwide principle should be assessed.

Some panel members also pointed to some loopholes which would subsist under the worldwide principle; for example, Luigi Spaventa mentioned the practice of coupon washing and Stephen Breyer indicated that 49%-owned joint ventures would be a safe alternative to fully owned subsidiaries. In principle, as pointed by Georges de Menil, the worldwide principle does not solve the problem of tax competition, as long as company headquarters can move. This would argue in favour of the abolition of corporate taxes, and sole reliance on individuals' taxation. Yet, as argued by Victor Norman, individuals could also move. This latter possibility was regarded by some panel members as less likely.

The amount of cooperation that would be required between countries to implement the worldwide principle was also discussed. Giovannini indicated that in principle some tax haven on a tiny exotic island could always be set up. Yet, it seemed that if Europe and the US could cooperate on this matter, their joint weight might be sufficient to deter potential tax havens. An alternative would be to pay them for not indulging in the provision of tax havens.

Appendix. A comparison of the worldwide and territorial principles

A1. Single-country case

The model (for a fuller treatment, see Giovannini, 1988b, 1989) used for the arguments presented in Section 5 describes investment and savings choices over two periods. Initial resources can be consumed or invested either in domestic capital or in a foreign bond with fixed return r^*. In the second period, output is produced and is allocated, together with gross income from foreign investment, to taxes and consumption.

The domestic (constant-returns-to-scale) production technology uses capital and a fixed factor (land or labour) that cannot be taxed. Of course, lump-sum non-distortionary taxes are not available. The government announces taxes in the first period, collects them in the second period, and uses the proceeds to provide a public good which affects the utility of the private sector. (I abstract from the problems raised by the incentives for the government to renege *ex post* on the announced tax rates).

Consider first the case of a small country in isolation. The analysis is around two distinct problems. In the first, the worldwide principle is applied, hence all income from savings is taxed. For the moment, let the tax rate be exogenous. Individuals solve the following problem:

$$\max U(C_1, C_2) + v(G) \tag{A1}$$

subject to:

$$C_1 + K + A = E \tag{A2}$$

$$C_2 = [f(K) + A(1 + \tau^*)](1 - \tau) \tag{A3}$$

Utility is separable in consumption and (second-period) government spending, G, which is taken as exogenous by consumers/investors. Initial resources E are allocated to first-period consumption and investment K. The first-order conditions are:

$$f'(K) = (1 + r^*) \tag{A4}$$

$$U_1(C_1, C_2) = (1 + r^*)(1 - \tau) U_2(C_1, C_2) \tag{A5}$$

When the territorial system is applied, the consumers' problem becomes:

$$\max U(C_1, C_2) + v(G) \tag{A6}$$

subject to:

$$C_1 + K + A = E \tag{A7}$$

$$C_2 = f(K)(1 - \tau) + A(1 + r^*) \tag{A8}$$

The first-order conditions are:

$$f'(K) = (1 - \tau)(1 + r^*) \tag{A9}$$

$$U_1(C_1, C_2) = (1 + r^*) U_2(C_1, C_2) \tag{A10}$$

A2. Tax policy interactions

There is a large set of identical countries which are individually too small to affect the world interest rate. I assume that these countries, as a whole, are isolated from the rest of the world. The assumption that countries are identical allows me to illustrate the optimal level of taxation using a 'representative country', while the assumption that countries are small allows me to neglect the optimal tariff incentives to manipulate the capital income tax. Since the whole set of countries is closed, the optimal level of capital income taxes is determined by solving a representative country's optimal tax problem, assuming no international capital mobility. Because all countries are assumed to be identical, the representative country is just the average of the whole region and, by assumption, does not trade in assets with the rest of the world. Notice that the optimal level of capital income taxes does not depend on whether the worldwide or territorial principle is adopted. Formally, the problem can be stated as follows:

$$\max_{\tau} U(C_1, C_2) + v(G) \tag{A11}$$

subject to:

$$C_1 + K = E \tag{A12}$$

$$C_2 = f(K)(1 - \tau) \tag{A13}$$

$$G = \tau f(K) \tag{A14}$$

$$U_1(C_1, C_2) = (1 - \tau)f'(K)U_2(C_1, C_2) \tag{A15}$$

The private sector's optimal decision rule (a constraint to the tax authority) is Equation (A15). The subscripts to the utility function indicate the partial derivatives with respect to first and second period consumption, respectively. The first-order conditions of problem (A11) – (A15) yield the following:

$$U_2(C_1, C_2) = \left[1 + \tau \frac{f'(K)}{f(K)} \frac{dK}{d\tau} \right] v'(G) \tag{A16}$$

The expression in square brackets is less than 1, since an increase in the tax rate decreases first-period investment, thus increasing the gross rate of return to capital. If the supply of capital was fixed, the optimal level of government spending would be chosen so that its marginal utility equals the marginal utility of consumption at time 2. With an elastic supply of investment, taxes are chosen so that the marginal utility of government spending at time 2 exceeds the marginal utility of consumption. Notice that the optimal (coordinated) taxation of capital is the same under both the territorial and worldwide taxation principle, since in the aggregate there is no international borrowing and lending.

In a Cournot–Nash equilibrium, when the territorial principle is followed, the problem is:

$$\max_{\tau} U(C_1, C_2) + v(G) \tag{A17}$$

subject to:

$$C_1 + K + A = E \tag{A18}$$

$$C_2 = f(K)(1 - \tau) + A(1 + r^*) \tag{A19}$$

$$G = \tau f(K) \tag{A20}$$

$$f'(K) = (1 - \tau)(1 + r^*) \tag{A21}$$

$$U_1(C_1, C_2) = (1 + r^*) U_2(C_1, C_2) \tag{A22}$$

Equation (A18) shows that, in every country, initial resources are used to purchase domestic capital and foreign assets. From an individual country's perspective, the world rate of return is fixed at r^*. When only income from domestic sources is taxed, consumption plans are undistorted: international portfolio diversification ensures that the after-tax rate of return on all assets equals the world rate of interest (Equations (A22) and (A21)). The first order conditions for the problem (A17) to (A22) yield the following equation:

$$U_2(C_1, C_2) = \left[1 + \tau \frac{f'(K)}{f(K)} \frac{dK}{d\tau} \right] v'(G) \tag{A23}$$

The difference between (A23) and (A16) is in the term $dK/d\tau$. In the Cournot–Nash equilibrium, $dK/d\tau$ is the perceived *outflow of capital* in response to a change in the tax rate: it is obtained by differentiating Equation (A21). By contrast, in the cooperative equilibrium $dK/d\tau$ is the decrease in the capital stock in response to a change in the after-rate of return to savings. The closer the function $f(K)$ is to linear, the larger the perceived capital outflow in response to a change in the tax rate, and hence, the lower the desired tax revenue. Indeed, the perceived decrease in savings can be arbitrarily large, as $f''(K)$ gets arbitrarily close to zero. By contrast, with smooth convex indifference curves, a linear production function does not give rise to an infinite response of savings to the tax rate in a closed economy. As a result, in a Cournot–Nash equilibrium with territorial taxation, the equilibrium tax revenue from capital income can be far below the optimal level.

Finally, the problem solved by individual countries when the world-wide system is applied is as follows:

$$\max_{\tau} U(C_1, C_2) + v(G) \tag{A24}$$

subject to:

$$C_1 + K + A = E \tag{A25}$$

$$C_2 = [f(K) + A(1 + r^*)](1 - \tau) \tag{A26}$$

$$G = \tau[f(K) + A(1 + r^*)] \tag{A27}$$

$$f'(K) = (1 + r^*) \tag{A28}$$

$$U_1(C_1, C_2) = (1 + r^*)(1 - \tau) U_2(C_1, C_2) \tag{A29}$$

Notice that, from an individual country's perspective, changes in the tax rate do not affect investment, which is determined, through Equation (A28), by the world rate of interest. Hence, the change in savings in response to a change in the tax rate is reflected, from an individual government's perspective, in a change in foreign asset accumulation, A. The first-order conditions for the problem (A24) to (A29) yield the following:

$$U_2(C_1, C_2) = \left[1 + \frac{\tau(1 + r^*)}{Y_2} \frac{dA}{d\tau}\right] v'(G), \tag{A30}$$

where $Y_2 = f(K) + A(1 + r^*)$ (second-period GNP), and $dA/d\tau$ is the response of savings to the rate of interest. This term can be positive or negative. Hence, when all countries follow the worldwide principle, the distortions from non-cooperative tax policies can lead to either excessive or too little capital tax revenue. The size of this distortion depends on the size of the response of savings to the real rate of interest.

References

Abrams, R. M. (1978). 'Tax Evasion and Swiss Banking Secrecy', *The Practical Lawyer*.

Adler, M. (1979). 'US Taxation of US Multinational Corporations: A Manual of Computation Techniques and Managerial Decision Rules', in M. Sarnat and G. Szego (eds.) *International Finance and Trade*, Ballinger: Cambridge MA.

Alworth, J. S. (1988). *The Finance, Investment and Taxation Decisions of Multinationals*, Basil Blackwell, New York.

Bovenberg, A. L. (1988). 'The International Effects of Capital Taxation: An Analytical Framework', mimeo, International Monetary Fund.

Dale, R. (1984). *The Regulation of International Banking*, Prentice Hall. Englewood Cliffs, N.J.

Darby, M. (1975). 'The Financial and Tax Effects of Monetary Policy on Interest Rates', *Economic Inquiry*.

Diamond, P. A. and J. Mirrlees (1971). 'Optimal Taxation and Public Production I: Production Efficiency', *American Economic Review*.

Feldstein, M. (1976). 'Inflation, Income Taxes and the Rate of Interest: A Theoretical Analysis', *American Economic Review*.

Giavazzi, F. and A. Giovannini (1989). *Limiting Exchange-Rate Flexibility: The European Monetary System*, MIT Press, Cambridge, MA.

Giovannini, A. (1988a). 'Capital Controls and Public Finance: The Experience in Italy', in F. Giavazzi and L. Spaventa (eds.) *High Public Debt: The Italian Experience*, Cambridge University Press, Cambridge.

—— (1988b). 'International Capital Mobility and Tax Avoidance', mimeo, Graduate School of Business, Columbia University.

—— (1989). 'International Capital Mobility and Capital Income Taxation: Conceptual Issues and Policy Implications for Europe', paper presented at the European Economic Association Meetings, Augsburg, September.

Gordon, R. H. (1983). 'An Optimal Taxation Approach to Fiscal Federalism', *Quarterly Journal of Economics*.

—— (1987). 'Taxation of Investment and Savings in a World Economy', *American Economic Review*.

Gordon, R. H. and J. D. Wilson (1986). 'An Examination of Multijurisdictional Corporate Income Taxation Under Formula Apportionment', *Econometrica*.

Gros, D. (1989). 'Tax Evasion and Offshore Centres', mimeo, CEPS.

Hall, R. E. (1988). 'Intertemporal Substitution in Consumption', *Journal of Political Economy*.

Hines, J. R. Jr. (1989). 'Transfer Pricing', mimeo, Harvard University.

Hines, J. R. Jr. and R. G. Hubbard (1989). 'Coming Home to America: Dividend Repatriation Decisions of U.S. Multinationals', mimeo, Columbia Business School.

King, M. and D. Fullerton (1984). *The Taxation of Income from Capital*, Chicago University Press, Chicago.

McLure, C. E. (1983). 'Assignment of Corporate Income Taxes in a Federal System', in C. E. McLure (ed.) *Tax Assignment in Federal Countries*, Canberra: Centre for Research on Federal Financial Relations, The Australian National University.

Nadelmann, E. A. (1985). 'Negotiations in Criminal Law Assistance Treaties', *The American Journal of Comparative Law*.

—— (1986). 'Unlaundering Dirty Money Abroad: U.S. Foreign Policy and Financial Secrecy Jurisdictions', *Inter-American Law Review*.

Organization for Economic Cooperation and Development (OECD) (1987). *International Tax Avoidance and Evasion*, Issues in International Taxation, No. 1, OECD, Paris.

—— (1988a). *Tax Consequences of Foreign Exchange Gains and Losses*, Issues In International Taxation, No. 3, OECD, Paris.

—— (1988b). *Taxation of Net Wealth, Capital Transfers and Capital Gains of Individuals*, OECD, Paris.

Papke, L. E. (1988). 'International Differences in Capital Taxation and Corporate Borrowing Behavior: Evidence from the U.S. Withholding Tax', mimeo, Boston University.

Salminen, T. (1988). 'Banking Secrecy Legislation in Western Europe', *Issues in Bank Regulation*.

Sinn, H. W. (1985). 'Why Taxes Matter: Reagan's Accelerated Cost Recovery System and the US Trade Deficit', *Economic Policy*.

—— (1987). *Capital Income Taxation and Resource Allocation*, North-Holland, Amsterdam.

—— (1988). 'The 1986 US Tax Reform and the World Capital Market', *European Economic Review*.

Stiglitz, J. E. (1986). *Economics of the Public Sector*, W. W. Norton & Co., New York.

Tanzi, V. (1974). 'Inflation, Indexation, and Interest Income Taxation', Banca Nazionale del Lavoro *Quarterly Review*.

Wahl, J. B. (1987). 'Taxation of Foreign Exchange Gains and Losses', U.S. Treasury Department OTA Paper No. 57, October.

Financial markets

Vittorio Grilli

Summary

One potential effect of the integration of European financial markets concerns the geographical location of financial 'hot spots'. It is likely that liberalization will tend to promote countries with already large and well developed international financial markets. Attracting the residents of smaller countries, these markets will become larger and more liquid, and thus even more appealing. It is very unlikely that other European countries could design policies apt to threaten London's supremacy as the main European financial centre. While the article focuses on the market for bank deposits, similar considerations apply to other financial markets. It appears that a large part of cross-country bank deposits are explained by country-specific factors, such as particular institutional arrangements in the areas of capital controls, tax regulations and secrecy laws. However, the relative importance of these factors varies between inter-bank deposits and non-bank deposits: taxation and banking secrecy matter for non-bank deposits while the very size of the economy influences inter-bank deposits. Finally, imperfect competition and switching costs imply that more intense competition will be felt primarily in the market for large deposits. Small deposit contracts will probably be unaffected by liberalization, at least in the short run.

Europe 1992: issues and prospects for the financial markets

Vittorio Grilli
Yale University and NBER

1. Introduction

The decision to remove barriers to the flow of goods and services among the members of the European Community by 1992 will have profound consequences in many different sectors of the economy, both in Europe and the rest of the world. There is a widespread belief (almost fear) that the impact of the integration process will be particularly powerful in the capital markets. Because transformations and innovations in financial markets usually occur suddenly and rapidly, economic policy corrections may be hard to implement.

In several European countries, financial market regulation has been so extensive that the national capital markets have been isolated, almost completely protected from foreign competition. The transition to a new open environment could produce radical changes and uncertainty about what will happen is, in itself, reason for concern. Structural changes could involve shifts in the location of some of the markets and, therefore, induce a geographical redistribution of business activity, employment and income. Notwithstanding such concerns, however, there is a general enthusiasm and optimism about the benefits that the process of integration of the monetary and capital markets will bring. This sentiment is not confined to Brussels, but is shared by a large portion of the population. For example, according to a recent poll by Eurobarometer, as reported in the box below, almost 80% of Europeans list the ability freely to make payments and carry money across borders as advantages of 1992. Some 70% also list the possibility of opening bank accounts anywhere in the community.[1]

Financial support from The Council for West European Studies at Yale University is gratefully acknowledged.
[1] Table 1 also reveals considerable differences in national attitudes toward 1992.

Box. Eurobarometer survey of Spring 1988 on the advantages of the Single European Market in 1992

Question: The coming into being of the single European market by 1992 will mean the free circulation of persons, goods and property within the European Community Countries. Some people think this will mostly be an advantage. Others think it will be a disadvantage. Can you tell me, for each of this single common European market which I am going to mention, whether you personally think it will be an advantage or a disadvantage?

	E12	Blg	Dnk	Fra	Ger	Gre	Irl	Ita	Lux	Ntl	Por	Esp	UK
					% answering advantage								
Make payments	79	78	69	88	78	64	79	84	80	75	61	77	74
Carry money	79	76	61	88	82	73	79	74	77	68	68	78	79
Buy products	77	79	51	81	77	71	79	82	76	76	71	81	72
Residence	77	76	59	84	76	75	85	85	79	70	75	85	63
Work	76	73	58	81	66	67	88	88	67	72	77	85	71
Bank account	70	70	39	71	71	61	78	71	66	58	65	75	70
Buy properties	68	70	27	73	70	51	69	72	65	59	60	76	64
VAT closer	66	71	74	84	54	60	84	74	42	80	49	63	54
Border control	64	77	54	71	74	73	71	57	65	59	67	77	42
Public works	52	50	38	56	48	50	58	55	46	50	56	58	47

1. Make payments: The ability to make payments without complication within the whole European Community.
2. Carry money: The possibility to take any amount of money with you when you travel to other countries of the European Community.
3. Buy products: The possibility to buy in one's own country any product lawfully sold in other countries of the European Community.
4. Residence: The opportunity for any citizen of a country within the European Community to go and live without limitation in any country of the Community for instance to retire there or to study there.
5. Work: The opportunity for any citizen of a country within the European Community to go and work in any other country of the European Community.
6. Bank account: The possibility to open a bank account in any country of the European Community.
7. Property: The possibility to buy land or property throughout the Community.
8. VAT closer: Bringing closer together the rates of VAT applied in the various countries of the Community so that products are sold under similar cost conditions.
9. Border control: Elimination of custom controls when crossing frontiers between countries inside the European Community.
10. Public works: The possibility for a contractor from another country to be in charge of public works (for instance, building a bridge or a road) in our country if his offer is cheaper at the same level of quality.

Much of this optimism is based, at least in the professional literature, on principles borrowed from basic trade theory under the assumption of perfect competition. Current discussions start from this not so much because it is an appropriate description of how financial markets operate, but rather because of the lack of a well developed alternative. In fact, there is a paucity of theoretical and empirical analysis in the area of international financial intermediation. Neither the industrial organization literature, nor the international trade and finance literature offers many insights into the issue of what determines the structure, trade flows, and prices in these markets. Obviously, I will not attempt in this paper to fill in these gaps by formulating a complete theory of financial structures in an integrated world economy. Instead, I will illustrate how, by applying frameworks other than perfect competition, we can obtain predictions which are far less optimistic than what is often heard. I will also focus on two specific issues.

The first issue concerns the effects of liberalization on the long-run structure of international financial markets, and in particular their geographic location. Nowadays, we are familiar with the idea and existence of 'financial centres' like London, New York and Tokyo, i.e. with the clustering of different types of financial intermediaries in specific locations. Recent years have witnessed considerable changes in the relative importance of these centres, as well as the emergence of new ones like Singapore, Hong Kong and the Bahamas. How can the existence of such 'hot spots' be explained? Will the events of 1990–92 induce modifications in their relative importance, possibly leading to the emergence of new ones? The sober conclusion will be that drastic locational changes are quite unlikely. The second issue concerns the specific market for international bank deposits. One of the most debated components of the integration programme is the possibility of opening bank accounts in any member country. To what extent will this new freedom affect the international flow of bank deposits and what kind of movement should we expect in deposit interest rates? The conclusion is that most of the significant changes and gains in this area are likely to be confined to particular segments of the market, effectively bypassing a large number of depositors.

2. The effects of liberalization on the location of financial centres

' ... I predict, very tentatively, that Brussels will emerge as the financial center of the European Community, for the following reasons: it serves as the headquarters for the Commission; it attracts foreign corporations and will ultimately attract foreign and European banks;

it tolerates the world intellectual medium of exchange, the English language.'
(C. Kindleberger, 'The Formation of Financial Centers: A Study in Comparative Economic History,' 1974.)

Even if Belgium (including Luxembourg) has an important role in the international banking industry, many would name London as the main European financial centre. However, even though recent developments in financial markets may prove Kindleberger's conclusion inaccurate, the question that he tried to address is now more relevant than ever. At the world level, in addition to the UK, the US and Japan host the largest financial centres. These countries' complex networks of financial markets and financial intermediaries (listed in Table 1) are not matched anywhere else in terms of manpower and volume of activity. Could the liberalization of European capital markets alter the relative importance and location of world financial markets? Will part of the business, now concentrated in these centres, move towards the newly liberalized markets thereby making the geographical distribution of financial activity more uniform? Or, instead, will the activity originated in the recently liberalized countries flow towards London, New York or Tokyo, widening the gap between the 'financially' developed areas and the rest of the world?

The real question is why financial activities tend to be highly concentrated. At the outset, it must be emphasized that we do not have a well-developed theory to answer this question. Clearly, regulations matter. 'Off-shore' centres like Nassau and the Cayman Islands, are examples of particularly favourable regulatory environments because of the absence of income, corporate, and capital gains taxes as well as because of bank secrecy. However, advantages in terms of regulation do not account for the dominance of a centre like London, where the tax structure is far less benevolent than in the off-shore centres. For such major centres the explanation is more likely to be the existence of increasing returns deriving from thick-market externalities, as described by Diamond (1982). By recognizing the dependence of a firm's productivity on the size of the market in which it operates, this approach can offer an appealing account of the growth and concentration of financial markets. The idea is simple and is formalized in Appendix A. Concentration arises whenever a firm's productivity directly benefits from the proximity of competitors or firms engaged in related activities. Each firm is more profitable, possibly larger, than if it were operating alone. On the surface, it looks as if there were economies of scale. Yet, these external economies are clearly distinct from the more traditional, internal, economies of scale.

**Table 1. Principal characteristics of the main
financial centres, 1987**

UK (London)
Stock Exchange
60% of Eurobond Market
London Futures and Options Exchange (FOX)
London International Financial Futures
    Exchange (LIFFE)
London Metal Exchange
International Petroleum Exchange of London
Baltic Futures Exchange
International Freight Futures Exchange
    (BIFFEX)
London Grain Futures Market
London Meat Futures Exchange
London Potato Futures Market
Soya Bean Meal Futures Market

US (New York and Chicago)
New York Stock Exchange
American Stock Exchange
Commodity Exchange (COMEX)
New York Futures Exchange (NYFE)
New York Mercantile Exchange (NYMEX)
Coffee, Sugar and Cocoa Exchange
New York Cotton Exchange
Chicago Board of Trade (CBT)
Chicago Mercantile Exchange (CME)
Mid-America Commodity Exchange (Chicago)

Japan (Tokyo)
Tokyo Stock Exchange
Tokyo Commodity Exchange for Industry
Tokyo Financial Futures Exchange

This idea is well suited to describe financial centres, since they are complicated networks of various types of intermediaries and specialized firms operating and interacting in closely related markets. As these markets become larger, communication channels are more developed, the number of agents operating in the market increases, and accordingly business opportunities and commercial partners are more easily found. In addition to this improved 'matching process' on the customer side, matching on the labour input side becomes easier as well. In fact, the existence of a large market guarantees the training, and thus the availability, of a skilled labour force, which is an essential element for success in this highly specialized market. Because the productivity of the financial industry depends so crucially on the size of the market, large industrialized economies probably enjoy a comparative advantage in attracting financial firms from the rest of the world. Such thick-market externalities explain why the size of the economy matters, and why the four largest international financial centres (London, New York, Tokyo and Paris) are also the financial centres of four out of the five largest economies.[2] This idea also suggests that public incentives to create a large financial market may be hard to design. Indeed, any particular firm's incentive to move largely depends upon other firms also moving to the same location. In the end incentives may be dispensed with if many firms have moved, but initially it may be very hard, and very expensive, to trigger the change.

Even if these forms of externalities can help us understand why financial activities are not uniformly distributed in space, and why, instead, they tend to be concentrated in a few 'hot spots', several other important questions are still left unanswered. For example, why are financial intermediaries so highly concentrated in London and in New York and not in Madrid or Boston? Can the location of these centres be altered, and will European integration have such an effect?

Explaining the precise geographical location of financial centres is a difficult problem. Because the economic and institutional environments are important, policy decisions in these areas must have contributed to the configuration of today's world financial scene. Moreover, strictly geographical considerations, like the time zone to which a country belongs, are also crucial. Yet, a whole series of historical events which span over several centuries have shaped the current situation. It is probably impossible to disentangle them, as Robert Hall has recently observed:

'... the distribution of economic activity is probably close to indeterminate, so the location of economic hot spots is largely a matter of historical accidents'.
(R. Hall, 'Noise Over Space and Over Time,' 1988 Arthur Okun Memorial Lectures.)

The type of market-size externalities considered here are known to imply the possible existence of a large number of equilibria and do not provide any clue to understanding, or predicting, which one actually

---

[2] The fact that Germany doesn't have a centre of the same importance does not necessarily contradict the theory proposed above. Rather, the manner in which financial markets evolved in Germany after World War II is largely responsible for this absence. For obvious reasons, following World War II, Berlin ceased to be the financial capital of Germany, leaving the country without a clear dominant centre. Dusseldorf, Hamburg and Frankfurt shared a similar moderate level of status in the banking industry for almost two decades. It was only in the 1960s that Frankfurt emerged as the clear market leader and thus, until then, Germany was not characterized by the same degree of market thickness as the other major countries.

occurs. The fact that there exists more than one possible configuration indeed suggests that market locations are determined by a wide variety of factors. Thick-market externalities can also produce considerable amounts of inertia in an industry because, by itself, a firm may not be able to take advantage of a more efficient environment unless a whole number of other firms also decide to move to the new location. This is a typical example where coordination is required: unless all firms agree to move together, none will move, and there is no mechanism to trigger such a collective action. This also implies that market sizes and locations may be rather difficult to change by policy actions once an equilibrium has been reached. Quite to the contrary, we should expect that liberalization will favour countries with developed markets, so that in the medium run at least, it is very unlikely that London's supremacy will be challenged. Indeed, this would require very aggressive behaviour by the other European governments, including the adoption of off-shore types of regulations which appear to be largely incompatible with a concerted liberalization. In the whole, the existence of externalities might prevent the industry from achieving a higher level of profits, i.e. from shifting to the locations made more efficient as the result of deliberate public incentives. (Excessive market inertia is shown by Farrell and Saloner, 1986 to arise in a situation similar to that described above.)

3. The market for international bank deposits

3.1. Some stylized facts

In advanced economies, the financial sector is an important contributor to both employment and output. In Europe, the banking sector alone employs between 2.5 and 7.0% of the labour force and its value added represents between 4.2 and 6.0% of GDP (Table 2). It is, therefore, understandable that a considerable amount of attention has been directed towards the evaluation of the possible consequences of 1992 on the future of this industry. The liberalization of 1990–92 may operate through two main channels. First, liberalization will necessarily imply symmetric treatment of domestic and foreign (European) banking institutions, especially in matters like the establishment of new branches or the acquisition of existing ones. Second, the elimination of exchange controls will give individuals the freedom to choose foreign banks for their deposits or their loans. In theory, both channels could provide a way to increase competition in some of the more restricted national markets.

Several elements, however, suggest that the primary effects of 1990–92 will operate through the second channel. This is not to say that

Table 2. Importance of the financial sector, 1985

	Banking		Banking and insurance	
	Employment (% of total)	Value added (a) (% of GDP)	Employment (% of total)	Value added (% of GDP)
Belgium	3.0	4.4	3.9	5.9
France	2.5	4.9	3.4	4.5
Germany	2.7	4.6	3.7	5.5
Italy	—	6.0	2.5	5.6
Luxembourg	7.0	—	7.7	14.0 (b)
Netherlands	2.5	4.2	3.5	5.4
Spain	—	4.8	3.9	6.1
UK	2.5	4.3	3.6	12.6

Source: Price Waterhouse, *The 'Cost of Non-Europe' in Financial Services*.
Notes: (a) 1983 data; (b) 1982 data.

Table 3. Summary of restrictions in financial markets between EEC countries

	Establishment of branches	Participation and acquisition	Exchange controls
Belgium	none	none	yes
France	none	>20%	yes
Germany	none	none	none
Italy	none	none	yes
Luxembourg	none	none	yes
Netherlands	none	none	none
Spain	yes	>50%	yes
UK	none	none	none

Source: Price Waterhouse, *The 'Cost of Non-Europe' in Financial Services*.

direct foreign investment in banking will not take place, or will occur only in limited amounts. On the contrary, this phenomenon is already present and is becoming increasingly important. However, this is part of a general worldwide trend towards financial integration, and is not necessarily related to 1992. The reason is that the existing discriminatory laws against non-resident EEC financial institutions which are currently in place, and bound to become void, are not actively enforced anyway. Table 3 documents these regulations. Spain has restrictions on the number of branches that a foreign institution may open (no more than three), and restrictions on the percentage of a Spanish bank that a non-resident may acquire without prior approval (no more than 50%). These restrictions have not been too strictly enforced since in 1986 there were already 37 foreign banks operating in Spain. In France, the

government has the general prerogative to cancel any foreign investment in a French company, if it exceeds a 20% share. In the specific
case of banks intervention by the authorities may occur even below the
20% limit. In practice, however, the French government has been less
and less inclined to intervene in these matters and, in 1983, there were
already 119 foreign-controlled banks out of a total of 289. In some
other European countries, foreign participation in the industry is
already quite substantial, and is likely to increase in the future, but
1992 does not appear to have a major role to play in this process.

This is why we shall concentrate on the second channel, trade in
international deposits. Table 3 also documents the existence of exchange
controls inhibiting the flow of funds. Belgium and Luxembourg still
operate under a two-tier exchange market arrangement. It is also
important to notice the presence in France, Italy and Spain, of various
restrictions which have prevented residents from holding bank accounts
abroad. One of the most direct consequences of European liberalization
on the banking sector will be the removal of these restrictions to capital
flows. The market for bank deposits is a critical market, given that
deposits are, by far, the most important source of funds for commercial
banks, as shown in Table 4. Depending on the country, they constitute
between 60 and 90% of total bank liabilities. In addition, in most of the
countries surveyed, non-bank deposits (as opposed to inter-bank
deposits) represent the largest share of total deposits. A different picture
obtains if we consider non-resident deposits, i.e. deposits received by
banks from agents resident in countries other than the one in which
the bank operates; the total amount of non-resident deposits was
$4,911 bn. in the second quarter of 1988, and almost 80% of these
deposits are the result of international inter-bank operations. Moreover,
the amount of international trade in deposits has increased considerably
over the last 15 years. If we use the total output of the OECD countries
as a unit of measurement, then between 1972 and 1986 inter-country
bank deposits have risen from 10 to 35% of output.

In Table 5 we present the geographical distribution (as of 1988Q2)
of these stocks, expressed as fractions of world totals. These tables reveal
a number of interesting features. First, the UK appears to be the single
favourite destination of non-resident deposits, in both the inter-bank
and non-bank markets. However, grouped together the large 'off-shore'
centres (the Bahamas, the Cayman Islands, Hong Kong and Singapore)
have the largest share of inter-bank deposits. Second, the US and
Belgium (including Luxembourg), and the UK seem to have a similar
role in both the inter-bank and non-bank markets. Third, some countries seem to have become specialized in particular segments of the
market. For example, Japan has established itself as the second largest

Table 4. Importance of deposits, 1985 (% of total liabilities)

	Total deposits	Interbank deposits	Non-bank deposits	Liabilities to non-residents	
Austria, large commercial banks	—	79.68	50.43	29.25	33.62
Belgium, banks	87.96	63.52	24.44	63.74	
Canada, banks	89.88	22.77	67.11	—	
Denmark, banks	71.42	23.21	48.21	27.27	
France, large commercial banks	80.35	41.33	39.02	40.48	
Germany, commercial banks	76.47	27.42	49.05	24.71	
Greece, large commercial banks	87.14	1.53	85.61	—	
Italy, commercial banks	59.22	10.26	48.96	13.56	
Japan, ordinary banks	75.85	—	—	—	
Luxembourg, banks	89.72	66.70	23.02	83.56	
Netherlands, banks	78.24	29.19	49.05	35.19	
Portugal, banks	78.59	1.59	77.00	4.69	
Spain, commercial banks	79.37	15.89	63.48	11.78	
Switzerland, large commercial banks	75.20	21.95	53.25	40.70	
UK, London clearing banks	91.65	—	—	—	
US, large commercial banks	72.46	8.75	63.71	—	

Source: OECD (1985).

market for total foreign deposits, and this position is due almost exclusively to its active role in the inter-bank market. Switzerland, on the contrary, has concentrated on the collection of deposits from non-banks.

The changes in the relative size of the most important geographical areas in the international market for bank deposits are described by Figures 1 to 3. The position of Belgium and Luxembourg has remained very stable over the years in all categories. Switzerland, on the other hand, lost almost half of its market share. The loss occurred mostly during the early 1970s, and affects particularly transactions with the non-bank sector. Part of this decline seems to have been deliberately self-inflicted with the imposition, in July 1972, of a negative interest rate on non-resident Swiss franc deposits.[3] Japan and the off-shore centres show a strong positive trend in both categories, with the exception of Japan, apparently unable, or unwilling, to attract deposits from non-banks. The UK shows a declining trend until 1978. At the time when Margaret Thatcher was elected and foreign exchange controls were removed, the decline was halted and a moderate growth in market share was observed, at least until 1985. It is worth noting that the reversal in the trend occurred earlier (1976) for deposits from non-banks. While the US share of inter-bank deposits shows a positive trend,

---

[3] This regulation was later removed in February 1980.

Table 5. Foreign deposits at domestic banks, 1988Q2 (% of world's total)

Non-banks' deposits		Banks' deposits		Total	
UK	20.8	UK	17.4	UK	18.5
Switzerland	14.7	Japan	16.7	Japan	13.4
Belgium–Lux.	8.8	US	12.9	US	11.9
US	7.5	Belgium–Lux. (c)	6.9	Belgium–Lux.	7.5
Cayman Islands	7.4	Hong Kong	6.3	France	5.5
France (c)	5.2	France	5.3	Hong Kong	5.0
Bahamas	5.0	Singapore	4.6	Cayman Islands (a)	4.8
Singapore	3.9	Cayman Islands (a)	3.9	Switzerland	4.6
Germany	3.4	Bahamas	2.7	Singapore	4.5
Canada (b)	2.9	Germany	2.1	Bahamas	3.2
Netherlands	2.8	Netherlands	1.9	Germany	2.5
Japan	0.7	Switzerland	1.6	Italy (b)	2.2
Italy	—	Canada (b)	0.9	Netherlands	2.1
Hong Kong	—	Italy	—	Canada (b)	1.4

Source: IMF *International Financial Statistics.*
Notes: (a) 1987Q4; (b) 1988Q1; (c) 1987Q3.

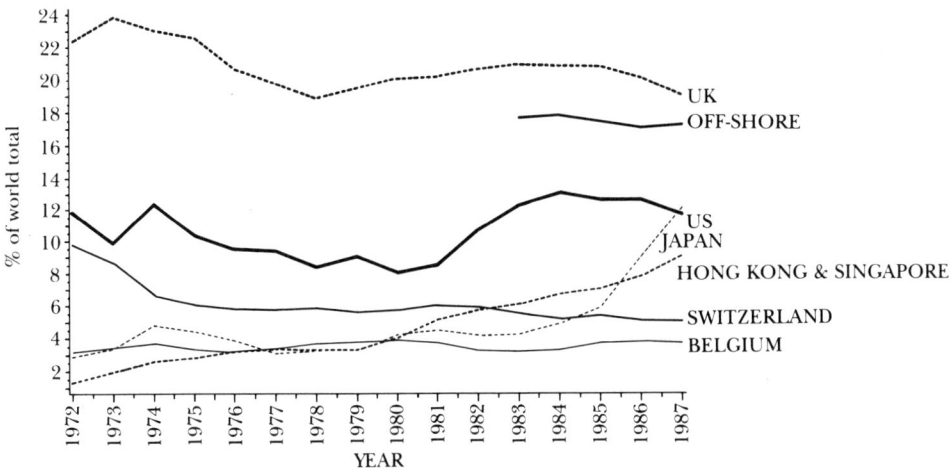

Figure 1. Total liabilities

deposits from the non-bank sector declined until 1981, and then increased substantially. It is not a coincidence that in December 1981 the international banking facilities (IBFs) were enacted. IBFs' regulations authorized US banks to operate separate books when accepting foreign Eurocurrency deposits to be lent abroad, making these funds free from reserve and insurance requirements. This allowed US-based banks to regain their competitiveness with respect to the off-shore centres, especially the Bahamas and the Cayman Islands.

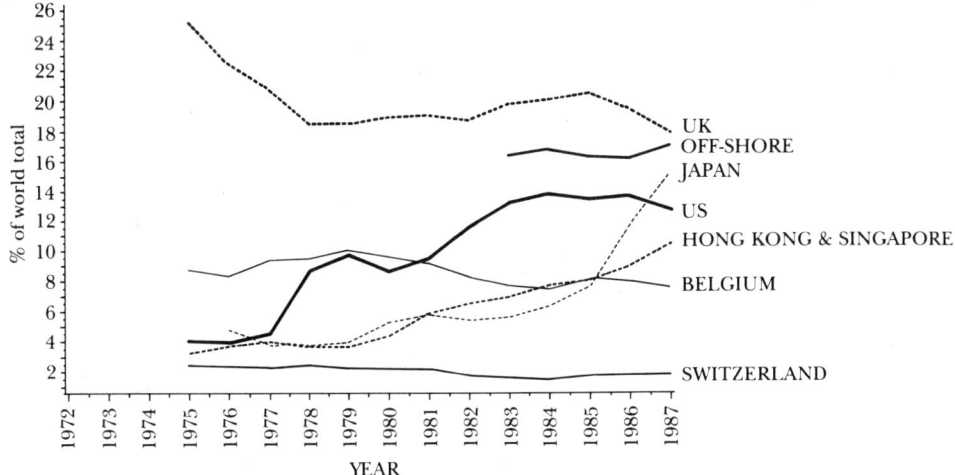

Figure 2. Inter-bank deposits

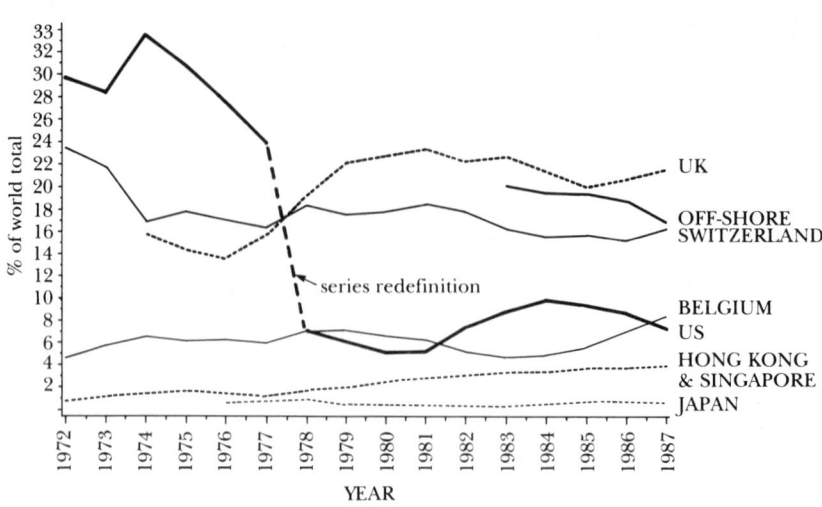

Figure 3. Non-bank deposits

3.2. The role of institutional factors in the international movements of bank deposits

As already stressed, we lack a well developed theory of international trade in banking services which could help identify the crucial elements responsible for the movements in international bank deposits described above. In principle, however, we should view the decision to deposit funds in different countries as part of a global portfolio optimization problem. Such a problem could be described as follows. Agents observe the interest rates (levels, variability and correlations) offered by the various banking systems, and hold views on the corresponding exchange rates (expected changes, variability and correlations). From this, agents deduce the expected returns and the associated risks on various international bank deposits. In principle, appropriate portfolio decisions could then be made. However, an empirical assessment of this approach requires data on the composition of foreign deposits in each country, broken down by the nationality of ownership and currency of denomination. Unfortunately, these data are not available, which prevents further analysis along these lines.

Because banks are highly regulated, the institutional environment plays an essential role in shaping international deposits. Factors like tax regulations, minimum bank reserve requirements, and secrecy laws are especially important in this context. The examples, already mentioned, of foreign exchange liberalization in the UK or the establishment of the international banking facilities in the US strongly suggest that purely regulatory factors may have strong effects on the direction of trade in bank deposits. The experiences of off-shore centres, like the Bahamas or the Cayman Islands, are other examples of the importance of such factors. Given that 1992 will operate essentially through the removal of technical barriers and the partial harmonization of regulations, it is important to determine, in more detail, the effects of these institutional elements on the performance of a country in attracting foreign deposits. Several regulations and practices may favour or frustrate the international movement of capital and, in particular, of bank deposits. In the following analysis we sort them into three different categories: capital controls, withholding taxes, and secrecy laws.

3.2.1. Capital controls. Under the generic label of capital controls, there is a large and diversified body of measures. They include the absolute legal or regulatory prohibition on making capital transactions, requirements of case-by-case authorization, restrictions on the timing of the operations, surrender requirements, prudential regulations and so on. Countries still differ considerably in this dimension. Discussions of capital controls also often implicitly refer to restrictions on capital *outflows* from a country, i.e. constraints imposed on residents' financial decisions. Indeed, countries like Italy and France have had very restrictive legislation of this kind throughout the 1970s and the 1980s. Others, like the UK and Japan, removed such restrictions at the end of the 1970s. At the same time, other countries like Germany and Switzerland have always had a very permissive attitude toward capital outflows but, from time to time, have limited the amount of capital inflows in order to maintain close control over monetary aggregates:

> '... restrictions have from time to time been imposed to ward off speculative inflows of foreign exchange and create greater room for maneuvers for monetary and fiscal policy at home. In 1972–3, for example, capital imports into the Federal Republic of Germany were restricted by a number of administrative measures.'
> (*Deutsche Bundesbank Special Series* No. 7., p.70.)

Some of these administrative measures have involved the imposition of particularly high reserve requirements on liabilities to non-residents. At one time, in 1978, the reserve requirement was virtually 100%. Another example, already mentioned, is the temporary imposition, in Switzerland, of a negative interest rate on non-resident Swiss franc deposits. In general, all types of restrictions on capital movement tend to isolate the domestic financial market and delay its development, thereby discouraging the inflow of deposits.

3.2.2. Withholding taxes. Another regulatory element that is crucial in international deposit decisions is the extent to which interest on bank

Table 6. Withholding taxes, 1988 (%)

	Bank deposits		Dividend income non-residents (d)
	Residents	Non-residents	
Belgium	25	25	25
Denmark	0	0	—
France	45	46 (a)	25
Germany	0	0 (b)	25
Greece	0	0	—
Ireland	35	0	—
Italy	30	30 (c)	32
Luxembourg	0	0	—
Netherlands	0	0	25
Portugal	15	15	—
Spain	20	20	—
UK	variable	0	0
Austria	0	0	—
Finland	0	0	—
Japan	20	35	35
Sweden	0	0	—
Switzerland	35	35	35
US	0	0	30

Source: Bank deposits: Banca d'Italia, *La Tassazione delle Rendite Finanziarie nella CEE alla Luce della Liberalizzazione Valutaria*; Dividend income: *Business International Money Report, Business Europe, International Tax Summaries.*

Notes: Special bilateral conventions to avoid double taxation may reduce the above rates for specific countries. For example, for Italian residents the withholding tax in Spain is 12%, instead of 20%; (a) checking accounts and special saving accounts are not subject to withholding tax; (b) starting 1-1-89 is 10%; (c) not subject to withholding tax if in foreign currency; (d) 1987.

deposits is subject to withholding taxes. As reported in Table 6, which describes the current situation on the matter, there are considerable differences in tax regulations regarding the treatment of non-resident deposits. In some countries, like Germany, Luxembourg, the Netherlands and the UK, deposits owned by non-residents are not subject to any withholding tax. Other countries, like Italy, Japan and Switzerland, apply heavy withholding taxes. The rates reported in Table 6 should be used with caution because special bilateral conventions can substantially reduce the tax rate applicable to the residents of the signatories. The rates in Table 6 apply in absence of a treaty. The difference between these statutory rates and special treaty rates can be quite substantial.

The location of deposits is obviously related to the net rate of return available in the various centres but also depends on net rates available on other assets into which bank deposits can be easily converted. Indeed, it is likely that foreign bank deposits are also used as convenient temporary parking for funds to be invested in other assets abroad. It is, therefore, important also to consider how income from other assets is taxed. Interestingly, countries which do not levy any withholding tax on bank deposits, like Germany or the US, instead impose high tax rates on dividend income.

3.2.3. Secrecy. Banking secrecy takes various forms, depending on the history, legal framework and customs of a country. Adherence to banking secrecy is analogous to the exercise of professional discretion which is typical of lawyers or doctors. This type of professional confidentiality does not legally extend to banks in all countries. When it does, bank secrecy is enforced to varying degrees. In some countries it is limited to the dissemination of information to other private citizens and institutions, in others it also extends to public authorities, either domestic or foreign. The demand for secret or hidden assets is believed to be quite substantial. It arises from different motivations, both legal and illegal. Walter (1985) offers five reasons underlying the demand for secrecy: personal confidentiality, business confidentiality, capital flight motivated by political reasons when secrecy is needed to preserve the safety of the owner, tax evasion and criminal activities.

Switzerland has the longest tradition of banking secrecy and the strictest legislation. Actually the legal basis of the Swiss banking secrecy can be found in its Constitution and Civil Code. Violations of bank confidentiality are met with severe punishment. Penalties include not only administrative and financial measures, but also criminal sanctions. In 1977, a Convention of Diligence was signed by all the major Swiss banks. The purpose of this action was to limit the role of banking secrecy in illegal activities. Though somewhat weakened by the Convention, bank secrecy is consistently maintained in Switzerland. In 1981, Luxembourg also passed strict bank secrecy laws, thereby becoming the EC country with the most protective legislation in this area. None of the other main industrialized countries has extensive secrecy laws. In some countries, like the UK and Germany, the principle of secrecy is recognized and applied to a certain (though limited) extent. Yet in others, like France and Italy, banks are 'required by law to be informers' (Chambost, 1983).

In order to investigate the influence of these various regulations on international bank deposits we use data from 10 countries (Belgium–Luxembourg, Canada, France, Germany, Italy, Japan, the Netherlands, Switzerland, the UK and the US) covering 16 years (1972-87). The previous discussion suggests the following relationship:

$$D_{it} = \alpha_0 + \alpha_1 TaxI_{it} + \alpha_2 TaxD_{it} + \alpha_3 CapitalIn_{it} + \alpha_4 CapitalOut_{it}$$

$$+ \alpha_5 Secrecy_{it} + \alpha_6 GNP_{it} + \alpha_7 Time_t + \varepsilon_{it} \qquad (1)$$

where D_{it} is the stock of non-resident deposits in banks of country i at time t; $TaxI$ is the withholding tax on non-resident bank deposits; $TaxD$ is the withholding tax on non-resident dividend income; $CapitalIn$ is a dummy variable representing restrictions on capital inflows; $CapitalOut$ is a dummy variable representing restrictions on capital outflows; and $Secrecy$ is a dummy representing the extent of banking secrecy. The exact values of the dummies are described in Appendix B, which also provides bibliographical references. GNP is the country's contribution to total OECD output: it is meant to capture thick-market externalities which, we argued in Section 2, are likely to be related to the relative size of the country. Finally, given the strong growth of trade in deposits, a time trend is also included. Table 7 reports the results of estimating (1) for *inter-bank* and *non-bank* foreign deposits separately. The distinction between inter-bank and non-bank deposits is very important since they seem to respond to very different incentives. Only controls on the inflow of capital appears to have a significant effect on both. Otherwise, inter-bank deposits are affected by the tax treatment of dividends and by the size of the economy. Non-bank deposits, on the other hand, respond to the withholding tax on bank accounts and to secrecy protection.

These results provide some interesting insights into what really motivates international bank deposits. For individual investors (non-banks), tax avoidance is probably the main motivation: this would explain why they seek bank secrecy and low levels of withholding taxes. By contrast, institutional investors (banks), while considering taxes, attach most importance to the dimension and development of the financial markets, at least if we accept that the GNP variable reflects the existence of thick-market externalities. Finally, we note the highly significant and negative effect that the withholding tax on dividends exerts on inter-bank deposits. This suggests that bank deposits are not made simply to earn interest income but are also used by banks as 'parking' in between other financial market transactions.

What are the implications of these results for the liberalization of 1990? By eliminating the existing restrictions on the free movement of capital, liberalization will definitely have an effect on the location of deposits. However, the tax treatment of interest and dividend incomes may play an even more powerful role in shaping the geography of bank deposits. Undoubtedly, the abolition of capital controls will favour

Table 7. Regression results (Panel data: 10 countries, 1972–87)

	Non-banks' deposits ($\bar{R}^2 = 0.53$)	Inter-bank deposits ($\bar{R}^2 = 0.68$)
Constant	1.69	3.96
	(3.40)	(11.86)
Interest tax	−4.04	−0.61
	(−4.97)	(−1.10)
Dividend tax	−1.01	−5.09
	(−1.01)	(−7.49)
Capital inflow	−1.22	−0.45
	(−3.70)	(−2.02)
Capital outflow	−0.30	0.19
	(−1.40)	(1.33)
Secrecy and offshore	0.66	0.10
	(8.64)	(1.97)
GNP	−0.11	0.22
	(−1.31)	(3.82)
Time trend	0.68	0.98
	(4.96)	(10.50)

Notes: *t*-statistics in brackets. The 10 countries are: Belgium–Luxembourg, Canada, France, Germany, Italy, Japan, the Netherlands, Switzerland, the UK and the US.

countries with low withholding tax rates. This problem is widely recognized but, to date, no decision regarding withholding tax levels has been agreed upon. Although EC governments are negotiating about some form of tax rate harmonization, there is still much discord and disagreement. As a result, it is difficult to predict the ultimate effects that liberalization will have through this channel. Similar arguments hold for the issue of bank secrecy. In this case, the possibility of harmonization may be even smaller. In fact, the revision or elimination of banking secrecy may involve changes in the fundamental structure of a country's legal system and is thus very difficult to implement.

4. Imperfect competition, switching costs and bank deposits

The evidence offered in the previous section supports the view that international bank deposits respond strongly to the institutional structure of national markets and various forms of controls and regulations. Other factors are likely to be important too, although difficult to capture empirically. Certainly, we expect that the relative efficiency of different national banking sectors has a role to play. Liberalization, by eliminating capital controls, will put banking systems with different levels of cost efficiency and quality of service in direct competition. This is why this section focuses on the differences in microeconomic factors, abstracting from the institutional environment. A prerequisite to pursuing this line of investigation is to agree on the proper way of characterizing the market structure of the banking sector. If it were a perfectly competitive market, and if depositors were intrinsically indifferent between using domestic or foreign financial intermediaries, then immediately following liberalization we should observe a massive flow of deposits toward the lower cost countries. The process would continue until prices were equalized through a general reduction towards the lowest levels in the Community. The less efficient, high cost intermediaries would either reshape or disappear. This characterization is quite extreme.

In what follows, we show that price convergence following liberalization will be limited and that the gains are not going to be uniformly shared by the whole population. In particular, if price reductions occur, they are likely to be confined to limited segments of depositors, while remaining consumers will be unaffected, or even harmed, by liberalization. The reason behind this assessment is essentially that the markets for bank deposits are characterized by segmentation and frictions that substantially reduce the extent of competition. Evidence that the banking industry is not perfectly competitive is provided by the casual observation that product differentiation is an important dimension of bank competition. Within the same country, where the institutional and regulatory environments are relatively homogeneous, the terms of a deposit contract vary substantially from bank to bank. Even within the same bank similar types of deposits are frequently remunerated differently, suggesting that banks have the ability to discriminate across customers (and the size of their deposits). Hence, banks have some market power stemming from product differentiation and it is preferable to describe the market for deposits as oligopolistic. Of course, the scope for product differentiation and price discrimination arises from the diversity of depositors. In particular, depositors are likely to respond very differently to interest rate incentives (technically, they differ in the interest rate elasticity of their demand for deposits). Such heterogeneity most probably arises because different customers have different levels of information about alternative forms of investment and they face different costs of acquiring, updating and processing such information. Not only does the cost of searching for better opportunities vary, but the cost of managing 'international' portfolios differs substantially among individuals as well. It is reasonable, at least for expository purposes, to assume that large depositors are more sensitive to deposit yields.

In this type of market, the best strategy for a bank is to price-discriminate among customers, offering low prices (e.g. high deposit

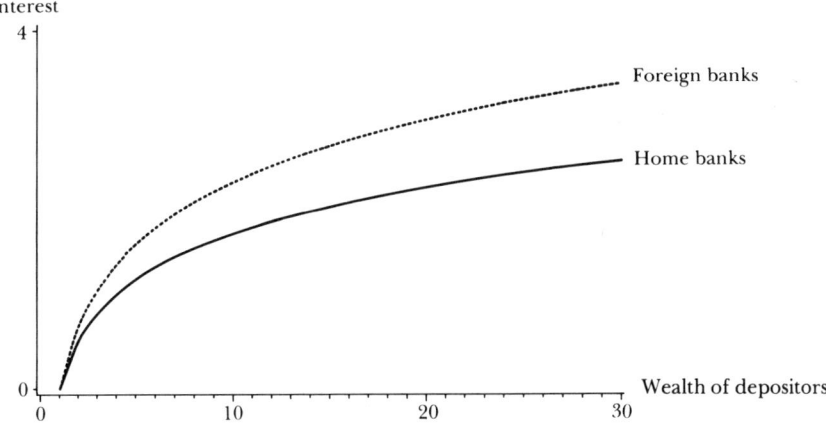

Figure 4. Interest offered and size of deposit

rates) to the more sensitive customers (e.g. the large depositors), and high prices (low deposit rates) to the less sensitive customers (small depositors). (Appendix A presents formally the implications of a departure from the assumption of perfect competition). This effect is described graphically in Figure 4, where customers are differentiated by their wealth (w), wealthier consumers being more sensitive to deposit yields. The interest rate schedules are upward sloping because banks offer better rates to larger customers.[4] Now suppose that the country opens its commercial banking market to foreign competition and that the country is small enough so that foreign banks do not change their strategies, i.e. they maintain their interest rate schedule unchanged. If the foreign banking system is more competitive and/or more efficient than the domestic one, it will be characterized by a higher deposit interest rate schedule. In the absence of any other market friction, capital market liberalization will lead to an outflow of deposits which will lead either to a global increase in the domestic interest rate, or to the failure of the domestic intermediaries.

However, if market imperfections exist and are important, the effects of capital market integration may be far less extensive. As mentioned above, collecting and updating information about alternative banking systems is costly and, even if we ignore the burden of this searching process, we still have to consider the costs, both monetary and non-monetary, of switching between domestic and foreign bank accounts. Moreover, maintaining a business relationship with a bank located

---

[4] The precise shape of the curve depends on the specific characteristics of the demand for deposits. In the case of Figure 4, we assume that the elasticity of demand increases with the size of the depositor, and does so at a decreasing rate.

abroad can be far more complicated than with a bank located 'around the corner'. Assuming that management costs are proportional to the size of the deposit, the foreign deposit rate effectively faced by domestic customers will be lower than its actual level. Graphically, this is represented by a downward shift in the foreign interest rate schedule. The foreign schedule will cross the domestic schedule at some level of w, say $\bar{w}$. Only depositors larger than $\bar{w}$ will face a foreign interest rate higher than the domestic rate and will, therefore, have an incentive to move their deposits abroad. As a result, only the market for large deposits will become more competitive (to the benefit of large customers), while small deposit contracts will be largely unaffected by liberalization. Nor is it any longer the case that domestic interest rates will equal the foreign rates. Foreign interest rates will still exceed the corresponding domestic rates. (These basic conclusions are not altered, under the alternative assumption that the 'switching costs' are fixed. In this case the shift of the foreign interest rate schedule will now be greater at a lower level of deposit size and it is, therefore, possible that the cut-off level $\bar{w}$ will be larger than in the previous analysis.)

It is even conceivable that small depositors could actually be worse off and face declining yields on their bank deposits. So far it has been implicitly assumed that the banking sector was characterized by fixed marginal costs. In this case, increased competition for large deposits will not have spill-over effects on smaller deposits. However, if the banking industry were characterized by decreasing marginal costs (internal economies of scale), negative spill-over effects would arise. Because the loss of market share to the foreign competitors would reduce the scale of operation of the domestic banks, their marginal cost would increase and they would lower the interest rate on those deposits which are smaller than $\bar{w}$.[5] Whether this last effect is likely to occur is an open question. Evidence from the US suggests that constant or increasing marginal costs are the norm (Benston, Hanweck and Humphrey, 1982, and Murray and White, 1983). However, it is interesting to notice what happened in the UK equity market after deregulation in October 1986. The Price Waterhouse (1988) report on the 'Cost of Non-Europe' shows that the commission costs for *large transactions* decreased after October 1986 while commission costs have actually increased for *small bargain* values (Table 8). To be sure the apparent existence of the negative spill-over effect may be related to other reasons

---

[5] In the opposite case, in which the banking industry is characterized by increasing marginal costs, the spill-over effects will be positive. Increased competition in the large deposit tier will tend to raise interest rates for small deposits as well.

Table 8. Commission rates on equities in the London stock exchange

Bargain values (pounds)	Pre-deregulation (%)	Post-deregulation (%)
1,000	1.53	1.63
5,000	1.26	1.60
10,000	1.02	1.25
20,000	0.60	0.63
50,000	0.53	0.34
100,000	0.39	0.28
5000,000	0.31	0.25
1,000,000	0.22	0.22

Source: Price Waterhouse, *The 'Cost of Non-Europe' in Financial Services.*

than decreasing marginal costs; it could be the result of cross-subsidization of larger deposits by small deposits. Yet, if the British experiment is a front-runner to EC-wide deregulation, there is some indication that small deposits may end up at the losing end.

So far we have assumed that the foreign banking sector did not change its interest rate schedule in response to the opening of the home market. It is possible, however, that in order to attract new depositors from the home country, foreign banks decide to raise their rates in order to capture a larger share of the domestic market (lower $\bar{w}$ in Figure 5). Of course such a strategy would reduce profits from the already established clientele. Therefore, the smaller the size of the domestic market, the smaller the potential gain in depositors and,

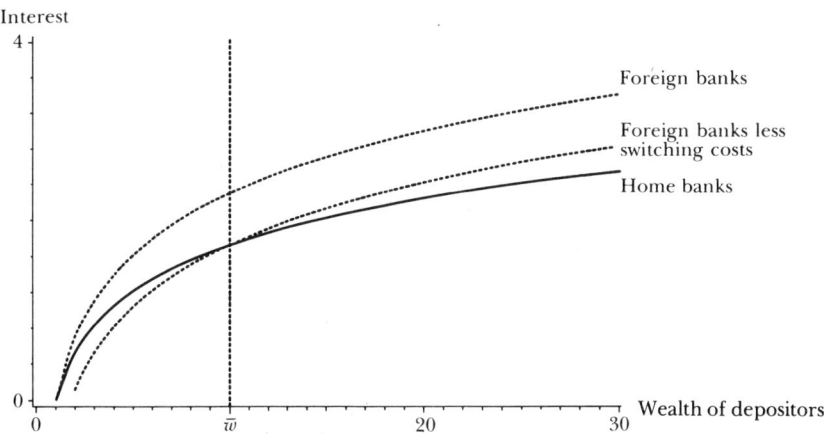

Figure 5. The determination of $\bar{w}$

therefore, the less likely it is that foreign banks will alter their pricing behaviour.[6] A related point was recently raised by Klemperer (1987), analysing the impact of switching costs on the strategic behaviour of firms. Because the existence of switching costs makes the demand for deposits less responsive to price changes, the best strategy for a bank would be to increase the deposit rate only temporarily. Then, after having increased its market share, they could exploit the fact that customers are partially 'locked-in' by the existence of switching costs and decrease the interest rate back to its original level. Thus, while on impact, the liberalization could produce considerable price adjustments, in the longer run these effects may tend to disappear. When most of the movements of deposits have taken place, and the market shares are firmly established, the banks could find it optimal to decrease the interest rates towards pre-liberalization levels. However, if depositors anticipate this type of behaviour, they may decide to limit the extent to which they reallocate their deposits. In this case, the liberalization will only produce an apparent price competition among financial intermediaries, without affecting much the cross-country movements of deposits.

5. Conclusions

Three main conclusions emerge from this article. The first concerns the geographical location of the main financial markets, the so-called 'hot spots'. It seems highly likely that the liberalization process will strengthen the already existing dominant markets, namely London and possibly New York. As residents of countries with relatively small financial markets find it more attractive to operate in developed centres, these markets will become even larger and more liquid, and thus yet more appealing. Of course some countries may be tempted to adopt policies designed to threaten London's supremacy as the main European financial centre but success is most unlikely. Indeed, such action would have to be quite aggressive, like the introduction of off-shore types of regulations. Even in the improbable case that a country takes these extreme types of measures, there is no certainty that they will have the desired effect as thick-market externalities tend to produce considerable amounts of inertia in the financial industry.

A direct empirical study of international bank deposits confirms the existence of external economies of scale or thick-market externalities. The finding that country-specific institutions go a long way towards explaining the observed international bank deposits underscores the

---

[6] Notice, however, that the rest of the analysis would still be valid even if the foreign banks were to increase their interest rate schedule. The only difference is that $\bar{w}$ would be smaller.

importance of the liberalization move for the industry. Of particular interest is the result that the inter-bank deposit market responds to a different set of regulations than the general public deposit market: both markets are of course quite sensitive to capital controls, but inter-bank deposits seem driven above all by the size of the economy – a measure of thick-market externalities – while non-bank deposits respond primarily to the tax treatment and to the extent of banking secrecy. These results imply that the wholesale market (inter-bank deposits) should follow the same trend as the 'hot spots'. While there is some scope for movement in the retail market (non-bank deposits) if countries try to change the regulatory environment, switching costs once again may frustrate these efforts. This is why the third main conclusion is that the increase in competition induced by the European integration will primarily affect the market for large deposits. Small deposit contracts will probably remain unaffected, at least in the short run. It cannot even be ruled out that the increased competition in the larger deposit market will have adverse spill-over effects on smaller bank customers.

Discussion

Charles Bean
London School of Economics

There is a school of thought according to which 1992 will have more profound implications in financial markets than in goods markets, which are already fairly integrated. The removal of remaining capital controls and restrictions on the location of banking activities will affect both the structure of financial markets and the functioning of macroeconomic policies such as the EMS. Much has been written on the latter topic, but little on the former, with the exception of the European Commission's 'Costs of non-Europe' exercise. Grilli has drawn welcome attention to some debatable assumptions in the Commission's report – particularly that of perfect competition.

In the first part of the paper, Grilli addresses the question why financial activity locates where it does and, therefore, whether financial liberalization will lead to a more homogeneous distribution of financial services throughout the Community. He points to economies of scale arising from 'thick-market externalities' as the main reason for the agglomeration of financial activity in a few centres. The focus is very much on physical externalities, such as those due to communication networks. However, a non-tangible externality in the form of a centre's general reputation for excellence may be equally important. Unlike physical externalities, such a reputation can be destroyed quite quickly by one or two financial scandals (Guinness?). It should also be said that

these externalities need not always be beneficial. Congestion externalities may be important, as in the bidding-up of the salaries of a small
number of financial experts with specialist expertise.

This line of argument predicts that the present pattern of financial
'hot spots' is unlikely to be affected by 1992. An individual firm will
not relocate in pursuit of small internal cost reductions, because of the
loss of the external benefits of staying where it is. Only if all firms move
together is a relocation likely to occur. Governments may provide
financial incentives to encourage such co-ordinated movement, but
Community regulations will limit the extent of such action. So, is
London's hegemony assured? Probably. But the current British attitude
to the EMS and the process of monetary unification raises the prospect
that the UK will be left on the sidelines as the rest of the Community
forges a common currency area and a system of central banks to
administer it. The resulting shift in focus away from London could be
exactly the push needed to ensure that financial firms centre their
activities in Paris or Frankfurt.

The rest of the paper looks at the market for bank deposits. Grilli
argues, probably correctly, that 1992 will not lead to major changes in
banks' direct investment, since foreign participation in the banking
sector is already widespread. The evidence presented suggests that,
while capital controls are important, the tax regime and the level of
bank secrecy are equally important, so the degree of harmonization in
these fields may be important in determining the reallocation of bank
deposits in the Single Market.

This analysis ignores difference in the efficiency of banks in different
countries. Price Waterhouse took the view in the Commission's report
that deposits would flow towards the most efficient financial intermediaries who could offer the most attractive terms to depositors. Grilli
argues that this will occur only for large deposits, since the market for
small deposits is subject to significant segmentation and frictions. While
I think this judgment is correct, the evidence is not entirely persuasive.
Deposit accounts and other instruments are typically bundles of characteristics. A cheque account may or may not have associated overdraft
facilities; a building society deposit account may make it easier to get
a loan, and so on. There may also be fixed costs or other non-linearities
in the costs of servicing an account: the apparent variation in the terms
offered (e.g. in Table 8) may reflect these features rather than a lack
of competitive behaviour *per se*.

Grilli also draws attention to switching costs that lock in existing
customers. It is worth emphasizing that these do not imply the absence
of competition, but rather that such competition occurs when customers
first open accounts. This is evident in the UK where there is intense

competition between the banks for student accounts through introductory offers.

Though I have considerable sympathy with the paper's general arguments, let me close by noting two shortcomings. First, I was disappointed that, having dismissed the analysis in the Commission's study as simplistic, Grilli did not attempt to furnish alternative estimates of the microeconomic gains from financial market integration. Are the issues discussed in the paper important or are they just second-order effects? Second, there is no discussion of the asset side of banks' balance sheets. Financial market integration could be just as important for the cost and supply of bank loans as in the market for deposits.

Jean-Pierre Danthine
University of Lausanne and CEPR

'There is a paucity of theoretical and empirical analysis in the area of international financial intermediation. Neither the industrial organization literature, nor the international trade and finance literature offers many insights into the issue of what determines the structure, trade flows, and prices in these markets.' This observation by the author gives the paper the right outlook. 1992 will indeed be as much of a challenge for the economics profession as it is likely to be for the European economies themselves. This paper squarely faces important issues that have not previously been addressed. It shows us how poorly prepared we are, as a profession, to produce convincing and insightful answers to the questions raised by the occurrence of a significant shock such as the completion of the internal market.

The paper tackles three issues. First, it argues that the supremacy of London as the dominant financial centre in Europe is likely to be unchallenged. It is on this point that Grilli's contribution is most convincing. The model he provides is useful to organize thoughts. Its prediction looks like a fairly safe bet, elegantly supported by the concept of thick-market externalities: even if Paris were to develop into an objectively more efficient financial centre than London, coordination problems could well prevent the emergence of the most efficient geographical distribution of activities and indeed would favour the status quo.

The second issue that the paper addresses relates to the institutional determinants of foreign bank deposits. Here Grilli's main conclusion is that the factors explaining inter-bank deposits (the level of the dividend tax, the existence of capital controls and the size of the economy) are quite different from the factors explaining non-bank deposits (the level of the interest tax, the presence of controls on capital outflows and the extent of banking secrecy and offshore facilities). While this is a plausible result, one should use the usual dose of caution in interpreting econometric estimates, such as these, derived outside a fully specified economic model. (In the absence of appropriate data, the economic determinants of international movements of deposits are not part of the regressions). Furthermore, the values given to some of the explanatory variables, notably the secrecy dummy, would deserve further discussion and a sensitivity analysis. The ranking of countries on the secrecy issue is debatable, as is, *a fortiori*, the index of secrecy ranging from −1 (for France) to +5 (for Switzerland).

Third, pursuing the question of international competition for deposits, Grilli develops a model suggesting that the assumption of perfect competition used in computing the gains from integration in financial markets is likely to lead to an overvaluation of these gains. Assuming an oligopolistic market structure with depositors differentiated by their interest rate elasticity, he obtains the result that an increased degree of competition between banks will favourably affect only the largest depositors. The small depositors could be left unaffected or could even be hurt if the loss in market share to foreign competitors reduces the scale of operations of domestic banks and increases their marginal cost.

I wonder about the significance of bank deposits in the context of 1992. Competition in international banking focuses less and less on deposits and increasingly on the range of services that the banks can offer to corporations. Yet the general message conveyed on this issue is undeniably important: let us be cautious about the benefits of the internal market when they have been computed on the basis of perfect competition models (even if we are not really in a position to produce comparable data under more realistic hypotheses). As to the specific conclusion that the biggest share of the benefits from financial deregulation and integration in Europe is going to accrue to the largest players in the markets, it conforms with the strategy of the large international banks; apparently they do not expect to make profits from small customers in foreign markets.

General discussion

Luigi Spaventa wondered whether the demand for deposits was determined on a portfolio basis. The main reason for holding deposits abroad was to facilitate investment in other assets: Belgium and Luxembourg were good countries in which to do so because of the absence of withholding taxes. Several other speakers pointed to the significance of arbitrage induced by differences in regulatory regimes. Denis Richard stressed the distinction between the liberalization of capital movements by 1990, which would not make a great difference since there was considerable movement of capital already, and the establishment by 1992 of the freedom to supply services, which could lead to a major shake-up of the regulatory environment and competition via product innovation.

This led to a discussion of whether the gains from 1992 in the financial sector had been exaggerated in the Cecchini Report. Victor Norman was puzzled by the magnitude of the estimated gains in relation to gains in the real economy. 1992 was not just about coordinating regulation but also about lowering transaction costs more generally. But these were already low in financial markets. Jacques Melitz thought the Report had attached too much significance to apparent price differentials for service products. Many banking services were joint products so that pricing decisions for any one product were largely arbitrary. He also pointed out that reserve requirements would not be unified. Damien Neven said that domestic and international banking were very different: the Price Waterhouse study of prices had included many products that were not internationally traded. Colin Mayer thought that many of the existing price differentials were exacerbated by informational problems faced by consumers. 1992 was about diminishing these problems, especially through the development of common regulatory standards. It would be important to know how much freedom of access financial institutions enjoyed in each other's markets. Jean-Pierre Lambert was worried by the effects of 1992 on concentration in the industry.

Mayer also said he was unconvinced by the arguments that London's preeminent position in Europe was secure. Two reasons why markets might move could be major differences in regulatory costs, and differences in the efficiency of the settlement process. Paris was already on the way to establishing a much more efficient settlement process than that in London, and it would take London some time to catch up.

Appendix A. The theoretical models

A1. Thick-market externalities, 'hot-spots' and financial centres inertia

Assume that the production function of a typical financial intermediary is given by:

$$y = \beta x^{\alpha} \qquad \alpha < 1 \tag{A1}$$

where y is the amount of financial services produced, and x is the amount of input. The financial firm is assumed to maximize profits:

$$\max \Pi = y - px \tag{A2}$$

where p is the price of input in terms of output. In the absence of any thick-market externalities, firms in different locations will have similar production decisions given by:

$$x = \left(\frac{\alpha\beta}{p}\right)^{1/(1-\alpha)} \tag{A3}$$

If we abstract from possible differences in the relative price of inputs at different locations, financial intermediaries in different countries will make similar decisions, i.e. they will be producing the same amount of services, and they will have the same level of profits.

Thick-market externalities mean that the productivity of a firm is positively affected by the size of the market in which it operates so that the production function of a financial firm in country i is given by:

$$y_i = \beta x_i^{\alpha} Y_i^{\gamma} \qquad \gamma > 0; (\alpha + \gamma) < 1 \tag{A4}$$

where Y_i is the total amount of financial services produced in country i. The larger the size of the market, the larger the firm's production for a given use of inputs. Let $Y_i = n_i y_i$, i.e. the product of the number of banks in country i multiplied by the amount of services offered by each firm. Therefore,

$$y_i = \beta^{1/(1-\gamma)} x_i^{\alpha/(1-\gamma)} n_i^{\gamma/(1-\gamma)} \tag{A5}$$

The production decision of the typical firm in country i is given by:

$$y_i = \left(n_i^{\gamma} \beta \left(\frac{\alpha}{(1-\gamma)p}\right)^{\alpha/(1-\gamma)}\right)^{1/(1-(\alpha+\gamma))} \tag{A6}$$

In the presence of thick-market externalities output and profits are affected by the size of the market. In a large economy, with a large number of firms, output and profit for each bank are greater than those in a small economy. If the various national markets become integrated, firms located in smaller markets will have an incentive to move towards larger markets.

The government can reduce the incentive for domestic financial intermediaries to relocate part of their activities abroad by acting as a market maker, i.e. by trying to broaden the dimension of the domestic market before the opening of frontiers. Even if there are initially only a few operators in a particular financial market, the government could substantially increase the degree of liquidity by actively participating in the market. A natural example would be futures and options markets for government securities. Let then $Y_i = g_i n_i y_i$, where g_i is an indicator of the participation of the government in the market. Now the output of the firm in the domestic market will be given by:

$$y_i = \left(g^\gamma n_i^\gamma \beta \left(\frac{\alpha}{(1-\gamma)p} \right)^{\alpha/(1-\gamma)} \right)^{1/(1-(\alpha+\gamma))} \tag{A7}$$

so that government intervention can compensate for the initially small size of the domestic market, and reduce the incentive for domestic firms to move abroad.

The model can also illustrate the potential inertia of markets characterized by agglomeration externalities. Suppose that a country, say France, introduces new measures which increase the efficiency of its domestic financial market. This is captured by an increase in the β coefficient in the production function. Firms which decide to locate in Paris will face a production function given by:

$$y_p = \beta^1 x_p^\alpha (n_p y_p)^\gamma \tag{A8}$$

where $\beta^1 = k\beta$, with $k > 1$, and the subscript p indicates the location 'Paris'. It is clear that if the whole market moved to Paris, the productivity of the sector could increase. However, whether this move will happen is an open question. Consider the case of a bank located in the current leading centre, say London, which is evaluating the possibility of a switch to Paris. The effects of the decision on bank productivity and profits depend on the actions of the other firms. Suppose that nobody else decides to move to Paris. It can be shown that the output (profits) of the switching firm will be greater than if it remained in London only if:

$$k > \left(\frac{n_L}{n_p} \right)^\gamma \tag{A9}$$

where n_L and n_p are the size of the London and Paris markets, respectively. The increase in productivity must be large enough to compensate for the differential in liquidity in the two markets. If this is the case, the move is always profitable, independent of the other firms' decisions, and the market will unquestionably move to Paris. However, if (A9) does not hold, a firm will decide to move to Paris only if it thinks that a large enough number of firms are doing the same. The outcome, therefore, depends on market expectations which, in this case, will be self-fulfilling. It is quite possible that the market will remain in London, despite the potential advantage of moving to Paris.

A2. Monopolistic competition in the market for deposits: an example

Suppose, for the moment, that marginal costs are constant and identical across firms. Potential depositors have different elasticities of demand for deposits. This difference derives from different levels of a characteristic variable, w, with which individuals are endowed. For convenience, we refer to this variable as wealth. There are N banks in the market, supplying a homogeneous product (deposit) to customers with identical characteristics. Therefore, they will offer the same interest rate to everyone in the same class of depositors. Finally, we make the standard Cournot assumption that firms compete by choosing a level of deposits and we look for a non-cooperative Nash equilibrium. With fixed marginal costs, banks will decide on the level of deposits for each class of customers, independently of other classes. Routine calculations yield the equilibrium level of interest rate for the customer class w, as:

$$r_d(w) = \left(\frac{N\varepsilon(w)}{1 + N\varepsilon(w)}\right)(\bar{r}_L - c) \tag{A10}$$

where c is the level of the marginal cost, $\bar{r}_L$ is the (exogenously given) rate on bank assets and $\varepsilon(w)$ is the interest rate elasticity of the demand for deposits of customers with wealth w.

First, notice that more competitive markets, i.e. markets with larger numbers of banks, will be characterized by a higher deposit interest rate, for all classes of customers. Second, the higher the marginal cost, the lower the interest rate. Given the opposite effects of competition and cost efficiency, it is possible that high cost banking systems can nonetheless offer high interest rates if they are characterized by a high degree of competition (i.e. large N). Finally, note the existence of price discrimination across customers: different classes of depositors will face different deposit rates. Under the reasonable assumption that larger depositors (high w individuals) have larger elasticities of demand, i.e. $\varepsilon' > 0$, they will be offered higher rates than small depositors.

A3. Monopolistic competition, switching costs and international trade in deposits

Suppose that the banking system of the rest of the world is completely identical to the domestic one, except for a lower (constant) marginal cost. In this case, it is easy to show that:

$$r_D^*(w) = r_D(w) + \left(\frac{N\varepsilon(w)}{1 + N\varepsilon(w)}\right)(c - c^*) \tag{A11}$$

where $r_D^*(w)$ is the foreign interest rate on deposits and c^* is the foreign marginal cost, and $c > c^*$. Therefore, the foreign interest rate is always higher than the domestic one, for all classes of deposits. Moreover, since $\varepsilon' > 0$, the difference between domestic and foreign rates is increasing in w. This is described in Figure 4. Now suppose that, for domestic residents, there is a positive cost of switching to a foreign bank and of managing foreign bank accounts. We represent these costs by assuming that the foreign interest rate effectively faced by domestic customers $(i_D^*(w))$ is given by:

$$i_D^*(w) = r_D^*(w) - s \tag{A12}$$

where s is the 'switching cost'. The $i_D^*(w)$ and $r_D(w)$ schedules intersect at a level of wealth $\bar{w}$ implicitly defined by

$$s = \left(\frac{N\varepsilon(\bar{w})}{1 + N\varepsilon(\bar{w})}\right)(c - c^*) \tag{A13}$$

Consequently, domestic customers who are smaller than $\bar{w}$ will face foreign effective rates which are below the domestic ones (Figure 5 in the text). The positive effects of liberalization are further reduced under the plausible assumption that smaller depositors face larger 'switching costs', i.e. if $s = s(w)$ and $s' < 0$. In this case, in fact, the intersection between $i_D^*(w)$ and $r_D(w)$ will occur at a higher level of w.

Finally, consider the case in which the marginal cost is not constant. It could be shown that in this case the interest rate equation would be given by:[7]

$$r_D(w) = \left(\frac{N\varepsilon(w)}{1 + N\varepsilon(w)}\right)(\bar{r}_L - c'(\tau)) \tag{A14}$$

where τ is the total amount of deposits sold to all classes of customers. If, because of foreign competition τ decreases, the marginal cost $c'(\tau)$ increases thus generating a decrease in $r_D(w)$, for $w < \bar{w}$.

Appendix B. Dummy variables used in the regression

Table B1. Restrictions on capital outflows

	72	73	74	75	76	77	78	79	80	81	82	83	84	85	86	87
Belgium	0	0	0	0	0	0	0	0	0	0	0	0	0	0	0	0
France	1	1	1	1	1	1	1	1	1	1	1	1	1	1	1	1
Germany	0	0	0	0	0	0	0	0	0	0	0	0	0	0	0	0
Italy	1	1	1	1	1	1	1	1	1	1	1	1	0	0	0	1
Netherlands	1	1	1	1	0	0	0	0	0	0	0	0	0	0	0	0
UK	1	1	1	1	1	1	1	1	0	0	0	0	0	0	0	0
Canada	0	0	0	0	0	0	0	0	0	0	0	0	0	0	0	0
Japan	1	1	1	1	1	1	1	1	0	0	0	0	0	0	0	0
Switzerland	0	0	0	0	0	0	0	0	0	0	0	0	0	0	0	0
US	1	1	0	0	0	0	0	0	0	0	0	0	0	0	0	0

Source: IMF *Exchange Arrangements & Exchange Restrictions*, Summary Table (restrictions on payments in respect of capital transactions); OECD *Controls on International Capital Movements*.

---

[7] For simplicity, we now assume that $N = 1$.

Table B2. Restrictions on capital inflows

	72	73	74	75	76	77	78	79	80	81	82	83	84	85	86	87
Belgium	0	0	0	0	0	0	0	0	0	0	0	0	0	0	0	0
France	0	0	0	0	0	0	0	0	0	0	0	0	0	0	0	0
Germany	1	1	0.7	0.5	0.5	1	1	0.5	0.5	0.5	0.2	0.2	0	0	0	0
Italy	0	0	0	1	0	0	0	0	0	0	0	0	1	1	0	0
Netherlands	1	1	0	0	0	0	0	0	0	0	0	0	0	0	0	0
UK	0	0	0	0	0	0	0	0	0	0	0	0	0	0	0	0
Canada	0	0	0	0	0	0	0	0	0	0	0	0	0	0	0	0
Japan	0	0	0	0	0	0	1	1	0	0	0	0	0	0	0	0
Switzerland	1	1	1	1	1	1	1	1	0	0	0	0	0	0	0	0
US	0	0	0	0	0	0	0	0	0	0	0	0	0	0	0	0

Source: Sarver (1987); OECD, *Controls on International Capital Movements.*

Table B3. Secrecy laws

	72	73	74	75	76	77	78	79	80	81	82	83	84	85	86	87
Belgium	0	0	0	0	0	0	0	0	0	1	1	1	1	1	1	1
France	−1	−1	−1	−1	−1	−1	−1	−1	−1	−1	−1	−1	−1	−1	−1	−1
Germany	0.5	0.5	0.5	0.5	0.5	0.5	0.5	0.5	0.5	0.5	0.5	0.5	0.5	0.5	0.5	0.5
Italy	−1	−1	−1	−1	−1	−1	−1	−1	−1	−1	−1	−1	−1	−1	−1	−1
Netherlands	0	0	0	0	0	0	0	0	0	0	0	0	0	0	0	0
UK	1	1	1	1	1	1	1	1	1	1	1	1	1	1	1	1
Canada	0	0	0	0	0	0	0	0	0	0	0	0	0	0	0	0
Japan	0.5	0.5	0.5	0.5	0.5	0.5	0.5	0.5	0.5	0.5	0.5	0.5	0.5	0.5	0.5	0.5
Switzerland	5	5	5	5	5	5	5	4	4	4	4	4	4	4	4	4
US	0	0	0	0	0	0	0	0	0	0	0	0	0	0	0	0

Source: Blum (1984); Chambost (1983); Sarver (1987); Walter (1985).

References

Banca d'Italia (1989). 'La Tassazione delle Rendite Finanziarie nella CEE alla Luce della Liberalizzazione Valutaria', *Temi di Discussione.*

Benston, G., G. Hanweck and D. Humphrey (1982). 'Scale Economies in Banking. A Restructuring and Reassessment', *Journal of Money, Credit, and Banking.*

Blum, R. (1984). *Offshore Haven Banks, Trusts, and Companies.* Praeger. *Business International Money Report*, various issues.

Chambost, E. (1983). *Bank Accounts. A World Guide to Confidentiality.* John Wiley & Sons.

Diamond, P. (1982). 'Aggregate Demand Management in Search Equilibrium', *Journal of Political Economy.*

Farrell, J. and G. Saloner (1986). 'Installed Base and Compatibility: Innovation, Product Preannouncements, and Predation', *American Economic Review.*

Hall, R. (1988). 'Noise Over Space and Over Time', in the Okun Memorial Lecture, Yale University, September.

International Tax Summaries, John Wiley, various issues.

Kindleberger, C. (1974). 'The Formation of Financial Centers: A study in Comparative Economic History', *Princeton Studies in International Finance.*

Klemperer, P. (1987). 'The Competitiveness of Markets with Switching Costs', *Rand Journal of Economics*.

Murray, J. and R. White (1983). 'Economies of Scale and Economies of Scope in Multiproduct Financial Institutions: A Study of British Columbia Credit Unions', *The Journal of Finance*.

OECD (1978). *Regulation Affecting International Banking Operations*. Paris.

—— (1980). *Controls on International Capital Movements*. Paris.

—— (1981). *Regulation Affecting International Banking Operations*. Paris.

—— (1984). *International Trade in Services: Banking*. Paris.

—— (1985). *Bank Profitability*. Paris.

—— (1987). *International Tax Avoidance and Evasion*. Paris.

Price Waterhouse (1988). 'The Cost of Non-Europe in Financial Services', in *Research of the Cost of Non-Europe*, Commission of the European Communities, volume 9.

Sarver, E. (1987). *The Eurocurrency Market Handbook*. Prentice-Hall.

Walter, I. (1985). *Secret Money*. Lexington Books.

Economic Policy   October 1989   Printed in Great Britain

EFTA and the internal European market

Victor Norman

Summary

The EFTA countries must come to grips with the EC's single market. This article contrasts two options. Under the first option, the EFTA countries do not change their current arrangements with the EC. Under the second option, they join the EC's common market. Since the EC is the EFTA countries' main trading partner, significant changes in cost, demand and market structures within the EC must substantially affect EFTA. The simulation results – focusing on the motor vehicle and pharmaceutical industries – confirm that 1992 is important for EFTA countries, not so much because of the threat that an internal EC market represents, but rather because of the opportunities that a larger European market offers. Generally, the EFTA countries would not seem to lose much if they decided to stay outside the internal market but they could share much of the gains if they chose to integrate themselves. Quantitatively, the gain accruing to EFTA is likely to be greater than the gain to the typical EC country. This is because EFTA home markets are small, so that the tradeoff between scale economies and competition is more severe than for the larger EC countries.

EFTA and the internal European market

Victor D. Norman

Norwegian School of Economics and Business Administration and CEPR

1. Introduction

The EFTA countries – Austria, Finland, Iceland, Norway, Sweden and Switzerland – must soon decide how to react to the establishment of the internal market within the European Community. They have several options. At one extreme, they could do nothing – trusting that the free trade arrangements they already have with the Community will protect them from overly damaging effects, and hoping that they may perhaps benefit indirectly from higher efficiency and demand within the EC. At the other extreme, they could join the Community or enter into individual or joint agreements with the EC about a larger 'European space', establishing an internal market of 18 countries in Europe. Between the two extremes are a number of less radical alternatives; for example, EFTA might selectively appeal to the Commission's reciprocity principle to become part of the European market. Only key products would be concerned and the EC directives for those goods would be copied. The purpose of this paper is to assess the consequences for EFTA countries of the establishment of the EC internal market under two extreme alternatives: the EFTA countries do not take part in the integration process at all and current trade impediments between EFTA and EC remain; or else the EFTA countries become part of the internal market, and trade impediments between EFTA and EC are reduced to the same extent as inside the EC.

At the micro level, Emerson *et al.* (1988) distinguish three principal effects of an internal European market: lower real trade costs, more

I am very grateful to Alasdair Smith and Anthony Venables who have developed the model used in a substantial portion of this paper, and who have given me the data used in their application of the model to EC industries. I also want to thank Harry Flam, Henrik Horn, Jan Haaland and Anthony Venables, as well as members of the *Economic Policy* panel and seminar participants at the Norwegian School of Economics, for valuable comments. Finally, thanks to Charles Wyplosz for both valuable comments and editorial assistance.

aggressive competition and lower unit production costs. Lower trade costs will result from the reduction or abolition of border controls and the harmonization of product standards. More aggressive competition will automatically follow: lower trade costs will promote exports, so that all producers will have less of a shelter at home, while also exporting more. The effect will, however, be significantly greater if the internal market brings to an end intra-EC price discrimination, i.e. if markets become truly integrated. Evidence of substantial price discrimination suggests that firms exploit large market shares in their home markets by charging higher prices at home, and selling at lower prices in export markets. If markets become fully integrated, such discrimination will no longer be possible and firms will not be able to capitalize on a dominant position in their home markets. Finally, more aggressive competition could reduce average production costs, because high-cost producers will lose market shares, and because a more competitive market could foster larger (possibly fewer) firms which take better advantage of scale economies.

Some of these benefits can accrue in all industries simultaneously; for example, trade costs can be reduced across the board or sales can be reallocated from export to domestic markets without affecting other markets. However, increases in industry output require a reallocation of resources in favour of the industries concerned. Such increases can clearly not occur in all industries simultaneously. Instead, we expect reallocation from industries where the competition effects of 1992 are small, to industries where they are large. Such general equilibrium repercussions should therefore dampen, but not eliminate, the benefits from the internal market.

If EFTA countries become part of the integrated market, they should qualitatively derive the same benefits as the EC countries. Quantitatively, the gain accruing to EFTA is, however, likely to be greater than the gain to the typical EC country; the reason is that EFTA home markets are small, and as a result EFTA countries experience a more severe tradeoff between scale economies and competition than the larger EC countries. The EFTA countries are very open, and their trade with EC countries is, in relative terms, far greater than trade between large EC countries like the UK and France. As a result, if EFTA countries remain outside, changes in cost, demand and market structures within the EC could have substantial spill-over effects on EFTA countries.

European integration will have two conflicting effects on the exports of non-member countries: on the one hand, greater efficiency and correspondingly higher real income within the EC could raise demand for non-EC country exports. As the EC is by far the most important export market of EFTA, such a demand effect could be significant. On the other hand, more aggressive competition in EC markets and lower transaction and production costs within the Community, could reduce the market shares and depress the export prices of non-EC producers. The two effects correspond roughly to the ideas of 'trade creation' and 'trade diversion' known from the literature on customs unions: lower trade barriers between some countries will generate more trade ('trade creation'), but will also divert trade from third countries to the members of the union ('trade diversion').

EC integration could also have spill-over effects in the home markets of non-EC countries. If, for example, EC and EFTA markets are less than perfectly segmented, increased competition within the EC will reduce profit margins in EFTA markets as well, to the advantage of domestic consumers. Similar effects will occur if 1992 lowers the marginal cost of EC producers. On the other hand, there could be adverse product-selection effects, because increased competition in export markets might force EFTA firms to abandon some of their products. As an example, we could imagine that Swedish car manufacturers would be forced to abandon some models. To the extent that Swedish cars have particular appeal to Swedish consumers, the loss of consumer surplus could be significant. The net effect on EFTA countries if they remain outside is, therefore, in principle unclear, but likely to be negative.

The paper is organized as follows. Section 2 gives some background information on the structure of EFTA production and trade. Section 3 presents the method of investigation adopted here, namely industry simulations. The following three sections present and interpret the results of a number of simulations for the motor vehicle and pharmaceutical industries. These simulation experiments deal with the reduction in trade costs, the integration of previously segmented markets, and a reduction in production costs. Section 7 considers the role of possible entry and exit of firms. Section 8 investigates the sensitivity of the welfare results to the modelling of market shares. In this respect, the respective weight given to non-tariff trade barriers and consumer preferences in explaining difference in market shares turns out to be important. Because these results are derived from partial equilibrium simulations, they may miss some important economy-wide effects. Section 9 indicates that general equilibrium interaction dampens the effects which were previously identified, but that does not alter the main conclusions. Finally, in Section 10, some policy implications are pointed out.

At the outset, it is also worth noting that the discussion focuses on the gains from integration which arise from improvements in industry structure and performance. It is based on the recent literature on trade and trade policy dealing with imperfectly competitive markets. An introduction to this literature is given in Helpman and Krugman (1989). Other sources of integration gains – notably gains relating to the integration of European factor markets – are ignored. The same is partly true for gains arising from comparative advantage – some comparative advantage effects are implicit in the general equilibrium analysis in Section 9, but a more detailed analysis of how 1992 could affect the exploitation of comparative advantage in Europe is beyond the scope of this paper. (For a study of comparative advantage between EFTA and EC countries, see Haaland and Norman, 1987). The paper draws on several recent studies of 1992 and EFTA countries. Krugman (1988) sketches many of the qualitative market structure effects analyzed more closely here. Flam and Horn (1989) give a detailed survey of possible effects for Sweden. Some of these effects are discussed in greater detail by Lundberg (1989), who also gives much relevant data and presents a highly interesting study of Sweden's comparative advantage *vis-a-vis* the EC.

2. The structure of EFTA production and trade

There are three aspects of EFTA production and trade to keep in mind when looking at the relationship between EFTA countries and the EC. The first is size: EFTA countries are very small. Taken together, all the EFTA countries add up to an economy only half the size of West Germany. The implication is that the EC is far more important to EFTA countries than EFTA is to the EC. The second is that intra-EFTA trade, with one important exception, is insignificant relative to the trade of individual EFTA countries with the EC. The third is that EFTA trade with the EC reflects significant inter-industry specialization, the Scandinavian EFTA countries in particular having substantial net exports of metals and forest products, and net imports of other manufactures.

The second characteristic is evident from Table 1, which gives the percentage distribution of EFTA trade across trading partners. The EFTA countries have been split into Alpine EFTA (Austria and Switzerland) and Nordic EFTA (Iceland, Finland, Norway and Sweden). It appears that there is hardly any trade between the two EFTA subgroups: only 1.5% of the total trade of EFTA is between the Alpine and the Nordic countries. Trade between Austria and Switzerland is not particularly important either. On the whole, the Alpine EFTA countries have 10 times more trade with the EC than with EFTA countries. Intra-Nordic trade is somewhat more important. Still, even the Nordic

Table 1. Composition of EFTA trade, 1986 (% of total EFTA trade)

Exports to from	Nordic EFTA	Alpine EFTA	EC	ROW	Total
Nordic EFTA	4.4	0.7	13.8	8.1	27.0
Alpine EFTA	0.8	1.2	12.6	7.6	22.2
EC	13.2	17.8			
ROW	7.1	5.5			
Total	25.5	25.2			

Source: *EFTA Trade 1986* (EFTA, Geneva).

EFTA members have about six times more trade with the EC than with each other.

The lack of significant intra-EFTA trade suggests that interaction between EFTA countries can be ignored when looking at the effects of 1992. One can thus concentrate on the bilateral interaction between the EC and each individual EFTA country. The one important exception is Sweden. Of the intra-Nordic trade, the dominant flows are between Sweden and Finland and between Sweden and Norway, the latter being particularly important. Sweden is Norway's largest trading partner, and the Norwegian market is the single most important export market for Sweden. When looking at the effects of 1992 on Sweden or Norway, the interaction between the two can thus not be ignored. The same is true, but to a lesser extent, of Sweden and Finland.

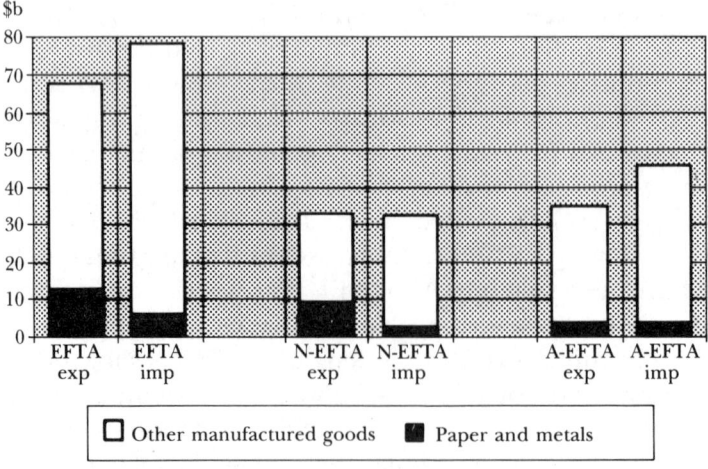

Figure 1. EFTA trade with the EC, 1986 ($b)
Source: *EFTA Trade 1986* (EFTA, Geneva).

The third characteristic concerns intersectoral specialization and trade. The exports of EFTA countries in general, and the Nordic EFTA countries in particular, reflect their comparative advantage in energy and raw materials-intensive production, with very substantial exports of metals and forest products. This is shown in Figure 1. Such specialization could be an important element of the benefits accruing to EFTA following the 1992 programme; indeed, if market integration has its primary direct effect on manufactures other than metal and forest products, we should expect resources within the EC to be reallocated into production of these other manufactures. In turn, more of the EC metals and paper markets will be left to EFTA producers.

3. The approach: industry simulations

3.1. The Smith–Venables model

One objective of this paper is to assess empirically the importance of the various effects that European integration could have on EFTA countries. To address this question, one methodology consists of calibrating a model to represent particular industries. The effect of integration is then simulated. For the EC countries, Smith and Venables (1988) have carried out a number of such simulation experiments. To make comparable assessments for EFTA countries, my model, presented in Appendix A, will be largely identical to the one they use. In the model, an industry is described by a number of firms, each of which produces various goods (which can be interpreted as brands or models). Each firm has a monopoly on its own brands, but different brands are close substitutes, so the market is one of monopolistic competition with economies of scale in the production of each variety, and economies of scope across varieties. Firms decide on the quantity of each variety that they will produce and on the quantity they want to sell in different markets. In the Smith–Venables study, firms can decide on the number of product varieties and there is free entry and exit. In what follows, I set the number of firms and the number of brands per firm. This enables me to study the effect of entry and exit explicitly. Each firm behaves as if the number of models and quantities produced by other firms were given and all firms sell in all markets. To capture the implications on intra-EFTA trade, I distinguish two EFTA markets, namely Sweden and Norway; the EC is divided into five identical submarkets, and the rest of the world is divided into three identical submarkets. This setup permits the effects of EC integration to be captured without having to model in detail each EC national market. There are national preferences, transport costs and other non-tariff barriers to trade between markets.

3.2. Two industries

The model describes two industries: motor vehicles (using 1985 data) and pharmaceutical products (using 1981 data). Motor vehicles provide an interesting case study for several reasons. First, at the European level, there is both significant product differentiation and oligopolistic interaction, so that the establishment of an internal EC market could have important effects. Second, because Sweden is a substantial exporter, the car market provides a good illustration of the effects of 1992 on EFTA exports to the EC. Third, other EFTA countries are significant net importers from the EC. Accordingly, motor vehicles should provide a good case study regarding the implications for EFTA imports. Fourth, Sweden is a major supplier of motor vehicles to other EFTA countries, and the interaction between EFTA and EC production in EFTA markets can thus be studied. Pharmaceuticals were chosen because they provide wholly different insights. First, in this market we observe both more product differentiation and more producers than in the motor vehicle industry. Accordingly, oligopolistic interaction should be less important. Second, international trade is very small compared to total production, suggesting that substantial gains can be reaped from integration. Finally, trade is mostly of an intra-industry nature, so that all countries will presumably experience the effect of integration both in the home and export market.

3.3. Calibration

Details of the calibration procedure are given in Appendix A. Only one point should be mentioned here, since it has an important bearing on the results. It concerns initial trade barriers. We typically find high market shares for domestic firms and brands, and low market shares for imports. In the absence of clear differences in production costs, such a pattern can reflect either consumer preferences for home-produced goods, or substantial non-tariff trade barriers. As both explanations are equally consistent with the data, an arbitrary choice has to be made. Practically, both trade restrictions and national preferences are captured as a tariff equivalent. This is nothing but the percentage *ad valorem* tariff which would produce the same effect. Following Smith and Venables, I arbitrarily attribute to non-tariff barriers a 10% tariff equivalent, the remainder of the difference in market shares being ascribed to consumer preferences. In Section 8, however, I assume that all of the market share differences are due to non-tariff trade barriers. Data describing the initial industry structures are shown in Table 2. The table also gives the tariff equivalents of trade restrictions and

Table 2. Calibration of industry simulations

	Pharmaceuticals (1981)				Motor vehicles (1985)			
	Nor	Swe	EC	ROW	Nor	Swe	EC	ROW
Sales ($m)								
Purchases from								
Norway	79	8	14	13	0	0	0	0
Sweden	44	225	134	116	230	3,483	1,464	2,466
EC	64	199	20,772	4,528	751	1,413	119,287	24,849
ROW	22	95	1,815	50,920	355	633	10,740	285,533
Tariff equivalents of national preferences and real trade costs (%)								
For imports from								
Norway	—	32	47	45	—	—	—	—
Sweden	37	—	40	38	20	—	25	21
EC	67	53	46	40	34	40	18	25
ROW	76	64	57	44	42	47	35	16
Market structure								
Submarkets	1	1	5	3	1	1	5	3
Domestic firms	3	6	78	60	0	2	18	12
Brands per firm	1	2	9	23	—	2	4	13

Note: The following values are given to technical coefficients: elasticity of substitution: 5.9 in pharmaceuticals, 11.1 in motor vehicles; price elasticity: 0.8 for pharmaceuticals, 1.5 for motor vehicles; ratio of marginal to average costs: 0.78 for pharmaceuticals, 0.84 for motor vehicles.

national preferences. As is seen, the tariff equivalents are quite high, emphasizing the importance of deciding whether market share differences are due to preferences or trade barriers.

4. Reduction in trade costs

4.1. Single industry effects

The first simulation experiment deals with a reduction in real trade costs, like, for example, transport costs or the costs of customs formalities. We need to have a key to interpret the simulation results. Hence, we shall first trace out the effects of a reduction in trade costs on a single industry. By so doing, we abstract from some important, but analytically difficult, aspects of inter-market competition. In our context, the reduction of trade costs within the EC will unambiguously lower prices. Indeed, foreign goods become cheaper, their sales and market share increases, the overall supply is raised and accordingly prices fall and the market as a whole is enlarged. Three main effects actually take place. First, some resources are saved: less is spent on unproductive trade costs, so that more resources are available to produce and buy goods, thereby improving the overall allocation of resources. Second, competition is enhanced as the disadvantage of foreign producers due to trade costs is lessened. Finally, and conversely, the domestic firms' market share is reduced since part of their initial competitive advantage, due to the trade costs incurred by foreign producers, is eroded.

It is clear from this decomposition of effects that there should be an overall gain, but that it will not be evenly distributed among the various parties involved. The appropriate welfare analysis is presented formally in Box 1. Quite obviously, the domestic consumers are net beneficiaries as they now purchase more goods at a lower price. The foreign producers also tend to benefit. Indeed, they appropriate part of the reduction in trade costs and they increase their sales and market share at the expense of domestic firms. As a result of the overall market expansion, price will, however, fall. Still, the negative effect of the price reduction falls short of the positive ones. Naturally, domestic firms are losers both because of the fall in prices and because of their loss of market share. It is not obvious, therefore, that the home country benefits from the reduction in real trade costs, as it depends on whether the consumers' gain more than offsets the producers' loss. It is not clear that the world at large benefits either, because total trade costs might increase. Indeed, the increase of the foreign firms' market share means that more goods are supplied by high cost producers given that trade costs are not incurred by domestic firms. This is but one instance where distortions, trade costs in the case at hand, may have negative effects on otherwise welfare enhancing measures.

The general result is that exporting countries are likely to gain from reductions in real trade costs while importing countries may gain or lose, and the world as a whole is likely to gain. A reduction of real trade costs between EC countries should, therefore, be beneficial to all countries involved; each will gain in their export markets, they could lose in their home markets but export gains should outweigh any losses at home, thereby giving each country a share in the total EC gains.

The situation is different for the EFTA countries. The position of EFTA firms selling in EC markets is analogous to the position of home market firms described above: they lose market shares and their profits decline since their marginal cost is unaffected by a reduction in internal EC trade costs. What about EFTA home markets? A reduction in internal EC trade costs need not have any effect in EFTA markets at all. If the two sets of markets are completely segmented, the population of firms is unchanged, and trade costs between EC and EFTA countries remain unchanged, there will be no domestic effect in EFTA countries.

Box 1. The effects of a reduction in real trade costs

The effects of a reduction in real trade costs within the EC are best illustrated for the case of a homogeneous good which is sold in segmented markets. Such a market is depicted in Figure 2 where competition is of the Cournot type (firms set output quantities). Two types of firms, foreign and domestic, operate in the market. Domestic suppliers produce at marginal cost b_h, and foreign firms at marginal cost b_f. Part of the marginal cost of foreign firms consists of real trade costs. For these initial conditions, there is an equilibrium with price p^0, total sales x^0, and sales by domestic firms x_h^0. Next, suppose that real trade costs are reduced, thereby lowering the marginal cost of foreign firms to b_f^1. The effect will be lower market price (p^1), increased total sales (x^1), and reduced sales by domestic firms (x_h^1). The welfare implications are straightforward: domestic consumers will gain – consumer surplus increases by ($A + B + C$). Domestic firms will lose – their profits fall by ($A + D + H$). Foreign firms will most likely gain – their profits rise by ($D + F + G - B$). This can be decomposed as follows; G is the reduction in real trade costs at initial imports, D is made of profits shifted from domestic firms as the result of a stronger market position by foreign firms; and ($F - B$) is the profit effect of increased total sales.

The net effect on the home country is ($B + C - D - H$), which may be positive or negative. The net effect on world welfare is ($C + F + G - H$). With trade cost reductions which are significant relative to the initial level of trade barriers, however, the net effect on world welfare will be positive.

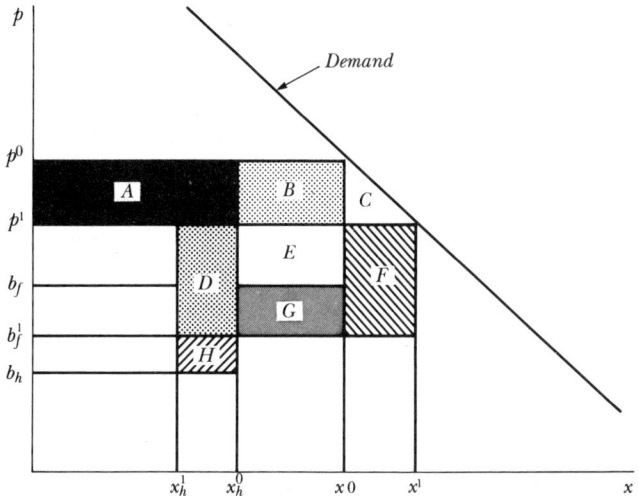

Figure 2. The effects of a reduction in real trade costs

In that case, therefore, there will be no domestic market gain compensating the EFTA firms' loss in EC markets.

In practice, spill-over effects are likely. Markets are not perfectly segmented and the marginal cost of EC sales to EFTA could be affected by what happens within the EC. We know, for example, that if border delays are reduced within the EC, transport costs to countries outside the EC will be reduced as well. If EFTA countries remain outside the internal market, such spill-over effects will of course be of a smaller order of magnitude than the effects in EC markets. Moreover, if there are spill-over effects to EFTA markets, there will also be spill-over effects to third markets where EFTA and EC countries compete. The gains that EFTA countries could obtain through spill-over effects in their domestic markets could, therefore, easily be outweighed by some fall in their exports to third country markets. On the whole, it seems quite likely that EFTA countries – if they remain outside the internal market – will lose from a reduction of trade costs within the EC, at least so long as we ignore demand effects and general equilibrium interactions. If EFTA countries join the internal market, they should benefit.

4.2. Simulation results

As in Smith and Venables, the cost reduction is set at 2.5% of the initial value of intra-EC trade, which is a modest estimate. The simulation assumes that markets remain segmented, and that there are no changes in marginal production costs or in the number of firms. Accordingly, EFTA countries will not benefit from lower trade costs within the EC if they remain outside. The results of the simulation are given in Table 3. (The effects on EC welfare are somewhat larger than those obtained by Smith and Venables – for pharmaceuticals 0.39–0.41%, compared to their estimate of 0.29%; for motor vehicles 1.39–1.42%, compared to 0.83%. The differences are probably due to market specification.)

Two remarks should be made about the results. First, and not surprisingly, Scandinavian participation matters very little to the EC – if Norway and Sweden join the internal market, the EC could make an extra gain of 0.02–0.03% of initial consumer expenditure. Second, real trade cost reductions are important to the Scandinavian countries. If they remain outside, lower trade costs within the EC would give them a modest loss. If they join, and we get comparable reductions in the real trade costs of Scandinavian exports and imports, they would reap quite significant benefits; for pharmaceuticals, the gains would be three times as large (in relative terms) as in the EC, whereas for motor vehicles gains would be of the same order of magnitude as in the EC. Table 3 also gives the reduction in real trade costs as a percentage of the total

Table 3. Effects of 2.5% lower real trade costs within the EC

	Pharmaceuticals				Motor vehicles			
	Nor	Swe	EC	ROW	Nor	Swe	EC	ROW
Scandinavia outside								
Production (%)	−0.32	−0.61	0.47	−0.08	0	−2.68	3.10	−0.49
Exports (%)	−0.88	−0.56	3.98	−0.31	0	−2.82	8.86	−0.55
Imports (%)	0	0	7.39	0	0	0	10.51	0
Profits ($m)	−0.1	−0.5	−3.5	−2.4	0	−17.5	−17.6	−43.2
Cons. surplus ($m)	0	0	21.4	0	0	0	403.0	0
Welfare ($m)	−0.1	−0.5	17.9	−2.4	0	−17.5	385.4	−43.2
Welfare								
(% of expenditure)	−0.02	−0.09	0.39	−0.01	0	−0.30	1.39	−0.04
Trade cost reduction								
(% of welfare gain)	0	0	61	0	0	0	56	0
Scandinavia inside								
Production (%)	0.14	2.68	0.49	−0.10	0	2.91	3.11	−0.55
Exports (%)	9.44	6.02	4.90	−0.62	0	5.35	10.10	−0.82
Imports (%)	4.33	4.58	7.79	0	3.31	9.39	10.83	0
Profits ($m)	−1.0	0.9	−3.7	−3.0	0.0	−24.7	−21.6	−37.4
Cons. surplus ($m)	3.8	7.3	22.6	0.0	30.1	75.2	415.1	0.0
Welfare ($m)	2.8	8.2	18.9	−3.0	30.1	50.4	393.5	−37.4
Welfare								
(% of expenditure)	1.25	1.46	0.41	−0.02	2.03	0.88	1.42	−0.04
Trade cost reduction								
(% of welfare gain)	101	64	61	0	91	57	56	0

welfare gain. For the EC, lower real trade costs account for around 60% of the total gain; the rest correspond to the induced efficiency gain explained in Section 4.1. It is worth noting that the induced efficiency gain to EFTA countries (if they become part of the internal market) might represent a much smaller fraction of their total gain. In the case of Norway and pharmaceuticals, there is actually a (small) efficiency loss, so the reduction in real trade costs amounts to more than 100% of the welfare gain.

5. Effects of market integration

5.1. Single industry effects

The second potentially important effect stems from the removal of international price discrimination. As before, an analysis of the case of a single industry is presented to serve as a background for the simulation experiment. Emerson *et al.* (1988) present convincing evidence of substantial price differences between EC countries. The differences between EC and EFTA countries are likely to be of at least the same order of magnitude. Consequently, a potentially important effect of 1992 is the integration of previously segmented markets. To assess the consequences of market integration, it is important to specify the structure of international price differences. The following analysis explicitly assumes that firms charge higher prices at home than abroad. This assumption is based on the reciprocal-dumping theory of intra-industry trade formulated by Brander and Krugman (1983). This theory suggests that because market shares are larger at home, the demand for their products is less elastic. Consequently, it is in their interest to exploit their domestic market power and discriminate across markets; they will charge higher prices at home than in foreign markets where they face a higher demand elasticity because of their lower shares.

Casual observation tends to confirm the Brander–Spencer hypothesis for many products. Fiat cars are sold in Germany at a price so much lower than that in Italy that significant reimportation to Italy takes place. Norwegian Jordan toothbrushes are sold in Hong Kong at half the price charged in Norway. Finnish Arabia tableware is 10–20% more expensive in Finland than in other Scandinavian countries. According to the producer, the typical sales price (to the producer) for a Norwegian DBS bicycle sold in Norway is NOK 2,000. The average export price is NOK 1,375. A similar price differential exists for Norwegian pharmaceutical products.[1] Still market share is likely to be only one of many determinants of price sensitivity of demand. For many goods, consumer product perceptions may be more important. The Swedish furniture chain IKEA is an example. In Scandinavia, it is perceived as a mass-consumer, low-price, medium-quality product. In North America it caters to a limited segment of young, design-conscious buyers. As a result, price sensitivity is likely to be higher at home than abroad. It is not surprising, therefore, that IKEA often charges higher prices in France and the US than in Scandinavia.[2] Yet IKEA and similar producers will be regarded as an exception: prices will be assumed to reflect market shares and thus to be higher at home than abroad.

Market integration then has two distinct effects. First, firms reallocate sales from market segments where they initially had to charge a low price (export markets) to market segments where they initially were able to charge a high price (home markets). Second, the market power

---

[1] Information about the price differentials for Fiat was provided by Luigi Spaventa. The DBS bicycle figures were taken from an unpublished student paper by Ingunn Lønning at the University of Oslo; and the information on Norwegian pharmaceuticals from an unpublished student paper at the Norwegian School of Economics and Business Administration. The casual data on toothbrushes and china is based on own observations.

[2] Information on IKEA prices was provided by Steinar Vagstad at the Centre for Applied Research, Bergen, who is currently engaged in a study of international price differences.

enjoyed by all firms will be weakened, margins will fall and total output will increase.

The first effect, namely the reallocation of output, is illustrated in Box 2. If as a result of market integration firms must charge the same price on domestic and foreign markets, they will lower prices at home and increase them abroad. Domestic consumers will benefit and their foreign counterparts will lose. The firms are necessarily worse off: they could have charged the same price in both markets before integration but had chosen not to do so. (Under segmentation the loss from their reduced market share abroad is more than offset by the higher price than they can charge on the domestic market.) Globally, however, there is a net welfare improvement. The gain to the domestic consumers outweighs the combined losses of foreign consumers and domestic firms, so that the exporting country benefits at the expense of the importing country. If both countries are simultaneously exporting to each other, both benefit if their exports are of the same magnitude. If there is a trade imbalance, the outcome might favour the country with positive net exports.

So far, in order to concentrate on the market reallocation effect, it has been assumed that total sales are given. However, market integration will also have an effect on total sales by each firm. The direction of change is, however, unclear. The ability to discriminate could induce firms to produce more when they face segmented markets than when they must price uniformly across different countries. A monopolist discriminating between different buyers in a single market would do exactly that. On the other hand, because the market power of any individual seller in a large, integrated market is smaller than in segmented markets, margins should be lower in an integrated market, and accordingly total production should be higher. In the benchmark case where domestic and foreign demands are equally sensitive to price changes, the only source of price discrimination must come from differences in market power at home and abroad: the effect of integration will be to reduce the market power of the dominant seller in each market segment, resulting in lower average prices, and larger total sales.

5.2. Simulation results

The results presented in Table 4 describe a simulation which allows for market integration (i.e. price equalization across markets) *in addition to reductions in real trade costs*. Again, the numbers for the EC are somewhat different from the corresponding estimates of Smith–Venables; for pharmaceuticals, I obtain 1.7% compared to 1.1%, whereas for motor vehicles, the Smith–Venables estimate is higher than the 2.8% gain

Box 2. The effects of market integration

Given that total output amount to x^*, a firm has to allocate sales between the home (x_h) and export (x_e) markets. This firm faces a home-market demand curve D_h and an export market demand curve D_e, with corresponding marginal revenue curves MR_h and MR_e. If the home and export markets are fully segmented, the firm will charge a price p_h at home and p_e abroad, with corresponding sales given by x_h^S and $(x^* - x_h^S)$. If price discrimination is impossible, the same price, p^I will be charged in both markets. Domestic sales will amount to x_h^I, the rest being shipped abroad.

Home consumers will gain $(A+B)$ from integration. Foreign consumers will lose $(D+E)$. The firm will obtain $(E-F)$ from its export sales; from its home sales it will lose A but gain $(C+D+F)$; the net effect on the firm's profits is, therefore, $(C+D+E-A)$ – which is necessarily negative (otherwise firms would not have undertaken price discrimination to start with). Summing all of these effects, we see that the world will gain $(B+C)$ from an end to market segmentation. Since foreign consumers lose, however, more than 100% of the gain goes to the exporting country – its total net gain is $(B+C+D+E)$. Of course, if the market is one of intra-industry trade only, and if exports and imports balance, each country will gain on its exports and lose on its imports. Export gains should outweigh import losses and each country should end up with a net gain equivalent to $(B+C)$.

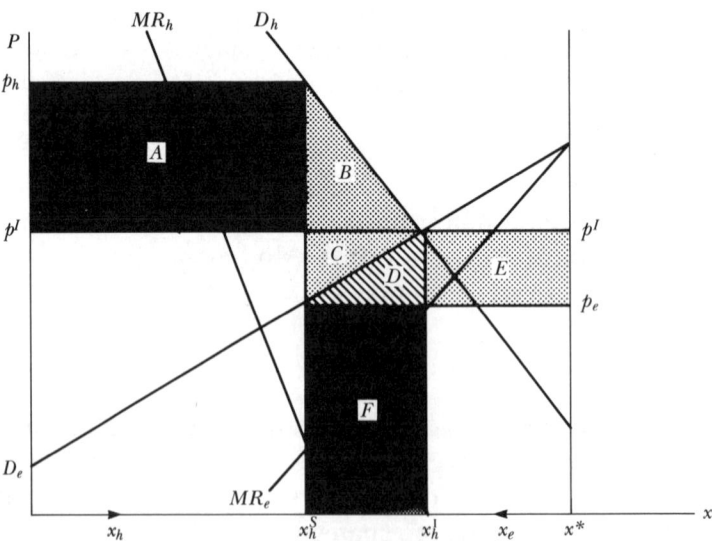

Figure 3. The effects of market integration

Table 4. Effects of market integration and lower real trade costs

	Pharmaceuticals				Motor vehicles			
	Nor	Swe	EC	ROW	Nor	Swe	EC	ROW
Scandinavia outside								
Production (%)	−3.34	−6.41	6.14	−0.86	0	−8.08	11.78	−1.48
Exports (%)	−9.32	−5.95	−2.97	−3.27	0	−8.51	−5.60	−1.66
Imports (%)	0	0	−16.18	0	0	0.00	−15.47	0
Profits ($m)	−0.6	−5.6	−173.7	−25.2	0	−52.4	−662.3	−129.1
Cons. surplus ($m)	0	0	253.5	0	0	0	1,446.4	0
Welfare ($m)	−0.6	−5.6	79.8	−25.2	0	−52.4	784.2	−129.1
Welfare								
(% of expenditure)	−0.26	−0.99	1.72	−0.13	0	−0.91	2.83	−0.12
Trade cost reduction								
(% of welfare gain)	0	0	39	0	0	0	66	0
Scandinavia inside								
Production (%)	6.51	2.53	6.16	−0.90	0	7.26	12.07	−1.66
Exports (%)	−6.61	−4.22	−3.27	−4.12	0	−22.69	−7.05	−2.51
Imports (%)	−6.53	−7.66	−16.24	0	3.82	−47.39	−15.90	0
Profits ($m)	−2.6	−9.7	−175.7	−26.7	0.0	−181.4	−699.1	−139.9
Cons. surplus ($m)	11.5	22.5	255.4	0.0	30.0	528.6	1,471.2	0.0
Welfare ($m)	8.9	12.8	79.7	−26.7	30.0	347.1	772.1	−155.5
Welfare								
(% of expenditure)	3.97	2.28	1.71	−0.14	2.02	6.03	2.78	−0.13
Trade cost reduction								
(% of welfare gain)	47	68	40	0	−6	32	68	0

given in Table 4. For motor vehicles, they however assume that there are some economies of scale at the margin, while the estimate in Table 4 assumes constant marginal cost. The results indicate very significant Scandinavian gains from participation in European market integration. For pharmaceuticals, the net gain from being inside rather than outside (the sum of the gain from participation and the loss from non-participation) amounts to 3.4% for Norway and 4.2% for Sweden. For motor vehicles the net gain is 2.0% for Norway and as high as 6.9% for Sweden.

6. Effects of lower EC production costs

Production costs can be affected through several channels. First, if marginal costs differ across firms, high-cost firms will lose market shares, because of more intense competition. As a result, the effective marginal cost of industry output will be lower. Second, larger total output, for a given number of firms, gives longer production runs per firm. If there are some economies of scale at the margin, lower marginal cost will result. This effect could be reinforced by the exit of firms from the industry, an issue directly studied in Section 7. Third, increased competition could reduce X-inefficiency. To capture the effects of lower

Table 5. Effects of 1.5% EC cost reduction, motor vehicles

	No EC cost reduction				1.5% EC cost reduction			
	Nor	Swe	EC	ROW	Nor	Swe	EC	ROW
Scandinavia outside								
Production (%)	0	−8.08	11.78	−1.48	0	−11.12	17.79	−2.86
Exports (%)	0	−8.51	−5.60	−1.66·	0	−12.27	2.55	−3.57
Imports (%)	0	0	−15.47	0	1.50	5.02	−14.58	2.07
Profits ($m)	0	−52.4	−662.3	−129.1	0	−97.9	−547.4	−376.0
Cons. surplus ($m)	0	0	1,446.4	0	13.3	40.5	1,856.3	222.9
Welfare ($m)	0	−52.4	784.2	−129.1	13.3	−57.3	1,308.8	−153.1
Welfare								
(% of expenditure)	0	−0.91	2.83	−0.12	0.89	−1.00	4.72	−0.14
Scandinavia inside								
Production (%)	0.00	7.26	12.07	−1.66	0.00	4.59	18.03	−3.01
Exports (%)	0.00	−22.69	−7.05	−2.51	0.00	−25.45	1.02	−4.36
Imports (%)	3.82	−47.39	−15.90	0.00	5.83	−41.86	−14.92	2.07
Profits ($m)	0.0	−181.4	−699.1	−139.9	0.0	−215.3	−587.2	−390.0
Cons. surplus ($m)	30.0	528.6	1,471.2	0.0	46.1	548.2	1,882.4	222.9
Welfare ($m)	30.0	347.1	772.1	−139.9	46.1	332.8	1,295.2	−167.0
Welfare								
(% of expenditure)	2.02	6.03	2.78	−0.13	3.10	5.78	4.67	−0.15

production costs, I simulate an exogenous reduction of 1.5% in EC marginal cost. For non-EC countries, no cost reduction is assumed. Since non-EC production goes down or increases by much less than EC output, the assumption of a reduction in EC costs alone seems reasonable. The results, for motor vehicles, are shown in Table 5. One observes that a reduction in EC costs raises EC welfare by an additional 1.9% of consumer expenditure. The total effect of a reduction in trade costs, market integration and cost reduction then adds up to a gain of 4.7%. The corresponding Smith-Venables estimate is 4.1%. In this case, Norway would reap an additional gain of roughly 1% of consumer expenditure, which originates from a fall in the price of cars in the Norwegian market. For Sweden, the net effect is small. Swedish producers get lower profits, which are almost exactly offset by gains to Swedish consumers from cheaper imports.

7. Effects through entry and exit

The simulations presented so far predict a considerable reduction in profits. In the integration case, for example, profits fall by some 3% of sales. As a result of this, firms might exit from the industry. Such exit will reduce, but not eliminate, the competitive effect of integration. At the same time, it will give further benefits in terms of lower average cost to EC countries. If EFTA countries remain outside the internal

Table 6. Effects of market integration, pharmaceuticals ($m)

| | Entry/exit | Norway | | Sweden | |
		Outside	Inside	Outside	Inside
Profits	None	−0.6	−2.6	−5.6	−9.7
	Free	0.0	0.0	0.0	0.0
Consumer surplus	None	0.0	11.5	0.0	22.5
	Free	−0.2	7.2	−2.3	14.3

market, the effects will again be ambiguous. EFTA firms will still lose in EC markets. In their home markets, however, they will face fewer EC competitors, and their domestic profits should rise. The overall effect on EFTA profits is, therefore, unclear. With free entry and exit, the effect on the number of EFTA competitors would accordingly be ambiguous. So is the effect on EFTA consumers. Having fewer EC products available entails a loss, but that could be offset by more domestic products if there is room for new EFTA entrants. Similarly, the degree of competition in domestic markets could rise or fall. Table 6 illustrates the effects of exit. It gives the welfare effects of market integration (reduction in trade costs plus an end to market segmentation, but without cost reductions) for pharmaceuticals, with or without free entry and exit. In the no entry/exit case, the number of firms is fixed at the initial level. With free entry and exit, the number of firms adjusts so as to restore zero profits.[3] The results are very much as expected: without entry or exit, there will be a substantial loss in profits, which, if the Scandinavian countries become part of the internal market, is more than offset by consumer gains. With free entry and exit, both Scandinavian and EC firms will leave the industry, restoring zero profits. However, the consumer gains from integration become correspondingly smaller; indeed, exit dampens the pro-competitive effect of integration and the consumer surplus is reduced as some brands disappear. The net effect of entry and exit is small.

8. Non-tariff trade barriers and demand composition effects

When there are trade restrictions, in the form of tariffs or non-tariff barriers, second-best effects must also be taken into account: trade restrictions produce a wedge between the domestic price and the import

---

[3] The integer constraint on the number of firms is ignored.

price of a good. This wedge is the difference between the marginal value of an extra unit of imports and its marginal cost to the importing country. An extra unit of imports will, therefore, give a welfare gain equal to the wedge. As a result, we shall not be indifferent between an increase in consumption of imports and an equivalent increase in the consumption of home-produced goods. Second-best effects of this type need not be considered if European integration involves the complete elimination of trade barriers. That seems unlikely, however.

This second-best effect raises particular problems when it comes to numerical assessment, because the trade impediments are unobservable and generally indistinguishable from (true) national preferences for own goods. An example can illustrate the issue. Casual observation suggests that Swedes buy more Volvos, and fewer Opels, than the Germans. Two interpretations are plausible. One is that Swedes prefer Volvos, while Germans prefer Opels. The other is that there are non-tariff barriers to imports of Opels to Sweden (and to Volvos to Germany). At the same time, it seems difficult to identify precisely the importance of non-tariff barriers. For example, how does one ascertain whether purchases of Volvos as company cars by Swedish corporations are due to true preference or to a feeling that Swedish officials will look more favourably on a company which 'buys Swedish'? Hence, in the absence of accurate information on non-tariff barriers, there is no way we can decide which interpretation is correct. The problem clearly only arises when domestic and imported goods are imperfect substitutes; if they are homogeneous, any difference in Volvo's market share in domestic and foreign markets must be due to transport costs or artificial trade barriers. Still, if we cannot separate the effect of national preferences from the effect of non-tariff barriers, we are not able to assess the second-best effect of European integration and, therefore, we are left with an important ambiguity.

Table 7 compares the welfare effects of integration in two cases: in the first case, (as in Table 4) market shares differences across countries are explained by consumer preferences in addition to a 10% tariff equivalent representing non-tariff barriers; in the second case, consumer preferences are identical and all of the differences in market shares are due to non-tariff barriers. The differences, particularly for Sweden, are striking. To understand why, let us illustrate the effects on Sweden of Scandinavia becoming part of the internal market. If Swedish purchases of Swedish cars reflect a real preference, Swedes will strongly benefit from an integration process which brings down the domestic price of their favourite cars. If consumption patterns are driven instead by non-tariff barriers, the benefit to consumers is much reduced. On the other hand, firms will experience a much more

Table 7. Consumer preferences versus non-tariff barriers: effect on the motor vehicle industry (change in welfare as % of initial consumer expenditure)

	Norway	Sweden	EC	ROW
1992 without Scandinavia				
Discrimination due to real preference	0	−0.9	−2.8	−0.1
Discrimination due to trade barriers	0	−0.7	−0.6	−0.1
1992 with Scandinavia				
Discrimination due to real preference	2.0	6.0	2.8	−0.1
Discrimination due to trade barriers	1.0	−0.1	0.5	−0.1

dramatic fall in profits following integration. Indeed, the rents accruing to firms are directly proportional to their ability to exploit consumer preferences. Finally, if initial trade patterns reflect non-tariff barriers, someone earns a pure rent from the wedge between consumer and producer prices, and that someone will lose when the wedge is reduced. Put differently, if high home-market shares reflect true preferences, there will be considerable welfare gains to be made from policies which lower the prices charged by firms in their home market and market integration has exactly that effect. If, on the other hand, dominance by home-market firms reflects non-tariff barriers, the important gains come from increased consumption of imports; to reap those, imported goods should become cheaper. Market integration, however, contributes to the opposite. With segmented markets, firms charge lower prices in the markets where they face trade barriers than they do at home. Integration forces them to charge the same price everywhere, so that imports become more expensive relative to home-produced goods.

9. General equilibrium effects

Market integration delivers three types of benefits. The first benefit is the direct saving of trade costs. The second benefit stems from a better allocation of resources within an industry. For example, as international price discrimination is reduced, sales will be reallocated from foreign to domestic buyers, and that could (but need not) be beneficial. Industry restructuring, which lead to fewer but larger firms could be another example, given that with scale economies a larger total output can be produced for a given amount of inputs. The third benefit results from better allocation of resources between industries. In general, imperfectly competitive industries tend to be too small, and highly competitive industries too large, by comparison with an efficient allocation of resources across sectors. The internal EC market should make all industries more competitive, but the impact should be greatest for those industries which are least competitive initially. As a result, we should expect a shift of resources in favour of less competitive industries.

We have found that a considerable part of the gains in the two industries considered above is associated with increased total output, and thus with reallocation of resources into these industries from the rest of the economy. For the estimation of these gains to be correct, two key assumptions need to be satisfied.[4] First, the rest of the economy must be perfectly competitive, so that marginal costs reflect the opportunity value of the extra resources used. Second, the industries concerned must be small, so that their expansion does not affect input prices. None of these assumptions is acceptable in the context of the 1992 programme. Indeed, the internal market will have significant effects only if market imperfections are widespread. That violates the implicit assumption that a couple of industries are imperfectly competitive, while the rest of the economy is perfectly competitive. It also means that 1992 will stimulate a large number of industries simultaneously. This will clearly have effects on input prices. If a large number of industries are deregulated simultaneously, income effects could also arise, which would affect the composition of demand and indirectly the allocation of resources.

A complete assessment of 1992 and its effects on EC and non-EC countries thus requires general equilibrium calculations capturing the interaction between simultaneous changes in market structure in all industries. No such calculations have been made. Emerson *et al.* (1988) have attempted to assess economy-wide effects for the EC; their approach is, however, far from a consistent general equilibrium evaluation.

9.1. A numerical general equilibrium model

To grasp the issues and to get a feeling for potential magnitudes, I have constructed a simple and highly aggregated general equilibrium model for the EC and EFTA. Even though the model is highly simplified, it should capture the more important general equilibrium effects of 1992. A systematic comparison of different models with the same structure and the same data base as the one used here does, however, indicate that general equilibrium predictions of trade policy effects are highly sensitive to the way in which imperfect competition is captured (see Norman, 1989). In particular, the relative weights assigned to product differentiation and oligopolistic interaction matter substantially.

---

[4] Strictly speaking, a third assumption is required as well, namely that the country pursues optimum trade policies for other industries. That need not concern us here, however.

This observation should serve as a general warning to treat the numbers in this section with great caution.

The model (presented in Appendix B) has three sectors of production, namely the production of metals and forest products, the production of other manufactures, and the production of non-tradeables (mainly services). Competition is perfect in metals and forest products and non-tradeables. Elsewhere, there is product differentiation and quantity competition much as in the partial equilibrium models discussed above. There are two sets of countries, namely the EC and EFTA. Each set consists of five identical countries. This is meant to represent Austria, Switzerland, Finland, Sweden and Norway in EFTA and UK, France, West Germany, Italy, and the remaining countries, for the EC. Markets for non-tradeables are purely national. There is one European market for paper and metals, and (initially) nationally segmented markets for the other manufactures. Quantities traded with the rest of the world are exogenous. There is free and costless trade in paper and metals. For other manufactures there are non-tariff barriers, set arbitrarily (as in the partial equilibrium models) as a tariff equivalent of 10%. All remaining differences in market shares are attributed to real preferences. The model is calibrated to actual 1984 production and trade data for the EC and EFTA (see Table 8).

9.2. Welfare effects: partial versus general equilibrium

I present simulations for the same experiments as those performed in Sections 4 and 5, namely a reduction in real trade costs and full market integration. As before, I look at the polar cases of EFTA remaining outside and joining the internal market. The welfare effects that I obtain are given in Table 9 and compared to the equivalent partial equilibrium effects (i.e. ignoring income effects in demand and general equilibrium effects on marginal cost and production structure). The main conclusion is that general equilibrium interactions significantly dampen the welfare effects of the internal market but substantial net gains remain. The general equilibrium calculations give estimated gains from full market integration which are around 60% of the corresponding partial equilibrium estimates. In the case of trade cost reductions only, the general equilibrium estimates are 50–55% of the corresponding partial equilibrium estimates. The estimated losses to EFTA countries if they remain outside the internal market are roughly the same. Similarly, general equilibrium interactions do not affect the relative gains to EC and EFTA. The conclusion that EFTA countries have more to gain from European integration than the EC countries is, therefore, still valid.

Table 8. Calibration of the general equilibrium model. Production/consumption matrix (value added, $b)

To	EFTA			EC			ROW		
From	Metals	Manufactures	Other	Metals	Manufactures	Other	Metals	Manufactures	Other
EFTA	14.8	51.6	181.2	2.2	12.6	—	1.1	10.8	—
EC	1.1	18.1	—	39.5	559.4	2,060.2	4.2	26.9	—
ROW	0.6	9.7	—	4.4	58.3	—	—	—	—

Note: Dashes represent trade flows which were not modelled.

Table 9. Welfare effects of the internal market: partial versus general equilibrium effects (change in real income)

	EFTA outside				EFTA inside			
	Partial equilibr.		General equilibr.		Partial equilibr.		General equilibr.	
	EFTA	EC	EFTA	EC	EFTA	EC	EFTA	EC
2.5% reduction in real trade costs								
% of total income	−0.02	0.11	−0.01	0.08	0.37	0.12	0.27	0.08
% of expenditures on good 1	−0.05	0.47	−0.03	0.25	1.28	0.53	0.69	0.28
Market integration (incl. 2.5% reduction in real trade costs)								
% of total income	−1.6	5.9	−1.5	3.8	11.8	5.8	7.6	3.8
% of expenditures on good 1	−5.7	25.1	−5.3	16.3	40.4	24.9	26.1	16.1

Note: Change in real income in the partial equilibrium case is the change in consumer surplus and profits. In the general equilibrium case it is the compensating variation.

Table 10. General equilibrium effects on production, trade and prices (% change)

	EFTA outside		EFTA inside	
	EFTA	EC	EFTA	EC
2.5% reduction in real trade costs				
Trade				
Metals and paper[a]	1.58	1.84	0.36	0.44
Exports, other manufactures	−0.36	−0.19	3.91	2.20
Imports, other manufactures	−0.34	−0.10	3.93	1.13
Production				
Metals and paper	0.10	−0.05	−0.02	−0.02
Other manufactures	−0.04	0.33	0.77	0.39
Other goods and services	0.00	−0.01	−0.05	−0.01
Prices				
Other manufactures	0.00	−0.36	−1.11	−0.42
Other goods and services	−0.05	0.02	−0.01	0.00
Factor inputs	−0.05	0.03	0.01	0.01
Market integration (incl. 2.5% reduction in real trade costs)				
Trade				
Metals and paper[a]	17.04	19.85	−16.30	−18.93
Exports, other manufactures	−4.14	−2.20	−10.28	−4.98
Imports, other manufactures	−3.93	−1.19	−8.90	−2.96
Production				
Metals and paper	1.09	−1.03	−1.97	−0.24
Other manufactures	−0.40	3.55	4.74	3.60
Other goods and services	0.04	−0.61	−1.03	−0.62
Prices				
Other manufactures	0.05	−3.99	−5.52	−4.44
Other goods and services	−0.52	0.21	0.48	−0.19
Factor inputs	−0.54	0.52	1.00	0.12

Note: (a) Change in EFTA net exports and EC net imports.

9.3. General equilibrium effects on production and trade

As mentioned above, general equilibrium calculations ensure consistency in welfare assessments, when deregulation occurs simultaneously in a number of industries. These calculations also indicate the effects of the internal market on the inter-industry pattern of production and trade. Table 10 shows that the inter-industry effects are quite large and highly dependent on how the internal market develops. If European markets remain segmented, and 1992 only involves a reduction in real trade costs for 'other manufactures', it will generally stimulate trade within Europe. Some of this trade stimulus will spill over into goods (paper and metals in the model) which are not directly affected by the 1992 programme. If the EFTA countries remain outside, EFTA trade with the EC will shift from products directly affected by the single market to some which are not directly affected. This accords with intuition and in particular, EFTA exports of paper and metals will increase.

If European markets are fully integrated, the effects are numerically larger and perhaps less obvious. Consider first the case where EFTA remains outside the internal market. Table 10 indicates a substantial increase in EFTA production and exports of paper and metals, and a corresponding decline in EFTA trade (exports and imports) in other manufactures. There are two forces at work. First, EC production of other manufactures being stimulated, the demand for factor inputs in the EC increases. Accordingly, the price of factor inputs rises and EC resources are reallocated from paper and metals production into production of other manufactures. Higher EC input prices also make EC products less competitive in EFTA markets, explaining the reduction in EFTA imports of other manufactures. Reduced EC production of paper and metals contributes to increased EFTA exports of those goods. The other force is the loss of EFTA market shares in EC markets for other manufactures. The excess resources shift into the production of paper and metals, while input prices decline.

If EFTA becomes part of integrated European markets, production of other manufactures is stimulated both in EFTA and the EC, raising input demand and prices. At the same time, however, firms shift their sales from export to home markets, so that trade in other manufactures declines and resources formerly absorbed by trade (transport and other real trade costs) become available. Some of these resources are used in the EC production of metals and paper, largely eliminating the initial negative impact. This causes a substantial decline in the volume of trade in metals and paper, reinforced by the reduction in demand due to a fall in the relative prices of other goods.

10. Conclusions

The numerical simulation results presented in the paper show that 1992 is important for EFTA countries, not so much because of the threat that an internal EC market represents but rather because of the opportunities that a larger European market offers. Generally, the EFTA countries would not seem to lose much if they decide to stay outside the internal market; the simulations suggest losses of less than 1% of initial consumer expenditures. The losses could be greater for those EFTA countries which export few products, like Finland with its high concentration in forest products, Norway with oil and metals, or Iceland with fish products. These countries could experience a significant deterioration in their terms of trade because they may be forced into even greater reliance on their staple products. Nevertheless, it does not seem that there is a basis for arguing that EFTA countries must participate in the European integration process to maintain their high real income levels. The EFTA countries could, however, gain significantly by becoming part of the internal market. The industry simulations indicate much larger potential gains from European integration for EFTA countries than for the current EC members. The gains to the average EFTA country could be two to three times as large as for the average EC country. In absolute terms, the typical EFTA gain could easily amount to some 2–4% of initial consumer expenditure.

Resource constraints could prevent EFTA countries from simultaneously reaping such sizeable gains in a large number of industries. General equilibrium interactions lower the estimated average gain by some 30–40%. Nevertheless, a fairly significant increase in real income would accrue to EFTA countries if they participated in a successful internal market. The effects on industrial structure are also worth noting. Should EFTA countries remain outside a fully integrated EC market, they would be forced into greater reliance on their traditional exports of metals, paper products and other semi-manufactured goods. If they participate in European integration, we should expect their industrial growth to be concentrated in other areas of manufacturing.

It should be emphasized that the calculations include only some of the effects that European integration can have on EFTA countries. Three omissions may be particularly important. First, the internal market might have an impact on firms' location. If EFTA countries remain outside the internal market, there could be large-scale exodus of firms. Second, we have assumed that some goods are non-tradeables and remain so. If 1992 successfully creates European markets for previously non-traded goods and services, there would be substantial additional gains. Finally, the industry calculations assume that European countries have already exploited their comparative advantage fully so that European integration will give no further 'classical' gains from trade. The general equilibrium simulations capture some comparative advantage effects. Still, a more detailed analysis of comparative advantage within Europe and its implications for the effects of European integration remains to be done.

Discussion

Henrik Horn
University of Stockholm

Norman's article assesses the possible consequences of the completion of the internal market for Norway and Sweden, using for the main part the methodology developed by Smith and Venables (1988). One particularly interesting aspect is the analysis of the motor industry since motor vehicles are a major Swedish export and make up a significant share of private consumption. Another appealing aspect of the paper is that it goes some way towards incorporating general equilibrium effects in the assessment of the internal market programme. Quite importantly too, the paper provides a very clear exposition of the issues at hand and in particular of partial equilibrium effects. I find that simulation models are ingenious constructs, which provide a useful tool. However, I do wonder whether these models should be used in the policy debate regarding the pros and (more seldom) the cons of the 1992 programme. In particular, I am sceptical about the validity of the predictions obtained from these models.

We know from the work of Smith and Venables that the internal market may lead to a significant increase in the welfare of EC countries *if* market segmentation is eliminated. One of the things we learn from Victor Norman's paper is that large gains could accrue to Sweden and Norway, at least for the two industries under review. Still, two conditions must be met actually to realize these benefits. First, firms currently discriminate in price between national markets to an important extent, and second they will *stop* doing so as a result of the creation of the internal market. As argued in the paper, there is strong empirical support for the first condition: there appear to be substantial price differences between different national markets in Europe. Yet, the analysis is also based on the crucial assumption that discrimination takes a particular form, namely that producers systematically charge higher prices in their home markets than in their export markets. Norman provides some examples in support of this assumption. More systematic evidence is, however, called for. In fact, it is relatively easy to find counter examples even in one of the industries under review; in particular, automobiles like BMW, Mercedes, SAAB and Volvo often sell at a higher price in the US than in the domestic markets of their producer. At the same time American automobiles are (or at least have been) substantially more expensive in Europe than in the US.

Even if price discrimination does in fact take the particular form assumed in the paper, one can still wonder whether the 1992 programme will eliminate it. Of course, a number of plausible arguments can be put forward; in particular, it will be easier for consumers and firms to arbitrage, taking advantage of price differentials across national markets. Still, we do not know the extent to which the observed price discrimination is the result of the obstacles to trade that the internal market is supposed to remove. As a result we cannot predict to what extent prices should converge. At the same time, firms have an interest in segmenting markets by means of implicit or explicit agreements. If anything, the internal market will also increase the incentives for firms to reach such agreements. In short, the assumption that the 1992 programme will turn segmented national markets into a fully integrated area is questionable. It is natural from an analytical point of view but yields extreme predictions for the real-world consequences of the 1992 programme.

Next, one can also wonder whether the market structure which is assumed in most studies of European integration is an appropriate description of real world competition. For analytical simplicity, these models consider that firms choose quantities, and sometimes prices, once-for-all. This assumption might not be valid for many of the industries which are likely to be affected by the internal market; in those industries a limited number of firms interact. These firms have sometimes co-existed for many years, and it seems reasonable to assume that they expect to co-exist with at least some of their competitors for some time in the future. One should thus expect the one-shot Nash equilibrium to be a poor description of such markets. The repeated character of the interaction should make other outcomes feasible and perhaps more likely. Accordingly, repeated games should be preferred as descriptions of firms' behaviour.

Another alleged source of welfare gain from the 1992 programme is a reduction of 'X-inefficiency'. While in the present paper this is only briefly referred to, it often plays a more prominent role in the policy debate. The concept should, however, be clarified and one should question the existence of the 'inefficiency' in the first place. Indeed, organizational slack, presumably taken as a sign of inefficiency, could be the result of an employment contract that takes into account employees' disutility of effort. Could we then be certain that a product market event that reduces this slack by making people exert more effort is welfare improving?

Finally, it seems that one should also consider how the trade relations and policies between EFTA and the rest of the world would be affected if EFTA joined the EC. The motor vehicles industry is a good case in point. The EC is more protectionist against Japan than is Sweden when it comes to imports of cars. First, the EC tariff on Japanese cars is 10% while the corresponding Swedish tariff is 6.2%. More importantly, many EC countries employ VERs against Japanese exports whereas Sweden does not. As a result the market shares of the Japanese producers are substantially higher in Sweden than in the EC countries: in 1987 the market share of Japanese producers in terms of newly registered cars was around 10% in EC9 and 21.7% in Sweden. The question then arises as to whether Sweden would have to align its trade policy *vis-a-vis* the rest of the world with the EC policy. The answer is probably yes. It is unclear, at this point, what such an alignment would entail, given that the future trade policies of Sweden and the EC (despite declarations by the European Commission), are not known. It is also unclear to what extent Sweden would be affected by, say, a 10% quota for Japanese cars for the whole of the internal market. Yet, it is not unrealistic to envisage a scenario where the internal market results in a reduction of trade barriers between Sweden and the EC, but where Sweden has to conform to more restrictive import policies *vis-a-vis* South Korea and Japan.

On the whole, one should stress that the numbers coming out of Norman's analysis are extremely imprecise for predictive purposes. It is unfortunate that this observation, which is obvious to economists, is lost on laymen, who often take them as authoritative.

Horst Siebert
Kiel Institute of World Economics

Victor Norman's paper presents an interesting analysis of the impact that the single European market will have on EFTA in two polar cases, namely that EFTA joins the EC or remains outside. In studying the effect of integration, Norman focuses on imperfectly competitive markets. He discusses the case of a given firm selling in two markets. This approach to market integration is somewhat narrow. At the same time, it can produce fairly odd results, such as the conclusion that imports become more expensive relative to home produced goods. One can think of two other important effects of market integration which are not analysed in the paper, namely the exploitation of comparative advantage and locational arbitrage by firms and capital. Indeed, the single market will provide more scope for exploiting comparative advantage, with, for instance, relatively labour-abundant countries specializing on labour-intensive production (see Haaland and Norman, 1987). In addition, the movement of capital and the relocation of firms will reduce factor price differentials among countries much more quickly than trade specialization. Capital movements and the relocation of firms respond to comparative advantage so that trade and location are substitute mechanisms of arbitrage in space.

The dynamic effects of factor movements should also be considered. Assume that a foreign country has a large endowment of some factor of production which is relatively immobile. For instance, one might think of a large endowment of unskilled labour, resulting in low wages. This country may be able to attract new capital and new technology as they flow more freely across the Community. As a result, the overall cost position of this country might be improved. Hence, with the mobility of some factors of production, competitiveness of a region for its export commodity may be improved. The efficiency gain might be larger than suggested by a static analysis.

The relocation of firms and capital outflows may be particularly relevant for the EFTA countries if they stay outside. EFTA countries might thus forgo an improvement in competitiveness. At the same time, EFTA specializes in products which are intensive in skilled labour, and it might be affected by the product cycle; some of the technologies used in manufacturing these products, once standardized, will be applied by lower wage countries. In response to cost differentials, and market segmentation, EFTA firms might thus like to locate inside the EC. EFTA countries would then lose out.

With respect to the partial equilibrium simulation undertaken for pharmaceuticals and motor vehicles, I wonder whether the effects of lower trade costs, market integration and lower production costs can actually be added up to obtain a complete estimate of the benefits. The author provides no guidance on this matter.

Next, it is interesting to note that in a general equilibrium context welfare effects are lower by comparison to what partial equilibrium analysis suggests. The reason is of course that not all industries can expand at the same time. The expansion of an industry raises factor prices, thereby reducing benefits in other sectors. The expansion of some industries with economies of scale also implies an appreciation of the currency, thereby deteriorating the competitiveness of other sectors. As an extreme case, if all sectors improved their competitive position by the same percentage, only the exchange rate would change. Similarly, considering capital outflow out of the EFTA might significantly affect the empirical results.

The effect of market integration on capital flows and competitiveness, should thus be very significant for overall welfare estimates. The main thrust of the paper is that EFTA may not'lose too much by not joining relative to the starting position, but could gain significantly by joining. This assertion can be backed by looking at the development of the last 20 years. Indeed, we observe that EFTA countries have not achieved a degree of integration with EC countries comparable to the degree achieved by EC countries between themselves. Figures 4 and 5 show the development of trade since 1970 between the 12 EC countries and the 6 EFTA countries. Trade has been influenced by several waves of integration. First, in 1977, a free trade area was established between EFTA and EC countries. This is basically a free trade area in manufactures dealing with tariffs and excluding other forms of segmentation such as regulated entry conditions. Second, the EC was successively enlarged from six to nine (UK, Denmark and Ireland, 1973), 10 (Greece

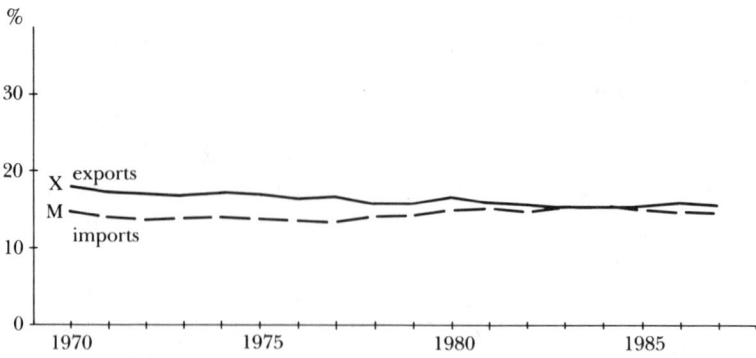

Figure 4. EFTA's share in EC exports to (imports from) EC and EFTA members

1981) and then 12 (Portugal and Spain, 1986) members. Figure 4 suggests that the EC's exports to the six EFTA countries have grown less rapidly than intra-EC exports and exports to EFTA taken together. Hence, it seems that EFTA has not been integrated with respect to the EC's exports to the same extent as EC members with respect to total EC and EFTA exports. As for EC's imports from EFTA, the proportion has not changed. EFTA has not lost competitiveness for its exports. One also observes (Figure 5) that EC exports to EFTA have declined relative to total EC exports. Judging from the absorption of EC exports

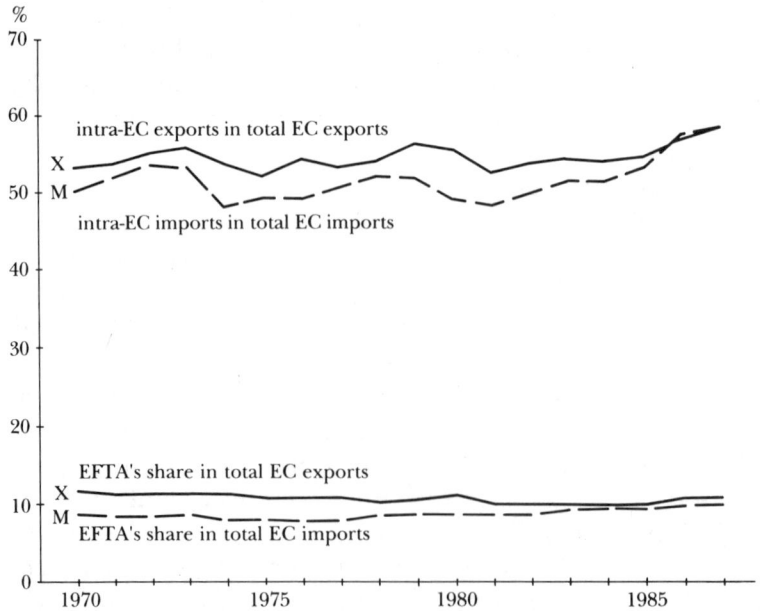

Figure 5. EFTA's share in total EC exports (imports) and share of intra-EC exports (imports) in total EC exports (imports).

by EFTA, we see that integration was, therefore, reduced. EC imports from EFTA in proportion to total imports rose slightly[5] so that by this measure integration has somewhat increased. However, intra-EC trade (exports went up from 53.36 to 58.66% and imports from 50.29 to 58.78%) clearly has increased more, so that the EC countries have integrated between themselves more than with EFTA. One may thus conclude that the establishment of a free trade area between the EC and the EFTA in 1977 has not been as successful in fostering trade between these areas as a full integration could have been. This outcome may be due to the fact that, in spite of the abolition of tariff barriers various non-tariff barriers to trade such as import quotas, subsidies or national regulation still exist between the EC and the EFTA.

Norman analyses the polar cases of EFTA joining or remaining out of the EC. However, potential forms of cooperation and integration between the EC and EFTA range from full-fledged membership to loose forms of consultation. Cooperation can also take place with EFTA as a whole or with specific EFTA members. In fact, a full-fledged membership of EFTA seems unrealistic because EFTA countries are not unanimously willing to allow the free movement of people, commodities, services and capital. For example, Switzerland is not inclined to change its agricultural and immigration policies. Sweden uses its exchange rates to make real wages flexible, which would not be possible in the EMS. Both countries would also like to continue their status of neutrality. Consequently, some mechanism of consultation may be found in which information on integration measures will be exchanged. Such a process, even making consultation compulsory, will still not affect the legislative and executive implementation of the internal market programme.

The paper does not deal with the process through which Europe is becoming integrated. This process is important for EFTA countries. Indeed, the European Commission has found that *ex ante* harmonization is widely impractical. As a result, integration occurs through competition between national institutional arrangements triggered by the principle of mutual recognition. This principle has been established by the verdict of the European Court on the famous case of the cassis de Dijon. In other words, harmonization occurs *ex post*. Competition among institutional arrangements is only possible if households and consumers have the option of spatial arbitrage. Relocation of firms forces the political

---

[5] Interestingly, EFTA's share in total EC imports in manufacturing has declined slightly since 1970. This outcome is all the more surprising as tariff barriers in manufacturing between the EC and EFTA were abolished in 1977.

process to harmonize the institutional arrangements. One may conjecture that EFTA members will take different attitudes with respect to institutional competition between national regulations. Thus, besides full-fledged membership of one or two countries, we can expect that specific countries will adopt those EC rules where they have a particular stake. The following areas can be distinguished. First, it seems that the border controls necessary to administer the differences in the tax system (value added tax) are likely to continue (except maybe in Austria and Norway). Second, technical standards, when harmonized in the EC, may be easily adopted by the EFTA countries. Indeed, EFTA countries export capital-intensive products where norms are particularly relevant and, therefore, have a particular stake in this matter. Next, the removal of entry barriers in the form of regulation in specific industries (electricity, banking and insurance) might be a matter of reciprocal negotiation between the EC and EFTA. For instance, creating new property rights with respect to transmission lines for electricity may require common action of all countries involved. But again, a country may try to establish a niche, for instance in the banking industry (Switzerland).

Finally, transportation infrastructure will presumably be affected in two ways. EFTA countries in the periphery will have an interest to improve their links to the heart of the EC area. Here the competitive process operates. For the Alps, representing a barrier to North–South trade, a bargaining solution will have to be found in which the EC's demand for improved traffic flow and the opportunity costs to the country involved have to be balanced.

General discussion

Can price differences across countries for a given product be taken as a good indicator of the lack of market integration? Or equivalently, can we anticipate that market integration will bring about a high degree of price convergence? This question was debated by various panel members. The matter is important because Victor Norman's estimates of the welfare gains from integration is very sensitive to the degree of price convergence that is assumed. Richard Baldwin first indicated that in the US there were substantial price differences across states and sometimes across nearby cities. He concluded that the large price differences observed in Europe today would possibly remain even after the completion of the internal market programme. Norman argued, however, that price differences in the US had been documented by the EC and turned out to be much lower than in Europe, where accordingly there is a scope for price convergence. In addition, price differences in the US occur between different economic units and not between administrative units, as in Europe. This suggests that price differences in Europe indeed stem from a lack of market integration and could, therefore, narrow down. Jacques Melitz also pointed out that flexible (or even quasi-fixed) exchange rates between European currencies would always maintain some price disparities.

Norman's analysis stresses that the welfare gains from market integration and price convergence crucially hinge on whether these price differences are due to a disparity of preferences or to the existence of non-tariff barriers. However, according to Anthony Venables, the distinction between preferences and non-tariff barriers is not fundamental; what matters is whether or not barriers involve real resource costs. Indeed, a difference in demand has the same effect as a non-tariff barrier involving a real cost. In turn, these will differ from barriers which simply generate pure rents. Still, the problem remains of assessing the respective role of both types of barriers in explaining the observed price differences. Venables argued that the main entry barrier in foreign markets stems from the sunk cost of setting up distribution networks. Since real resources are used in setting up distribution networks, barriers involving resources should *a priori* be considered as relatively more important. Jorge Braga de Macedo added that one should be careful about the endogeneity of the implicit barriers stemming from differences in demand; he thought that as Europe becomes more integrated, tastes and cultures will also converge, thereby reducing demand differences.

Damien Neven wondered about the choice of the pharmaceutical industry, as an interesting benchmark to estimate the benefits of integration; indeed, prices in this industry are subject to government control and arbitrage is inherently difficult because a third party is usually paying for the products. Norman argued that arbitrage could still take at the wholesale, rather than retail, level where this latter difficulty does not appear. Stephen Breyer added that certification procedures would still be a significant impediment to competition.

With respect to the general equilibrium analysis, Baldwin indicated that the estimates of the welfare gains could be significantly biased downwards; indeed, the model assumes that the supply of factors is fixed and that factors are fully utilized. In this context, an increase in the output of one industry happens entirely at the expense of output in another industry. Consequently, the general equilibrium estimates of the welfare gains tend to be very much lower than what a partial equilibrium suggests. Still, most European countries experience high unemployment rates and the labour supply could be further expanded. As a result, outputs in different industries are not direct substitutes and the total welfare effect of integration is likely to be higher than what the model suggests.

Jean-Pierre Danthine also reflected on the magnitude of the welfare effects in general; he thought that the estimates of the gains were very small, at least by comparison with the perception that the general public holds about them. The fact that the general public seems to be misled was, in his opinion, worrying because companies are today taking strategic decisions on the basis of wrong perceptions. Norman concurred, indicating that according to opinion surveys, a large majority of businessmen seems to expect increased profits from the 1992 programme. Surely, the marketplace will impose some consistency in their views and lead to a more sober approach.

Appendix A. Structure and calibration of the industry models

The partial equilibrium model used is similar to the Smith–Venables (1988) model, so only a sketch will be given here.

A1. Equilibrium in each market segment

Demand in a market segment is derived from an expenditure function defined over the price index for the industry, p, and the consumer utility level u,

$$e(p, u) = Ap^{1-\varepsilon} + u \tag{A1}$$

where the price index is a CES aggregate of individual product prices

$$p = \left[\sum_j n_j m_j a_j p_j^{1-\sigma} \right]^{1/(1-\sigma)} \tag{A2}$$

where n_j is the number of country-j producers selling in the market, m_j is the number of brands per firm from country j, and p_j is the price charged by country-j producers. The elasticity of substitution is σ.

Total industry demand will be

$$c(p) = (1 - \varepsilon)Ap^{-\varepsilon} \tag{A3}$$

and the demand for a country-j product variety becomes

$$x_j = c(p)a_j \left(\frac{p_j}{p} \right)^{-\sigma} \tag{A4}$$

A country-j firm has a cost function

$$b_j = b^j(x_j, m_j) \tag{A5}$$

displaying both economies of scale and economies of scope, i.e. (letting subscripts denote partial derivatives) with

$$b^j_x < (b^j/x_j)b^j_m < (b^j/m_j)$$

In the simulations, the cost function is assumed to be linear both in m and x.

A country-j firm faces trade barriers in the form of *ad valorem* tariff equivalents t_j. Thus, its profits will be

$$\Pi_j = m_j p_j (1 - t_j) x_j - b^j(x_j, m_j) \tag{A6}$$

For given m_j, the firm chooses x_j so as to maximize (A6), taking the number of models and quantities produced by other firms as given, giving the condition that marginal revenue equal marginal cost. If we let s_j denote the market share of firm j (i.e. the share that all the models of firm j constitute in the industry aggregate), we can write the condition as

$$(1 - t_j)p_j = \left(\frac{\sigma}{\sigma - 1}\right) \frac{1}{1 - \dfrac{s_j}{\varepsilon}\left(\dfrac{\sigma - \varepsilon}{\sigma - 1}\right)} \left(\frac{b^j_x}{m_j}\right) \tag{A7}$$

We have a Cournot market equilibrium for a given number of models when (A7) is satisfied for all firms.

A2. Market segments; simultaneous equilibrium in all segments

There are H market segments, each described by equations like (A1)–(A7). Letting x^h_j denote sales by a firm from country j in market h, and using corresponding notation for other variables, the full set of equilibrium conditions can then be written as:

$$c^h = (1 - \varepsilon^h)A^h(p^h)^{-\varepsilon^h} \tag{A8}$$

$$p^h = \left[\sum_j n_j m_j a^h_j (p^h_j)^{1-\sigma^h}\right]^{1/(1-\sigma^h)} \tag{A9}$$

$$x^h_j = c^h a^h_j \left(\frac{p^h_j}{p^h}\right)^{-\sigma^h} \tag{A10}$$

$$(1 - t^h_j)p^h_j \left(\frac{\sigma^h - 1}{\sigma^h}\right)\left[1 - \frac{s^h_j}{\varepsilon^h}\left(\frac{\sigma^h - \varepsilon^h}{\sigma^h - 1}\right)\right] = \frac{b^j_x}{m_j} \tag{A11}$$

Equations (A8)–(A11) give us $H(2n+2)$ equations to determine prices and outputs from each firm in each market, and aggregate sales and the industry price index for each market.

A3. Calibration

For pharmaceuticals, production data were taken from the official statistics for Norway, Sweden, the EC and the US (the latter as a proxy for the rest of the world; ROW production being assumed proportional to US production), while trade data were taken from UN trade statistics. For motor vehicles, Norwegian and Swedish data were taken from official statistics, while GATT data were used for the EC and the rest of the world. Data on market structure in the EC (Herfindahl indexes) were provided by Smith and Venables; as were the price and substitution elasticities used. Market structure data for Sweden and Norway are guesstimates, based on different sources.

Calibration involves solving a fairly complex set of simultaneous equations. In the description given here, the simultaneity aspect is ignored and the process is described as a sequence of steps. The reader, therefore, should not take the description literally; the purpose is only to convey the important issues involved in calibrating the model.

Data on the number of firms can be obtained from Herfindahl indexes of industry concentration – if all national firms were identical, the Herfindahl index would simply be the inverse of the number of firms; so the inverse of the Herfindahl index can be used as a proxy for the number of domestic producers. From production and trade statistics we have data on the value, at producer prices, of sales by different countries in different markets. Combining the two, we get data on sales per firm in different markets. To proceed to data on sales per firm per model, we need to know the number of models produced by each firm. Model data do not exist, but we can normalize by setting the number of models produced per firm in a particular country equal to one, and then proceed by assuming that total output per model is the same for firms in all countries. In this way, we can arrive at figures for sales per model for a firm from country j in market h; i.e. the revenue per model that firm j receives in market h.

The other essential piece of information we need is marginal cost. Again, that is generally not known. We know total revenue and total output per firm per model, however; and thus average revenue. If we assume zero profits, we then know average cost (= average revenue). Using empirical estimates of economies of scale in the industry, we can then compute marginal cost.

The industry price elasticity, ε^h, is assumed to be the same in all markets, and is taken from literature studies; market shares are known from production and trade statistics; so (A11) can be used to compute the producer prices $(1-t_j^h)p_j^h$ consistent with marginal revenue = marginal cost, as a function of the elasticity of substitution, σ^h. But we can, by appropriate choice of units, set the average producer price (across all firms and markets) equal to one; assuming the elasticity of substitution to be the same in all markets, we can then find the common value of σ^h. All producer prices are then found from (A11).

Consumer prices could be found directly from the demand functions (A10), if we knew the preference parameters a_j^h: from (A10) we could find relative consumer prices (p_j^h/p_1^h) from relative demands (x_j^h/x_1^h) and the ratios of preference parameters (a_j^h/a_1^h); with no trade costs for home-produced goods the consumer price of the home-produced product varieties would equal the producer price, so one consumer price in each market would already be known, fixing the levels of all prices.

Unfortunately, we do not know a_j^h. All we can obtain from (A10), therefore, are the products $a_j^h(p_j^h)^{-\sigma}$.

Thus, all we know are the producer prices, $(1-t_j^h)p_j^h$, and $a_j^h(p_j^h)^{-\sigma}$. From these we can find $(1-t_j^h)(a_j^h)^{1/\sigma}$. We also know that there are no trade costs for home-produced varieties, so $t_h^h = 0$. By appropriate choice of units in the industry demand functions (A8) we can always set $a_j^h = 1$ for one set of products; it is natural to do so for the home-produced varieties. If we do that, we can interpret $(1-t_j^h)(a_j^h)^{-\sigma}$ as a measure of 'effective discrimination' against goods of origin j in market h: with no trade costs and no preference for national goods, t_j^h would be zero and a_j^h one, so $(1-t_j^h)(a_j^h)^{1/\sigma}$ would be one. The higher the trade costs, or the lower the preference for good i relative to the home good, the lower will $(1-t_j^h)(a_j^h)^{1/\sigma}$ be. Generally, therefore, $[1-(1-t_j^h)(a_j^h)^{1/\sigma}]$ can be used to measure the tariff equivalent of trade costs and national preferences – it says how much lower the producer price of a country-j product must be if it is to sell the same quantity as a home-produced product variety. These tariff equivalents are all that can be determined through calibration.

Appendix B. Structure of the general equilibrium model

Each country has a production possibilities frontier defined over total outputs from the three industries and production of transport services. Demand at the industry level is generated from a Cobb–Douglas utility function defined over the three sets of outputs, while demand for individual products in the imperfectly competitive industry reflects a constant elasticity of substitution between product varieties. The model is closed by the requirement that demand expenditure in each country equal the value of production, less exogenous trade surpluses (included to calibrate the model to data).

The general equilibrium model differs from standard CGE models only in assuming imperfect competition in some of the production sectors. The structure of the model is very similar to a family of such models discussed in Norman (1989).

B1. Preferences and technology

Let c_i^h denote consumption of good i in country h, p_i^h its (consumer) price, and u^h the (one-consumer) utility level of country h. Demand in each country is then generated from a Cobb-Douglas expenditure function

$$e^h(p_1^h, p_2^h, p_3^h, u^h) = \left(\prod_1^3 (p_i^h)\alpha_i^h\right)u^h \tag{B1}$$

with (compensated) demand functions $c_i^h = (\partial e^h/\partial p_i^h)$. Uncompensated demands are found from the requirement that expenditure equal income, y^h,

$$e^h = y^h \tag{B2}$$

Goods 1 (paper and metals) and 3 (non-tradeables) are homogeneous. Good 2 (other manufactures) is an aggregate of differentiated products, similar to the industry aggregate in the partial equilibrium model. Thus, product differentiation is captured by making the price of good 2 a CES price index defined over the prices of different product varieties; dual to this is a proper quantity aggregate of consumption of the differentiated products.

The production technology is one of constant returns – apart from fixed costs in the production of good 2 – so each firm faces constant marginal cost. Through implicit, general-equilibrium effects on relative factor prices, however, the industry marginal cost curves are upward-sloping. This is captured through a CET production frontier:

$$\sum_i \frac{1}{\gamma} A_{ij}(x_{ij}+f_{ij})^\gamma \le v_j - v_{lj} \tag{B3}$$

where x_{ij} is output of good i in country j, f_{ij} are any fixed input requirements associated with the production of good i in country j, and $(\gamma-1)$ is a measure of how convex the production frontier is; i.e. how sensitive the opportunity cost of good i is with respect to the quantity produced of the good. On the right-hand side, v_j can be interpreted as a fixed resource constraint in the country; while v_{lj} denotes the resources that go into transportation or other sources of international trade costs. The production frontier gives general equilibrium cost functions for good i in country j:

$$b_{ij} = (w_j/\gamma)A_{ij}(x_{ij}+f_{ij})^\gamma \tag{B4}$$

where w_j is the resource shadow price in country j.

B2. Product markets

Goods 1 and 3 are produced in perfectly competitive sectors. There is free, costless trade in good 1, and European markets for that good are fully integrated. It is used as numeraire. There is no trade in good 3. Good 2 is produced in oligopolistic industries, identical to the one described in the partial equilibrium model; markets for good 2 are (initially) segmented; and there are real trade costs associated with it. Trade costs take the form of *ad valorem* tariff equivalents t_{ij}^h that have to be paid by country-j producers of good i selling in market h.

Thus, product market equilibrium conditions for sectors 1 and 3 consist of straightforward market clearing conditions and conditions that marginal cost equal price; while the product market conditions for good 2 are identical to those in the partial equilibrium model (except for an added subscript denoting good 2). The exact conditions need not be spelled out.

The trade costs incurred by country-j producers will be:

$$b_{tj} = \sum_h t_{2j}^h p_{2j}^h x_{2j}^h \tag{B5}$$

B3. Factor markets and income definitions

Factor market equilibrium obtains when (B3) holds as an equality i.e. for that w_j which gives:

$$\sum_i \frac{\partial b_{ij}}{\partial w_j} + v_{tj} = v_j \tag{B6}$$

where

$$v_{tj} = \frac{b_{tj}}{w_j} \tag{B7}$$

are the input requirements associated with the trade costs b_{tj}.

The model is closed by the income identity

$$y_h = w_h v_h + \text{profits}_h \tag{B8}$$

B4. Calibration

EC data were taken from the official EC statistics, while EFTA data were constructed on the basis of production and employment statistics for the Nordic countries, employment statistics for Austria and Switzerland and EFTA trade statistics. We have data on values of consumption and production, and thus on values of factor inputs. The number of firms in a representative good-2 industry is set exogenously, as are tariff equivalents of real trade costs. Choosing units so as to give initial marginal costs of 1, we obtain consumer prices from marginal costs and tariff equivalents. Knowing marginal costs and consumer prices, we obtain quantities produced and consumed, and quantities employed of factor inputs. What remain are demand function parameters (the distributional shares a_i^h in the Cobb–Douglas expenditure function, and the substitution elasticity σ_2^h and the preference parameters a_{2j}^h in the CES sub-utility function for good 2); and the parameters of the production frontier (γ_j and A_{ij}).

Of these, the substitution and transformation elasticities σ_2^h and γ_j are set exogenously. The value of γ_j is set arbitrarily at 1.5, which in the competitive case gives a price elasticity of supply of 2. The good-2 elasticity of substitution is set at 4.

The Cobb–Douglas shares are obtained directly from income and expenditures. The CES preference parameters, given exogenously specified tariff equivalents, follow from the computed quantities and prices, in the same way as in the partial-equilibrium model. The production frontier parameters A_{ij} can be found from quantities and prices, using the definition of marginal cost.

When calibrating the model to actual production and trade data, third-country trade must be accounted for as well. That is done in the simplest possible manner, by assuming exogenous trade flows, at fixed (world market) prices between third countries and EFTA and the EC. Exogenously given trade surpluses are then also included in the income–expenditure equations.

References

Brander, J. A. and P. R. Krugman (1983). 'A reciprocal dumping model of international trade', *Journal of International Economics.*

Emerson, M., with M. Aujean, M. Catinat, P. Goybet and A. Jacquemin (1988). 'The Economics of 1992', *European Economy.*

Flam, H. and H. Horn (1989). 'Ekonomiska konsek marknad', in *Svensk ekonomi och Europaintegrationen*, Stockholm.

Haaland, J. I. and V. Norman (1987). 'EFTA and the world economy', EFTA Occasional paper, No. 19.

Helpman, E. and P. R. Krugman (1989). *Trade policy and market structure*, MIT Press.

Krugman, P. R. (1988). 'EFTA and 1992', EFTA Occasional Papers, No. 23.

Lundberg, L. (1989). 'Svenskt näringsliv och den europeisk integratione', *Svensk ekonomi och Europaintegrationen*, Stockholm.

Norman, V. (1989). 'Assessing the trade and welfare effects of trade liberalization', mimeo (paper prepared for the 1989 International Seminar on Macroeconomics).

Smith, A. and A. J. Venables (1988). 'Completing the internal market in the European Community', *European Economic Review.*

Economic Policy   October 1989   Printed in Great Britain

███████

The appropriate level of regulation in Europe: local, national or community-wide? A roundtable discussion

The theoretical rationale

Manfred J. M. Neumann
University of Bonn

Government interferes with private activity in three ways: it sets and enforces rights and rules that define and constrain private production and exchange in markets for goods, services and assets; it provides public goods; and it appropriates taxes and seigniorage to finance its protective and productive activities and to provide for redistribution.

What is an appropriate division of these functions among different levels of government? In searching for a tentative answer we may draw on public choice reasoning about federalism, a body of thought previously concerned almost exclusively with the provision of public goods and the power to tax. There are two main lines of thought.

First, there is the traditional 'public interest' approach to government (Musgrave, 1959; Oates, 1972). It assumes benevolent government and relies on the efficiency norm in deriving lower bounds on the level of decision making. Each level of government should be assigned those functions that in principle it can perform best. The public interest approach is guided by the maxim: if in doubt, assign to a higher level of government. It favours centralized interventionism.

The second line of thought is the 'leviathan' view of government (Simons, 1948; Buchanan, 1975). Politicians are self-interested rent-seekers who exploit citizens by maximizing power and revenue, and by redistributing income and wealth to special interest groups. Given free migration between local jurisdictions, local governments – in contrast to central government – are forced to compete with one another. Competition between jurisdictions reduces the potential for exploitation. Consequently, the leviathan view of government suggests an upper bound on the level of government: if in doubt, assing to a lower level of government. The basic idea is to guarantee constitutionally decentralization of decision making with respect to domestic policy issues, hence putting competitive pressure on government intervention, wherever and as much as possible.

In discussing the proper jurisdictional level for different regulatory activities, I will lean towards the individualistic approach of government competition. I am concerned with a long-run framework and will not consider short-run problems of adjustment.

1. Competition and the regulation of markets

The EC Treaty rests on the conviction that dynamic competition is the most successful form of market organization to enhance the welfare of EC citizens in terms of personal freedom and the provision of goods and services. Workable competition requires free entry as well as free exit. In line with this, the Community promises free migration between jurisdictions for people, capital, finance, goods and services. With the completion of the internal market, the competitive structure will have to be protected by central institutions of the Community against industry-specific and national interests in protectionist regulations. Internal competition policy is to be monopolized by the Community.

However, the principle of workable competition does not imply that any type of regulatory activity is to be denied to lower level government. Regulation by local government may not reduce the degree of competition among producers but rather meet specific preferences that prevail among consumers in a local community. Local government alone should have the right to set opening and closing times for shops, to announce public holidays, or to decide which type of industry may settle in its jurisdiction. Local government alone should have the right to set minimum safety standards for construction of local buildings. Within the Community, mobility costs are sufficiently low as to allow Community-wide competition of local jurisdictions that will guarantee the avoidance of arbitrary paternalistic regulation.

Generally, for goods, services and assets that do not create significant adverse externalities, minimum standards to protect the physical, mental and financial health of the consumer must not be set at the Community level. In the comparatively rare cases where public standards can be justified, they may be set at the national level for products *originating* from that jurisdiction. This substitution of the origin principle for the destination principle creates a welfare-enhancing competition of safety standards by extending the range of choice for the consumer. However, the Community may consider assisting consumer choice, both by setting an EC-standard on minimum product information and by providing, in various ways, information about differences in national standards.

Matters are different for substantial adverse externalities (actual or potential) that cross the borders of national jurisdictions, for example pollution of the air by heating, cars or power plants. Environmental protection justifies Community establishment of uniform minimum standards for admissible emissions. There is, nevertheless, a case for supplementary regulatory competition. National governments must not be hindered from setting more demanding standards for their own jurisdictions: such standards do not create permanent barriers to entry that would undermine the Community's competence in protecting competitive markets.

Finally, we have to consider the threat of Fortress Europe, really a threat to the European consumer. Given a worldwide tendency towards protectionism and the need for international bargaining to avoid trade wars, the Community is entitled to bargain with its trading partners on the rules of international trade. As the Community has more bargaining power than its constituent Member States, this will minimize barriers to entry into foreign markets. By the same token, however, this institutional solution may lead to higher EC entry barriers when EC industries succeed in lobbying at the Community level. Therefore, it is advisable to raise the costs of lobbying for protective measures by requiring that any EC decision designed to introduce or raise entry barriers has to win unanimous, not merely majority, support of member governments.

2. The supply of base money

It is widely held that the supply of money is a natural monopoly. In principle it seems justified to create a European central bank for the supply of a uniform European currency; but this may be a matter for the long run.

Given the flagrant disparities in the levels and speeds of economic and social development among EC member states, it would be premature to forgo the elegant instrument of realignment of intra-Community real exchange rates. In comparison to the alternative measure of large-scale transfer payments to the less developed EC countries, parity adjustments do not discriminate among producers or consumers, do not set incentives to seek and capture rents and avoid the waste of resources on additional central EC bureaucracy.

During the transition, until the time is ripe for a single European currency, it is advisable to raise the degree of competition among member currencies in order to deepen the understanding that the provision of monetary stability, in terms of purchasing power, is the most important service of monetary policy. Forms of currency discrimination are still with us: for example, all obligations which have to be notarized or enter the land register still have to be written in the national currency; and governments accept payments only in their own currency. A radical solution is to declare all member currencies to be legal tender. In addition, one might consider abolishing the rule that weights of national currencies in the ECU are to be readjusted every five years.

National governments appear to accept the vision of a European central bank which (i) is committed to the objective of price stability, (ii) does not lend to public authorities and (iii) is independent of instructions from governments of all levels. If this is not just lip service, national governments should be ready to grant their national central banks the status of independence now. This reform would put all member currencies on an equal footing and result in currencies of equal quality. From there it will be a small step to complete monetary union once the need for large adjustments in real exchange rate parities is gone.

Where to regulate?

Michael Emerson
Commission of the European Communities

The question is deceptively simple. In reality, the founding fathers of the EC created a set of legal mechanisms that allows for very fine graduations in the degree and manner that policy functions can be assumed by institutions. This gives ample opportunity, if care is taken, to 'regulate from Brussels' in a way that fits naturally into the landscape of Europe's political economy. With the considerable expansion of the EC's regulatory functions entailed in the completion of the internal market – with 300 items of legislation of the 1985 White Paper – it is an urgent matter that all participants achieve a good understanding of the effective flexibility offered by the Treaties.

1. The basic toolkit

A framework is needed. I suggest a matrix in three dimensions:

Form of the legal act	Role of the institutions	Nature of the public activity
Regulation	Commission	Legislation
Directive	Council	Supervision
Decision	Parliament	Enforcement
Coordination	Court of Justice	
Mutual recognition	Committees	

Fortunately, not every cell in this three-dimensional matrix is a real possibility. Nonetheless, it is a helpful schema, and some basic political choices have already been made. First, where EC law is adopted it takes precedence over any conflicting national law. Second, mitigating this centralizing principle, the institutions give increasingly explicit support to the principle of subsidiarity: responsibility is assumed at EC level only when the function can be better discharged there than at national level. Third, preference is for decentralization of policymaking, execution and supervision. These principles of subsidiarity and decentralization are set out in the Padoa Schioppa Report (1987) and are regularly taken up in official documents such as the annual work programme addressed by the Commission to the Parliament.

Let me comment in more detail on the three directions of the matrix. 'Regulation' is a specific term of art in the law of the EC, and since economists use the term more widely it is as well to be clear. Article 189 of the 1957 Treaty defines a Regulation, a Directive and a Decision. A Regulation is binding in its entirety and directly applicable to Member States. It is typically used for trade policy law which has to be absolutely precise. By contrast, a Directive is more decentralized, specifying the result to be achieved, leaving national authorities to choose form and method in subordinate legislation. This is used typically for legislation governing what economists would call regulation, such as in financial services. A Decision is binding upon those to whom it is addressed, and is typically used where the Commission has to 'decide' whether various subsidies are legal or illegal under competition policy.

'Coordination' must also be clearly understood within the framework of EC institutions. It means joint and interdependent actions without legal force: renegers cannot be taken to Court. The most important example is the EMS in which participants behave according to agreed rules which are unenforceable in EC law.

'Mutual Recognition' refers to legislative acts which are national responsibilities but recognized and enforceable under EC law. It is applicable typically to standards and norms, and assumed prominence after the landmark judgment of the Court of Justice in the *Cassis de Dijon* case in 1978, and more recently by politically sensitive cases concerning German beer and Italian pasta. These judgments affirmed that in given areas of internal market law national norms are automatically acceptable in all other Member States. This decentralized form of legislation has lain at the heart of the Commission's recent progress in dismantling technical non-tariff barriers.

The evolution of EC regulatory responsibilities cannot be understood without taking into account the games between at least three institutions:

the Commission, the Council and the Parliament. The Single European Act has changed their behaviour. The key point here is that the contents of the two voting baskets (the 'unanimity' basket and the 'qualified majority' basket) were changed in 1987, with a lot of internal market legislation being passed from the former to the latter. The Parliament was also given some capacity for amending legislation and influencing the final outcome where Member States are not strongly united.

A final word on the triptych legislation-supervision-enforcement. Supervision seems likely to be predominantly a national responsibility, even with respect to EC law, at least where the operating agent to be supervised is in the private sector. Enforcement may also offer greater scope for decentralized action than is currently the case. National courts are in principle empowered to take disputes under EC law, but they do so relatively little. The Commission and Court of Justice, on the other hand, have long traffic jams piling up: with some minor modifications, national courts could do far more to enforce EC law at a decentralized level. This kind of model is much in evidence in the US.

2. Economic principles to guide the use of the toolkit

Professor Neumann took, to my taste, a rather negative view of what economics has to offer. The principle of spill-overs is enormously powerful and practical. It underpins the principle of federalism, that the efficient jurisdiction is that whose geographical coverage internalizes the major costs and benefits of the public policy in question.

Spill-over theory, however, is not sufficient. Public choice theory complicates matters by introducing the paradigm of competition between jurisdictions. The threat of leakages (of labour, capital or tax revenue) to other jurisdictions creates a pressure for efficient regulation. We have a potential conflict. Typically we cannot adopt efficient regulation at the outset: we have to experiment with different forms of regulation. Yet competition between rules without agreed minimum standards may threaten a competitive depreciation of public goods such as consumer safety. The alternative paradigm cannot have a free run.

Fundamentally, the difficulty in agreeing where to regulate in the EC can be traced to the conflicting advice of these two simple principles, the spill-over principle of federalism and the competition between jurisdictions arising from public choice theory. Where and how to regulate promises to remain a rich field to plough for students of Western European integration.

The case of financial services

Colin Mayer
City University Business School, London

Financial services provide a vivid illustration of many of the issues raised in this roundtable discussion. I want to examine what economics has to say about how it should be regulated.

I set out the Commission's approach, then briefly describe the characteristics of the industry relevant to the design of its regulation. I emphasize differences in risk which argue for diversity of regulation: in some regulation cases should be minimal, in other cases extensive. In some circumstances investors should be free to choose their preferred form of protection; in others, common levels of regulation will be required. I conclude that the degree of harmonization currently being sought by the Commission is excessive.

1. Regulating financial services in Europe

This is being guided by the principle of home country authorization: institutions licenced in one Member State should be free to operate elsewhere, thus, it is hoped, allowing the free flow of financial services between Member States. To ensure acceptable levels of protection, minimum standards of regulation are being sought of all Member States. These relate to individuals involved ('fit and proper' rules), to institutional performance ('conduct of business' rules) and to financial condition of firms (capital requirements).

It is clear that there will be significant differences by class of financial institution. The second Banking Directive lays down rules for deposit-taking institutions; other directives lay down different rules for insurance companies and mutual funds. But there is a tendency towards similarity of regulation, both across institutions and across countries. Minimum standards for capital adequacy and competence criteria will be set at the Community level, and will imply extensive regulatory harmonization in financial services.

2. Characteristics of financial institutions

Regulatory policy should be based on the activities of firms not on their institutional classification. However, for this discussion, it is convenient to contrast three classes of institution: banks, brokers and dealers, and investment managers.

Banks play the key roles of performing transactions, transforming maturities, and evaluating creditworthiness. Broker-dealers provide immediacy and liquidity in securities markets. The importance for the economy of investment managers is less transparent: they allow investors to diversify portfolios with specialist advice, but many securities markets operate quite successfully with fairly rudimentary forms of investment management.

Interlinkages involving banks are both direct (a bank failure threatening its counterparties) and indirect (the reputation of one institution affecting another, and a bank run prompting runs elsewhere). Similar interlinkages apply to broker-dealers. Financial institutions are heavily exposed to their counterparties whose failure can have widespread effects when financial integration is sophisticated. In contrast, interlinkages or externalities are much less significant in investment management: if managers do not take positions on their own accounts, risks of failure are small; if they do not hold client monies, the costs of failure are small even if it occurs. The final characteristic of relevance is the institution's clientele.

3. Market failures

From the above, it is easily seen that bank failures have systemic consequences. Failures of broker-dealers have consequences for securities markets, whose significance depends on the importance of securities markets in the operation of the economy. Few systemic risks arise from investment management.

However, investment management is prone to asymmetric information and the associated problems of moral hazard (fraud and negligence) and adverse selection (incompetence). Information is likely to be particularly deficient when investors are dispersed and holdings small. Thus, free riding in information collection will be most pronounced in institutions with private clients (banks and private client investment managers).

These distinctions are deliberately stylized but serve to emphasize the diverse nature of institutions and the varied regulatory responses that are required.

4. Regulation of financial services

Systemic risks are financial in nature: they come from bank runs and insolvency. A financial response is, therefore, appropriate. Since risks are correlated across institutions, they cannot be pooled. Capital must, therefore, be held against such contingencies by individual institutions. That is why capital adequacy is legitimately required of banks and broker-dealers but not of investment managers.

Asymmetric information is not a financial problem, but relates to the quality of individuals and management systems, and the activities of firms. The appropriate response is screening and monitoring: 'fit and proper' and 'conduct of business' tests. Often this could be done privately. Disclosure requirements may be enough to allow quality to be established, possibly with the aid of credit rating agencies. But private monitoring will not be adequate in relation to fraud. The need for information disclosure (through policing and public prosecution) and the application of criminal penalties necessitates public jurisdiction.

Regulatory requirements vary from a combination of capital adequacy and supervision of banks, through capital requirements for broker-dealers, to supervision for fraud and disclosure requirements for private client investment managers. A national response is required where serious externalities exist between firms: this is the case for banks. Elsewhere, regulation can be delegated to private bodies (private auditors, and rating agencies for the quality of broker-dealers or investment managers).

Should institutions be regulated in similar ways (e.g. capital adequacy) be subject to similar criteria when they face similar risks? Obviously not. Because of their greater linkages with the rest of the economy, banks should face more onerous capital requirements than broker-dealers, and requirements for the latter should be more onerous in the market-based UK economy than elsewhere in the EC. Investment managers with private clients should be more carefully scrutinized than those with professional clients.

5. International harmonization

By identifying market failures and establishing their magnitude, we can determine the appropriate level of regulation and the need, if any, for harmonization.

Investment managers with institutional clients should be almost free of regulation. At the other extreme, the central role of banks in all countries suggests there is a strong case for harmonization of bank regulation. In between lie broker-dealers whose operations create market-wide risks with differing consequences in different countries. Equity and bond markets are central to the operation of the UK economy but of minor significance in Portugal and Greece. There is no case for harmonization in this instance. For investment managers, international cooperation is required to police fraud, but quality evaluation can be left to private institutions. In fact, institutions could be encouraged to signal their quality by joining clubs offering different levels of protection or standards or care. Provided investors understand the protection and care offered by each club, competition between clubs should not only be permitted but encouraged.

A US perspective

Stephen Breyer
Circuit judge, US Court of Appeals, First Circuit

What is the appropriate level of economic regulation: local, national or community? The question posed is broad. I shall simply make four comments, hoping that they will prove helpful to those searching for answers.

1. The shift in institutional power

My first comment is a prediction. We shall see a shift in the balance of institutional influence from the European Court of Justice towards the European Commission. Before the Single European Act, the primary burden of testing local regulation against the 'free market' EC standard fell upon the European Court of Justice. Article 30 of the Treaty, for example, says 'quantitative restrictions on imports and all measures having equivalent effect shall . . . be prohibited between Member States.' This provision is subject to the reservation, in Article 36, that Member States may, nonetheless, regulate to protect public morality, public policy or public security, and for the protection of health and life of humans, animals or plants, national treasures, and industrial and commercial property. Prior to the Single European Act, the Court determined the lawfulness of particular national regulations, and struck down such local regulations as the German regulation of the contents of beer and the Italian regulation of the ingredients of pasta, reasoning that these acted as barriers to trade without sufficient justification.

By amending the Treaty of Rome, Member States have in effect created a legislative body, giving the Council the power to take 'legislative' measures to perfect the market, sometimes by majority, sometimes by qualified majority or by unanimity. This body intends to legislate, through regulations, directives or decisions, in respect of a vast number of economic activities.

My prediction of a shift in influence from the Court does not rest on the law itself. Articles 30 and 36 remain. The Court is still empowered to examine German beer regulations or Italian pasta regulations, to see whether or not they unduly restrict trade between Member States. Rather my prediction rests upon a judicial tendency (perhaps a human one) not to examine a matter too closely when another, better informed body, is also empowered to deal with the problem (see Lenaentz, 1988).

I speak of a shift in power towards the Commission rather than the Council because I suspect that the details of much regulation, though embodied in Council-enacted rules, will in fact be written by EC civil servants and recommended by the Commission to the Council. The substance of regulation (what metal can be used to make lawn mower blades) is often too detailed and too industry-specific to be fit for discussion at a meeting of the Council which may tend to accept most Commission recommendations.

2. Less regulation?

Whether a shift in regulatory authority, from national to community level or from Court to Commission, means less regulation will depend on the particular subject area. In some areas there will be increased reliance on rulemaking as a substitute for informal consensus, with increased bureaucracy.

Suppose the therapeutical drug approval system in country A relies heavily on informal consultation among a relatively small group of professionals who know and trust each other, but country B has more elaborate rules and regulations for determining when drugs are safe. Suppose doctors in Country A do not trust the results of Country B's approval system. Any community-based system that allows A to ignore B risks permitting A in effect to erect a trade barrier under the guise of safety regulation. But any community-based system that requires A *automatically* to admit B-approved drugs may expose A's citizens to dangerous drugs. The result of this 'regulatory stalemate' is likely to be some kind of compromise, with the development of community-based drug-approval standards or a community system for selecting an appropriate drug-approval system. Any such system, however, is likely to be more bureaucratic, more rule-and-regulation based, than the original system in Country A. As a practical matter, it is difficult to authorize a 'trust-and-confidence based' system among physicians, scientists, and manufacturers from many different community nations. Thus, it is more likely that A's system will become more bureaucratic than it is that the systems of other countries will become less bureaucratic.

3. The global 'which level' question has no interesting answer

I am skeptical about finding any simple theory that will help significantly to determine the appropriate level of regulation. Many special cases will arise that will force the authorities to make the level of regulation decision upon political grounds or which will require exceptions to individual programmes.

Consider a (simplified) candidate for a 'which level' decision rule: 'Look to the object of the regulatory scheme; determine whom the scheme is supposed to protect and why; thus decide which level of regulation is appropriate.' For example, town planning rules to protect local persons should be in the hands of local regulators; if, however, the object is to protect all community residents (such as an anti-acid-rain program), then regulate at a community-wide level.

This obvious rule cannot easily dispose of many real-world instances, for one cannot easily define regulations so local that they could not act as trade barriers or have community-wide impact. Consider safety regulation of lifts on construction projects. It is difficult to imagine a regulation more localized. Yet suppose the regulation specifies a particular metal only produced in that locality. It may amount to a trade barrier. The Community will have to have a method for balancing safety needs and economic consequences and for deciding what is lawful.

This example is meant to illustrate the kinds of problems that federal courts in the US face when they deal with cases concerning the power of state versus federal regulators to enact rules concerning, say, telephone or electricity regulation: local incentives, apparently a matter for local regulators, will in fact affect the number and types of firm then offering interstate services. Spillovers cannot be contained locally.

Similarly, federal statutes that permit states to require local electric power generating systems also permit states to force such firms to buy power for resale from small co-generation facilities. As a result, some states have developed rules that are currently attacked as forcing purchase of unnecessarily expensive electric power. If so, the rules will divert power flows between states into paths they would not otherwise take.

Whether or not interstate effects are substantial presents difficult questions of fact and of prediction. In the US one would normally look to federal regulators for the answer.

All this is simply to say that any effort to divide community-wide, national, and local responsibilities is likely to provoke a very crude first attempt; time and circumstance will soon create pressures that break down any initially simple system. The Community will have to devise mechanisms, probably on a case-by-case basis, to determine whether, where, and when community-wide effects are significant.

4. Procedural solutions

One type of answer in the US is procedural. Federal rules, for example, govern the safety of interstate trucking. But the states may still regulate in respect of local safety. Suppose a state imposes very severe rules (trucking dynamite through the state permitted only between 3 a.m. and 4 a.m.). Do those rules burden interstate commerce? Rather than have the courts answer directly or have a federal agency enact all rules on dynamite carriage, federal law creates a bureaucratic 'approval procedure'. The federal agency will itself examine the state rule which any party may present to the agency. It will then decide whether an individual state rule is, or is not, too restrictive. And the courts will probably respect the result.

I suspect that, given the vast number of regulatory rules and the virtually unforeseeable number of ways in which they might have community-wide or trade impacts, the Common Market will develop and rely on similar procedural devices to separate permissible regulation from impermissible trade restrictions. But that is only a guess.

General discussion

A number of panelists discussed whether optimal regulation necessarily required uniformity of standards across countries. Horst Siebert focused on environmental policy, and distinguished the use of environmental quality standards from the particular policy instruments designed to achieve those standards. Uniformity of the first (the goals) need not imply uniformity of the second (the means). Indeed, since different national environments could be thought of as immobile endowments it was natural to expect differential pricing at the optimum.

Manfred Neumann questioned Colin Mayer's preference for uniform capital adequacy standards across countries. Since information was readily available about capital standards in different countries, he wondered why consumers could not make up their own minds. Banks could be rated for capital adequacy, much as other institutions were rated. Mayer replied that capital requirements were a form of insurance, and it was well known that insurance markets were prone to market failure.

The discussion moved on to considering whether effective regulation could be achieved by competition between national regulators. Horst Siebert thought environmental policy could be decentralized by imposing controls on diffusion of pollutants between regions, and allowing regions to set their own internal standards, based on the costs of regulation in different environments. Current controls on air quality used a licensing system, which was subject to long delays and inefficiencies. But provided price incentives were allowed to operate instead he saw no major drawbacks in a decentralized policy. Richard Baldwin said that, in respect of trade policy, there were advantages in centralization because it tended to reduce pressures for protectionism. More of

the costs as well as the benefits of protection were borne by the decision-
making unit. However, in many other respects the US experience
showed that competition between localities had worked. Stephen Breyer
was more sceptical. As soon as it became possible to regulate at the
highest level, he said, it became necessary to regulate in the greatest
detail. When there was competition between 'laboratories of experiment', there would be great, but often hidden pressures for regulators
to protect producer interests in their locality. He returned to his example
of elevator safety regulations: though these might appear to have purely
local impact, they could easily be framed in such a way as to favour a
local supplier of elevator equipment. In the face of such pressures, he
thought that the pressure for accretion of power at the highest level
would be hard to resist.

Richard Portes thought the Tiebout approach to regulation, relying
on competition between localities providing public goods, was in serious
tension with the European Community's emphasis on restricting state
aids to industry. Michael Emerson agreed, and said there were several
reasons why competition between localities was less likely to work in
Europe than in the US. The US was a more competitive regulators'
market, with 50 states instead of a handful of major economies; Europe
was effectively a regulators' oligopoly. Furthermore, the geographical
distribution of major firms was more even, whereas in Europe a number
of major national champions such as Fiat were concentrated in particular
Member States. And experience had shown the scale of the pressure
for state aids: in Italy state aids in one form or another almost equalled
the budget deficit.

Jean-Pierre Danthine was puzzled by Manfred Neumann's argument:
did he want local consumer protection or no consumer protection at
all? Neumann replied that this would be up to consumers and voters
in their respective localities, where they could unite to achieve whatever
level of consumer protection they wished. Richard Portes emphasized
the great cultural differences between European countries, which would
tend to limit the degree of uniformity to be expected. Horst Siebert
pointed out that one consequence of attempting to harmonize standards
was that it would give rise to claims for transfer payments to cover the
costs to some countries of meeting standards. Stephen Breyer took this
as another instance of the pressure for centralization, though he thought
the EC's powers remained highly limited so far. Colin Mayer cited
another example, that of merger control: there was considerable pressure to reduce the discretionary element in the process, by making
merger scrutiny by the Commission automatic for all mergers above a
certain size. Paul Seabright added that while the decision as to which

agency should scrutinize mergers might be non-discretionary, merger investigation itself would remain very much a discretionary matter. The pressure for central control was due to the fact that it was difficult for Member States to monitor the competition authorities of other countries, and to be sure they were not colluding in forms of industrial protection. In the case of non-discretionary regulation, by contrast, centralization was due either to externalities between countries or (as under the Drinking Water Directive) to a judgment by the EC that UK voters had not got the government action they implicitly desired.

In conclusion, Manfred Neumann accepted that the ability of regulatory competition to work depended on the removal of rigidities in labour markets: citizens had to be able to vote with their feet. Michael Emerson thought that the limitations on the powers of the EC had been overemphasized: the Community was already more centralized than, for example, Canada. In many areas, however, it was important to retain flexibility: competition policy should be able to draw on economic expertise rather than just legal skills; and it would be a mistake to impose uniformity in social policy. There remained great diversity even in the US between elegibility levels for public health care, for instance. Not all of these divergences were necessarily desirable, but they indicated that the EC should not hope for standardization in such areas.

References

Buchanan, J. M. (1975). *The Limits of Liberty,* Chicago University Press.
Lenaentz, K. (1988). *Two Hundred Years of U.S. Constitution and Thirty Years of EEC Treaty: Outlook for a Comparison,* European Community, Brussels.
Musgrave, R. (1959). *The Theory of Public Finance,* McGraw Hill.
Oates, W. E. (1972). *Fiscal Federalism,* Harcourt Brace Janovich.
Padoa Schioppa, T. *et al.* (1987). *Efficiency, Stability and Equity: A Strategy for the Evolution of the Economic System of the European Community,* Oxford University Press.
Simons, H. C. (1948). *Economic Policy for a Free Society,* Chicago University Press.

Oxford Review of Economic Policy

Editor: **Christopher Allsopp,** New College, Oxford

The Oxford Review of Economic Policy, a leading journal in its field, presents balanced, non-technical appraisals of theoretical and empirical research, and evaluates the implications for economic policy. It contains commentary, forecasts, and articles on economic policy in the UK, and places economic policy questions in an international context.

Institutions and professionals in the worlds of business and economics are among the wide readership for whom the **The Oxford Review** provides impartial authoritative policy analysis in a readily accessible, non-technical form.

Forthcoming issues will include articles on:

- Health
- The EEC (including the implications of 1992)
- Exchange Rates
- Corporate Strategy
- Poverty and Social Insurance

Subscription rates for 1989 (Volume 5):
Institutions: **UK £60.00;** N. America **US$110.00;** Elsewhere **£68.00**
Personal: **UK £30.00;** N. America **US$55.00;** Elsewhere **£34.00**
ISSN: 0266-903 X, quarterly

---✂--------

Order Form *(please use block capitals)*

Payment may be made by cheque, credit transfer or major credit card—please give account number, expiry date and signature when ordering.

☐ Please enter my subscription to **The Oxford Review of Economic Policy,** Volume 5, 1989

☐ I enclose the correct remittance (cheques should be made payable to Oxford University Press)

☐ Please send me a **FREE** sample copy

Name ....

Address ....

Postcode............................... Country ....

Send to *Journals Subscription Department, Oxford University Press, Pinkhill House, Southfield Road, Eynsham, Oxford OX8 1JJ, UK*

OXFORD JOURNALS

MILLENNIUM

Journal of International Studies

Published three times a year at the London School of Economics

Recent articles include:

Immanuel Wallerstein   *The Reagan Non-Revolution*

Robert S. McNamara   *Reducing the Risk of Nuclear War: Is Star Wars the Answer?*

Fred Halliday   *State and Society in International Relations*

Forthcoming articles include:

Paul Teague   *The British Trades Union Congress and Membership of the European Community*

Michael C. Williams   *Rousseau, Realism and Realpolitik*

Special Issue   *The International Relations of Japan*
Winter 1989

Subscription information:

Individuals £13.00 per annum
(overseas £15.00, US $28.00,
Canada $32.00)

Students £7.00 per annum
(overseas £9.00)

Institutions £25.00 per annum
(overseas £30.00, US $60.00,
Canada $70.00)

Enquiries to:

MILLENNIUM: Journal of
International Studies
London School of Economics
Houghton Street
London WC2A 2AE
United Kingdom

ECONOMICA

Edited by Frank Cowell and David Webb
Managing Editor: Hugh Wills

Economica is devoted to economics, economic history, statistics, and closely related problems and over many years has established a reputation for thoughtful and important papers in all these areas. Papers taking both a theoretical approach and those dealing with problems of application are encouraged.

Economica is recognized as one of the world's leading journals in economics, appearing high in the rankings published by the **Journal of Economic Literature.** In addition to the main papers which make up each issue, there is an extensive and well-regarded review section, covering a wide range of recently published titles at all levels. From time to time special issues on selected topics are published, and are available as either single or back issues or, if published in the current year, are included in the annual subscription.

Recent articles include:

The Foreign Exchange Market: A Random Walk with a Dragging Anchor
CHARLES GOODHART

Edward West and the Classical Theory of Distribution and Growth
ANTHONY BREWER

Equilibrium Existence in the Linear Model of Spatial Competition
SIMON P. ANDERSON

On the Consistency of Libertarian Values
PRASANTA K. PATTANAIK

--✂------------------------

Economica is published in February, May, August, and November
Subscription Rates Volume 56, 1989
Individuals: £12.50 (UK) £12.50 (overseas) US$25.00 (N. America)
Institutions: £22.50 (UK) £31.00 (overseas) US$62.00 (N. America)
☐ Please enter my subscription to Economica/send me a sample copy

☐ I enclose cheque/money order made payable to Basil Blackwell

☐ Please charge my Access/American Express/Barclaycard/Diners Club/ Mastercharge/Visa account number:

.... Signature ....

Card expiry date ....

☐ For payments via the National Giro Bank, the Basil Blackwell account number is 236 6053

Address ....

....

....

If address registered with card company differs from above, please give details.
Please return this form together with your payment if applicable to:

Basil Blackwell · Journals Marketing Manager,
108 Cowley Road, Oxford OX4 1JF, UK or Journals Marketing Manager, 432 Park Avenue South, New York, NY 10016, USA.

Limiting Exchange-Rate Flexibility
The European Monetary System
FRANCESCO GIAVAZZI &
ALBERTO GIOVANNINI

The most comprehensive analysis to date of the
European Monetary System. The authors
highlight and discuss significant theoretical,
empirical and institutional aspects of the EMS.
£24.75   320pp   0-262-07116-9

The Insider-Outsider Theory of Employment and Unemployment
ASSAR LINDBECK &
DENNIS J. SNOWER

An accessible, balanced account of the insider-outsider theory of labour
market activity. The book examines the effect of insiders' activities on
wages, employment and unemployment, discusses the associated policy
implications, and relates the insider-outsider theory to other theories of
labour market activity.
£24.75   304pp   0-262-12139-5

Trade Policy and Market Structure
ELHANAN HELPMAN and PAUL R. KRUGMAN

A compact guide to the implications of trade policy under a number of
different market structures – from one of pure competition to imperfectly
competitive models. The authors synthesize the arguments of important
economists in the field and offer original insights of their own.
£22.50   cloth   0-262-08182-2   224pp
£10.95   paper   0-262-58099-3

Exchange-Rate Instability
PAUL R. KRUGMAN

Drawing on current theories of international finance, trade and industrial
organization, Paul Krugman presents a provocative analysis of the
extraordinary volatility of exchange rates in the 1980s.
£15.75   136pp   0-262-11140-3   *Lionel Robbins Lectures*

The World Trading System
Law and Policy of International Economic Relations
JOHN JACKSON

A clear and accessible introduction to the intricacies of the General
Agreement on Tariffs and Trade, a reference to its features and precedents,
and a reflective evaluation of its future.
£40.50   400pp   0-262-10040-1

THE **MIT** PRESS
126 Buckingham Palace Road London SW1W 9SA

CATALOGUE AVAILABLE

INTERNATIONAL REVIEW OF ECONOMICS AND BUSINESS

Rivista Internazionale
di Scienze Economiche e Commerciali

January 1989, Vol. XXXVI

T. Oberhofer: Two Hundred Years of Economics – M. Kadhim: Saint-Simonism and Its Relevancy to Third World Development – N.H. Assar and K.O. Kymn: The Impact of the Declining Saving Rate on the Great Ratios of Economics – G. Petrovich: Politiche fiscali e frazionamento del lavoro – M. Ziliotti: Controllo dell'impresa e struttura finanziaria ottimale – M. Moretto: L'impresa, l'accumulazione e il controllo esterno del tasso di rendimento

February 1989, Vol. XXXVI

G. Fodella: Internazionalizzazione economica e scenari anni 90 – R. Dore: Meritocracy, Employment and Citizenship in Japan and Elsewhere – C. Moriguchi: Economic Structural Adjustments and Macroeconomic Balance of Japan – C. Zanier: Japan as a Newcomer in the World Silk Market – N. Doi: Enterprise Groups and Market Performance in Japanese Manufacturing Industries – A. Lauria: New Rules in Labour Organization: The "Bunsha" System – K. Holbik: Japan's Internal Economic Inefficiencies and Its Trade Balance – C.C. Lai: Development Strategies and Growth with Equality. Re-evaluation of Taiwan's Experience

March 1989, Vol. XXXVI

A.N. Rugina: The Quest for Independence of Principia Logica. Toward a Third Revolution in Logic – A. Lanza: Considerazioni su un metodo per lo studio dei linkages in un contesto input-output – G. Signorino: Trasformazioni dei dati e verifica della stabilità strutturale in modelli con errori AR (1) – N.A. Yannacopoulos: A Graph-Theoretic Interpretation of a Proposition of the Theory of Monetary Exchange – C. Leipert and U.E. Simonis: Environmental Protection Expenditures – C.C. Mai: Technological Uncertainty and International Market Share Rivalry

A monthly journal. Subscription rate: Lire 130.000 (Italy); Lire 170.000 (abroad). - Complete set of back issues available (1954-1988). Address: R.I.S.E.C. - Via Teuliè 1 - 20136 Milano (Italy).